D1000972

University of London Historical Studies

XXVI

UNIVERSITY OF LONDON HISTORICAL STUDIES

I. HUGH TINKER. *The Foundations of Local Self-Government in India, Pakistan and Burma.* 1954

II. AVROM SALTMAN. *Theobald, Archbishop of Canterbury.* 1956

III. R. F. LESLIE. *Polish Politics and the Revolution of November 1830.* 1956

IV. W. N. MEDLICOTT. *Bismarck, Gladstone, and the Concert of Europe.* 1956

V. JOHN LYNCH. *Spanish Colonial Administration 1782–1810: The Intendant System in the Viceroyalty of the Rio de la Plata.* 1958

VI. F. H. W. SHEPPARD. *Local Government in St. Marylebone, 1688–1835.* 1958

VII. R. L. GREAVES. *Persia and the Defence of India, 1884–1892.* 1959

VIII. M. J. SYDENHAM. *The Girondins.* 1961

IX. MARGARET HOWELL. *Regalian Right in Medieval England.* 1962

X. N. M. SUTHERLAND. *The French Secretaries of State in the Age of Catherine de Medici.* 1962

XI. GWYN A. WILLIAMS. *Medieval London: from Commune to Capital.* 1963

XII. CHARLES DUGGAN. *Twelfth-century Decretal Collections and their Importance in English History.* 1963

XIII. R. F. LESLIE. *Reform and Insurrection in Russian Poland 1856–1865.* 1963

XIV. J. A. S. GRENVILLE. *Lord Salisbury and Foreign Policy.* 1964

XV. P. W. J. RILEY. *The English Ministers and Scotland 1707–1727.* 1964

XVI. J. F. BOSHER. *The Single Duty Project: A Study of the Movement for a French Customs Union in the Eighteenth Century.* 1964

XVII. JOAN MCDONALD. *Rousseau and the French Revolution 1762–1791.* 1965

XVIII. IAN H. NISH. *The Anglo-Japanese Alliance: The Diplomacy of Two Island Empires, 1894–1907.* 1966

XIX. WILLIAM URRY. *Canterbury under the Angevin Kings.* 1967

XX. PHYLLIS M. HEMBRY. *The Bishops of Bath and Wells 1540–1640: Social and Economic Problems.* 1967

XXI. N. M. FARRISS. *Crown and Clergy in Colonial Mexico 1759–1821: The Crisis of Ecclesiastical Privilege.* 1968

XXII. DEMETRIOS I. POLEMIS. *The Doukai: A Contribution to Byzantine Prosopography.* 1968

XXIII. JUKKA NEVAKIVI. *Britain, France, and the Arab Middle East 1914–20.* 1969

XXIV. G. G. HARRIS. *The Trinity House of Deptford 1514–1660.* 1969

XXV. J. T. CLIFFE. *The Yorkshire Gentry from the Reformation to the Civil War.* 1969

XXVI. JAMES L. STURGIS. *John Bright and the Empire.* 1969

JOHN BRIGHT
AND THE EMPIRE

This volume is published with the help of
a grant from the late Miss Isobel Thornley's
Bequest to the University of London

JOHN BRIGHT AND THE EMPIRE

by

JAMES L. STURGIS

UNIVERSITY OF LONDON
THE ATHLONE PRESS
1969

Published by
THE ATHLONE PRESS
UNIVERSITY OF LONDON
at 2 Gower Street London WC1

Distributed by Tiptree Book Services Ltd
Tiptree, Essex

Australia and New Zealand
Melbourne University Press

U.S.A.
Oxford University Press Inc
New York

485 13126 9

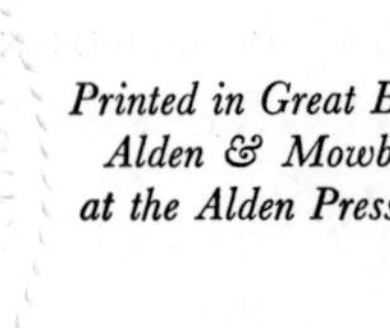

Printed in Great Britain by
Alden & Mowbray Ltd
at the Alden Press, Oxford

PREFACE

THIS BOOK is based upon a thesis which I completed at the University of London in 1963. There are many people to whom I am deeply indebted for encouragement and aid. Professor G. S. Graham of King's College, London, and Professor J. Flint of Dalhousie University were both helpful in various ways during the course of research and writing. I should like to mention, too, the kindness of Professor J. B. Conacher of the University of Toronto in allowing me to read a chapter on India from his forthcoming book on the Aberdeen administration. My friends, R. J. Stewart, E. O. Boyanowsky, and J. Jensen, have also helped me in numerous ways.

To the librarians and archivists of the various institutions in which I consulted reference material I should like to express my appreciation. In particular I wish to mention Miss Olive Goodbody of Friends' House, Dublin, who aided greatly in locating manuscript material in Ireland. I should also like to thank Mr Russell Ellice of Invergary, Scotland, for kind permission to quote from the Ellice papers deposited in the Scottish National Library.

Professor N. Mansergh of St John's College, Cambridge, read the manuscript and offered helpful suggestions, particularly in regard to Ireland. Dr S. R. Mehrotra of the School of Oriental and African Studies generously undertook the same task on the Indian chapters. Professor I. R. Christie of University College London, has offered so many valuable and insightful suggestions that my debt to him is incalculable. Nor can I measure how much I owe to Dr Mary Cumpston of Birkbeck College, whose tireless aid in my behalf went far beyond the duties of a tutor. Lastly, I wish to thank my wife for her grammatical suggestions and, above all, for having shared seven years of married life with the subject of this book.

I should also like to acknowledge the financial assistance of the Central Research Fund of the University of London which enabled me to carry out research in Birmingham, Manchester, Dublin and Belfast.

Publication has been made possible with a generous grant from the late Miss Isobel Thornley's Bequest to the University of London.

Birkbeck College, London J. S.
1968

CONTENTS

ABBREVIATIONS

Add. MSS.	Additional Manuscripts in the British Museum
Bell	John Dickinson, *Last Counsels of an Unknown Counsellor*, ed. E. Bell
Bright Papers, U.C.	Bright Papers, University College, University of London
Hansard	Hansard's Parliamentary Debates, Third Series (unless otherwise stated)
Leech	*The Public Letters of John Bright*, ed. H. J. Leech
P.M.H.S.	*Proceedings of the Massachusetts Historical Society*
Walling	*The Diaries of John Bright*, ed. R. A. J. Walling

Introduction

On 27 March 1889, there occurred in Britain the death of a statesman who earned the following tribute from W. E. Gladstone: 'His name remains indelibly written in the annals of this Empire...upon the hearts of the great and over-spreading race to which he belonged—that race in whose wide expansion he rejoiced, and whose power and pre-eminence he believed to be full of promise and full of glory for the best interests of mankind.'[1] The man upon whom this eulogy was bestowed was John Bright, who, for over half a century, had taken a leading part in the political and economic affairs of Britain and the Empire.

The aim of this book is to examine the ideas and activities of John Bright in relation to the British Empire and Ireland between 1843 and 1889. It will also attempt to assess his methods, the nature of the support he received for his ideas, and the contribution he made to imperial and Irish affairs. The more immediate task is to outline the early life of Bright, to give some idea of his character, and to place these within the framework of material conditions and the state of political parties in the Victorian age.

John Bright was born on 16 November 1811. His father, Jacob Bright, had established himself in the cotton spinning business in Rochdale. John Bright took an active part in this business from 1827 to 1841, after having attended several Quaker schools which, by his own admission, left little intellectual mark upon him. To make up for his lack of formal schooling, the young Bright took it upon himself to fulfil a programme of self-education by intensive reading, especially of Milton and the Bible. His literary tastes also extended to

[1] Hansard, vol. 334, 1173.

Byron, from whose writings he could recite long passages.[1] But his attachment to Milton was more revealing. His high regard for Milton represented his engrossment with the political struggles of the seventeenth century.[2] Various surviving religious disabilities were also constant reminders of inequalities yet to be overcome.

The controversy over the 1832 Reform Bill excited Bright's political curiosity, and he soon began to play a prominent part in the 'Rochdale Literary and Philosophical Society'. He became active as a local politician, and supported the Liberal candidate for Rochdale in 1837. About this same time, he first met Richard Cobden, and by late 1838 he was enrolled as a member of the 'Provisional Committee' of the Anti-Corn Law Association, which was shortly to become the famous 'League'. In 1840 he formed a branch of the League in Rochdale which attracted a great deal of support.[3] In 1841, even before the death of his first wife, he began to devote himself to the repeal of the corn laws.[4] From this point onward Bright moved out of local politics and became a full fledged agitator for the Anti-Corn Law League. In 1843, he decided to enter Parliament, and by 25 July had successfully contested one of the Commons seats for Durham.

Then, as later, Bright's physical appearance gave an observer an impression of unbounded vitality. An American journalist portrayed him in 1866:

> His hair even then was grey, though abundant, the complexion florid, and the rather irregular but powerful features gave you at first sight an impression of singular force and firmness of character. So did the whole man. The broad shoulders, the bulk of the figure, the solid massiveness of his masterful individuality, the immovable grasp of his feet upon the firm earth, his uprightness of bearing, the body knit to the head as closely as capital to column—all together made the least careful observer feel that here was one in whose armour the flaws were few.[5]

[1] Sir Austen Chamberlain, *Down The Years*, p. 258.
[2] J. Vincent, *The Formation of the Liberal Party 1857–1868*, pp. 162–3.
[3] G. M. Trevelyan, *The Life of John Bright*, pp. 7–32.
[4] D. Read, *Cobden and Bright*, p. 79.
[5] Quoted in A. Briggs, *Victorian People*, p. 206.

His striking appearance was allied with a character of equal forcefulness. His nature was one of absolute honesty and independence. No reward of office nor any long-standing friendship could stand in the way of his holding to opinions that he believed to be true. He was willing to take advice and to study a problem; but once he had command of the facts and had made up his mind on the subject, no one could be more immovable.

That he was a Quaker often led people to assume that he was pietistic. In the appropriate setting, no doubt he was, but many of his contemporaries could attest to the essentially combative side of his character. Commenting on various members of the Radical party, J. A. Roebuck wrote, 'The only man of metal and pluck was Bright, the pugnacious Quaker.'[1] Illustrative of this quality is the *Punch* cartoon which shows Bright with gloves on, dealing out vicious blows to a bag marked 'Aristocracy'.[2]

Bright had a wide curiosity which he satisfied by travel, reading and extensive intercourse with learned and expert men. Essentially he was gregarious, though the fact that he kept a diary indicates a certain degree of introspection. He had abundant determination, of which his struggle to repeal the corn laws is witness. He was a man who revered the idea of liberty; this was certainly one principle of Quakerism that he valued. Particularly in his early years he was strongly egalitarian in his outlook, and intolerant of either a landed or a commercial aristocracy. In a way his transfer from Manchester to Birmingham in 1857 was indicative, as Cobden pointed out, of a growing realization that Birmingham was more democratic than Manchester.[3] Lastly, he tended to see issues in terms of black and white, or right and wrong. A moral fervour characterized almost everything Bright did or said, because of his belief in justice, liberty and similar absolutes.

That Bright had faults is certain. To a remarkable degree he found it difficult to excuse what he regarded as political misdemeanours. Very often memories of past disagreements

[1] *Life and Letters of John Arthur Roebuck*, ed. R. E. Leader, p. 230.
[2] See *Cartoons by Sir John Tenniel*, pp. 30–1.
[3] J. Morley, *The Life of Richard Cobden*, p. 663.

remained wedged in his mind long after one would have assumed it normal to have either forgiven or forgotten. He was short of patience at times, particularly with poor penmen and the chronically unpunctual. He was often too outspoken. His diary reveals a self-righteousness that manifested itself on many occasions. His opponents resented the fact that Bright regarded his own views not only as self-evident, but as having descended from on high.

However, behind Bright's formidable exterior resided a soul that was often tormented by self-doubt. He suffered from two lengthy illnesses, the first one occurring shortly before the end of the Crimean War, and the second during his term of office in the first Gladstone administration. These 'breakdowns' may have represented the difficulty Bright unconsciously felt in moving from the Quaker milieu to the centre of the stage at Westminster. They may also have arisen from the tensions created by an inner personality that could endure neither self-effacement nor frustration coming into conflict with the uncertainty and complexity of political life.

Because Bright occasionally suffered from lack of confidence, Professor Ausubel's description of him as a man who relished praise and recognition seems accurate. He argues that Bright did worry considerably over his political fortunes and that his stand on the Crimean War was not taken without his casting an anxious eye on the possible political cost,[1] though the important point surely is that it in no way caused him to alter his opinion. It is further argued that his election for Birmingham in 1858 'worked wonders for Bright's morale',[2] but to say this is perhaps only to admit that he had a thoroughly human reaction. Generally, he found it difficult to adjust to the often carping and critical tone of politics, even though his natural instinct was to strike back when attacked. No matter how much it might have improved his health to have retired from Parliament, the fact was that he was too much obsessed by political life to withdraw.

Bright's character was formed in large part by his religious beliefs. In 1880 he wrote: 'I was, as I now am, a member of the Society of Friends, I knew something of their history and

[1] H. Ausubel, *John Bright, Victorian Reformer*, pp. 66–8.
[2] Ibid., p. 88.

of the persecutions they had endured, and of their principles of equality and justice.'[1] The emphasis on justice that pervades Bright's political speeches, if followed to its source, would probably derive from his religion.

There are several significant examples of the connexion between Bright's political actions and the ideas of the Quakers. Bright believed in the Quaker principle that the moral laws which applied to individuals applied also to nations.[2] He adopted the same position in regard to the Crimean War as was taken by the Friends' yearly meeting in London in 1854.[3] One reason why he hoped that Britain would extend better government to India was that he thought that nations could atone for their past mistakes by good deeds.[4] An enlightened attitude towards Indians and Africans flowed naturally from a religion that emphasized the brotherhood of man. Finally, his antipathy to war was part of his religious beliefs.

However, the very fact that Bright became a politician involved a certain degree of compromise with Quaker principles. Many of his sect disagreed with the view that politics was a suitable employment for a young man. Bright, for his part, often criticized some actions and ideas of the Friends,[5] and he never once stood up at a meeting of worship to pray.[6] The man who has commented most meaningfully on this problem of Quakerism and politics is Frederick B. Tolles. He thinks that it is possible for a Quaker like Bright to achieve success in politics, but only at a price—'the price of compromise, of the partial betrayal of his ideals'. If, on the other hand, he disdains politics and upholds his pure life, this too is achieved at 'the price of isolation....Let me call the two positions the relativist and the absolutist. And let me suggest that perhaps each one needs the other. The relativist needs the absolutist to keep alive

[1] Walling, p. 11.

[2] Hansard, vol. 272, 723.

[3] *Christian faith and practice in the experience of the Society of Friends*, London Yearly Meetings of the Religious Society of Friends. No. 634.

[4] *The Times*, 2 August 1883, p. 6, col. d.

[5] Bright upheld the idea that the spread of Quaker beliefs could be hindered by insisting on 'minor testimonies and peculiarities'. (J. T. Mills, *John Bright and the Quakers*, ii, 7–8.)

[6] Mills, op. cit., i, 374.

and clear the vision of the City of God while he struggles in some measure to realize it in the City of Earth.'[1]

One example of this compromise in Bright was his attitude towards war. Though believing that war was the worst disaster for mankind, he did not believe in pacifism. He wrote, 'I have never advocated the extreme peace principle, the non-resistance principle in public, or in private.'[2] His stand was that each person had to decide in every individual case.[3] This enabled him to uphold the North during the American Civil War because of the great moral victory that would result in the defeat of the South.

Bright's religion affected him in other ways. Perhaps because of his early opposition to church rates, he had always been much opposed to the idea of a State church. To his mind, any church in this position was only weakening itself. This was to have special importance in Bright's career in regard to Ireland.

Another important influence on his character was his association with Rochdale and Lancashire. Lancashire has sometimes been described as 'America-and-water',[4] and Bright imbibed deeply of this democratic mixture. His earliest political struggle took place in Rochdale against compulsory church rates. The Anti-Corn Law League was a northern growth, the success of which inspired Bright to believe that causes could be won by the harnessing of public energy.[5]

Bright travelled widely. He had begun by visiting Ireland in 1832.[6] In 1857 he visited Rome, and his comments on that city are illuminating as to the effect of travel and reading on him: 'I write this surrounded by the ruins of the once mistress of the world, and from her history, and indeed from all history, I learn that loud boasting, great wealth, great power, extended dominion, successive conquests, mighty fleets and armies, are not immovable foundations of national greatness. I would

[1] Friends Reference Library (Euston). 050 Social II (10a) F. B. Tolles, *Quakerism and Politics*, p. 20.

[2] Sturge Papers. Add. MSS. 43, 723. Bright to J. Sturge, 24 September 1857, f. 85.

[3] M. E. Hirst, *John Bright*, pp. 94–5.

[4] Briggs, op. cit., p. 213.

[5] Bright, like most Leaguers, exaggerated the importance of the League's efforts. See N. McCord, *The Anti-Corn Law League 1838–1846*, p. 208.

[6] Walling, p. 15.

rather rely on an educated and moral people, and on a system of Government, free at home, and scrupulously moral and just in its dealing with every other Government and people.'[1]

An extreme emphasis on morality was not unique to Bright. Predecessors in the House of Commons such as Edmund Burke had stressed the need for morality in dealings with other countries, particularly Ireland and India. Indeed, Burke in 1788, with India in mind, had reminded Members that rules of morality did not change with geographical location. He had also stressed that British rule in India was in the nature of a 'trust' for which Parliament was responsible.[2]

Another profound influence in Bright's outlook was the political philosophy of free trade. In 1776 Adam Smith had published his work, *The Wealth of Nations*, in which he attacked the idea that duties and a protection system for either agriculture or manufactures was a wise policy.[3] He also set up the principle that any individual could direct his own economic affairs and that the combined operation of individuals acting in this way would be to the general good of society. The introduction of commerce had its moral side too: 'whenever commerce is introduced into any country probity and punctuality always accompany it'.[4] Though Adam Smith had nothing very much to say about the prevention of war,[5] Bright and Cobden firmly believed that universal free trade would end war.[6] With increased trade, the greater wealth of all nations which would result would invalidate the reasons for war.

Adam Smith also wrote critically of colonies. He charged that the interests of the home consumer had been sacrificed for the interests of the producer by making the former pay for the upkeep of an Empire. He also thought that the East India Company was unfit to govern a great Empire, and that its sovereign and commercial duties were incompatible.[7]

[1] Ibid. p. 218.

[2] G. Bennett, *The Concept of Empire*, pp. 52–3.

[3] Adam Smith, *The Wealth of Nations*, ed. E. Cannan, i, 418–62.

[4] Ibid., p. xxiv.

[5] He suggested that payment for war within the year of its occurrence would be the best means of ending it. (A. Smith, op. cit., ii, 411.)

[6] In Bright's case see Leech, p. 37.

[7] A. Smith, op. cit., ii, 160, 243, 304.

The theoretical writings of Adam Smith in support of free trade were supported by the discovery of practical men of business that protection was not suited to their needs. Henry Ashworth[1] believed that while few men had read Adam Smith's work, many had been influenced by writings in the press on free trade.[2] The special contribution of the Anti-Corn Law League was to accept the validity of Book IV, Chapter V of *The Wealth of Nations* on the corn laws, and to show the country that the corn laws were, in Ashworth's words, 'a flagrant scheme of the landlords to enrich themselves by a legal authority which oppressed all other portions of the community'.[3]

It should be remembered that progress towards free trade had begun well before Bright and Cobden adopted the cause. Within the Board of Trade there was a tradition of anti-protectionism which attracted adherents of free trade. William Huskisson, while President of the Board of Trade from 1823 to 1827, was responsible for reductions in the tariff level of important articles such as raw wool and silks. In addition, he reduced the restrictions on colonial trade for foreign countries, provided reciprocal measures were passed. Poulett Thomson, who had been much influenced by Ricardo and the Benthamites, was President of the Department from 1834 to 1839, when extremely competent officials were appointed who were sympathetic towards free trade. It was one of these officials, Deacon Hume, who is thought to have suggested the idea of the select committee of 1840 whose findings did much to strengthen free trade opinion.[4]

The philosophy of free trade was admirably suited to Britain's business community in the early nineteenth century. Britain was truly the 'workshop of the world', and whatever developments occurred elsewhere, confidence was supreme. The slogan 'Britain Can Make It' had its roots in the Exhibition of 1851, and no phrase better typified the opinion of the Victorian

[1] ASHWORTH, HENRY (1794–1880). Vigorous supporter of the Anti-Corn Law League; managed extensive cotton mill at Turton; a Quaker; on especially good terms with Cobden.

[2] H. Ashworth, *Recollections of Richard Cobden M.P.*, p. 10.

[3] Ibid. pp. 10–11.

[4] Lucy M. Brown, *The Board of Trade and the Free-Trade Movement 1830–42*, pp. 2–3, 21–2, 71, 214–16.

business community.[1] The development of railways and better production methods, through such innovations as the Bessemer method of producing steel, helped to supply a world greatly dependent on Britain's productive capabilities.[2] Between 1815 and 1850 there occurred perhaps 'the most rapid rate of development of domestic resources throughout the whole of Britain's economic history'.[3]

One of the fastest growing industries was the manufacture of cotton textiles, which usually accounted for 30 to 40 per cent of Great Britain's total exports. In the ten years between 1846 and 1856 the value of cotton exports rose by 60 per cent. This phenomenal expansion put heavy pressure on manufacturers to acquire a steady supply of the raw material. Within Britain, the industry was concentrated almost entirely in Lancashire, north-east Cheshire and Yorkshire's West Riding.[4] This fact tended to make such an important national industry appear to be a narrow geographical interest group when it brought its difficulties to the attention of the nation.

Because of the aristocratic bias in government which still remained after the 1832 Reform Act, 'millocrats' gave their support in many cases to Radical politicians. Whigs and Tories, though perhaps distinguishable, seemed to be members of the same caste. But the Radicals faced numerous problems in the years following 1830–2, during which time it had seemed that a new political era was at hand. Surface progress masked an otherwise deteriorating position as the conservative elements in society re-asserted themselves. The further the Radicals receded from the seat of power, the more the lack of party cohesion became a problem.[5] S. Maccoby writes: 'The fact was that the Radical membership of 1835 and long afterwards was singularly unhomogeneous, singularly hard to unite on any practical course, and singularly given to riding individual hobby-horses.'[6] Then, too, the growth of Chartism—a move-

[1] J. Summerson, '1857—a New Age, a New Style', *Ideas and Beliefs of the Victorians*, p. 63.

[2] G. C. Allen, *British Industries and their Organization*, pp. 90–2.

[3] W. W. Rostow, *British Economy of the Nineteenth Century*, p. 19.

[4] A. W. Silver, *Manchester Men and Indian Cotton 1847–1872*, pp. 1–5, 76–82.

[5] N. Gash, *Politics in the Age of Peel, passim.*

[6] S. Maccoby, *English Radicalism 1832–1852*, pp. 432–3.

ment which embraced many points held by the Radicals in 1833, but made more dangerous by the open invitation to revolt by Feargus O'Connor—divorced the Radicals in Parliament from the working class.[1]

A new Radical party grew up with the appearance of the Anti-Corn Law League. Even though it developed a forward-looking political technique, the electoral system inhibited its effectiveness. But all of the Radicals' difficulties could not be blamed on a narrow franchise, rampant bribery and corruption, or lack of the ballot. More important, perhaps, was the desire to return to normality after 1846. Peel, by defusing the corn law issue, removed a potent source of unity on the political left.[2] The advent of prosperity reinforced this tendency to plane down the rough edges of society. In the short run both 1832 and 1846 proved disillusioning to the Radicals, for at the same time as they caught a glimpse of the promised land, their followers retreated into more familiar territory.

The repeal of the corn laws in 1846 produced a chaotic political situation in which the fledgeling party system of the 1830s and 1840s broke down almost completely. Sir Robert Peel's decision to repeal the corn laws broke asunder the rival elements within the Tory party which only his skill and popularity had kept intact to that point.[3] Before 1832 the Crown had been a stabilizing influence within Parliament in the same way as the increased electorate was after 1867. But in the intervening years, ministries rose and fell with bewildering rapidity. The Peelites, the Irish and the Radicals were usually to be found on the Whig side, but could easily be alienated by measures inimical to their interests.[4] It was not until the meeting in Willis's Rooms in 1859, when an alliance was patched up among the old Whigs, Liberals, Radicals and the leading Peelites, that some appearance of order was substituted for the formlessness of the preceding period.[5]

Before 1867 only one-seventh of the adult males in Britain

[1] *Chartist Studies*, ed. A. Briggs, p. 13. [2] McCord, op. cit., p. 212.

[3] See N. Gash, 'Peel and the Party System', *Transactions of the Royal Historical Society*, 5th series, i (1951), 62–3.

[4] R. Blake, *Disraeli*, pp. 270–8.

[5] J. B. Conacher, 'Party Politics in the Age of Palmerston', *1859: Entering an Age of Crisis*, eds. P. Appleman *et al.*, pp. 179–80.

had the right to vote, which meant that the preponderant political power remained with the aristocratic and landed elements. This system, in Bright's opinion, led to undue political privilege for the upper classes which expressed itself in unnecessary wars and monopolies such as the corn laws. He saw the remedy in a liberal reform bill which would then allow Parliament to speak for the nation and not a class.[1] Behind this advocacy was an assumption on his part that the broad masses of the people would share his political outlook. He believed that freer trade, a less bellicose foreign policy and lower taxes would find support among those who as yet had no vote.

Bright's personal political hold on the country grew out of the leadership he gave to the Nonconformist element within the population. Religious beliefs were closely allied with political affiliation. 'In fact, by the second quarter of the nineteenth century religion had received so political a shape, or politics so religious a shape, that it was for many people almost impossible to separate the two.'[2] The other source of political strength was the increasing support that Bright received from the working classes. This was enhanced by his defeat in 1857 at Manchester which marked the final rupture with the business elements in that city. It was true that during the 1840s Bright was distrusted by working-class leaders, but this feeling mellowed in the more prosperous 1850s and 1860s. It should not be assumed that Bright's position as a manufacturer ruined his chances for giving leadership to the working classes, especially to their élite. Many of the trade union leaders had come to share the same political and social outlook as the middle class.[3] John Vincent ably sums up the reasons for Bright's political effectiveness: 'He stood at the confluence of the working-class movement and of political Dissent. Both

[1] A paraphrase of Bright's speech at Glasgow, 16 Oct. 1866. (Trevelyan, op. cit., p. 368.) Bright's public statements on democracy lead to a certain confusion regarding his commitment to the cause. (Read, op. cit., p. 162.) Whatever his theoretical views really were, it is enough to note here that his practical efforts for reform were always steadier and more determined than Cobden's.

[2] G. Kitson Clark, *The Making of Victorian England*, p. 162.

[3] R. Harrison, *Before the Socialists*, p. 57. Vincent says both the working and middle classes 'had to work a parallel passage' before turning 'to face each other'. (Vincent, op. cit., p. xxx.)

movements failed to produce an inspiring leader in their own mould, and had to learn to accept Bright, cast in the mould of the League's social theories, which were only moderately sympathetic either to the working class or to militant Nonconformity.'[1]

Nevertheless Bright did not use the loyalty of his followers as a lever to gain personal power. As early as 1861 he had pointed to Gladstone as the man destined to lead the Liberal party.[2] While there was no objection to office *per se*, what was inadmissible was the acceptance of official position before the ideas for which he stood were generally subscribed to. This was not only ideologically but politically judicious. He was much less interested in representing the general will than in converting the populace to a new orthodoxy. If this sometimes coincided with self-interest then it only indicates that he was no more successful than politicians of any generation in separating the strands of public and private good.[3] What is clear is his certainty that there was no incompatibility between his own convictions and public acceptance of them. Their conjunction, however, required on his part constant effort. Hence the need for political teaching and action.

[1] Vincent, op. cit., p. 161.

[2] W. E. Williams, *The Rise of Gladstone to the Leadership of the Liberal Party*, pp. 47–8.

[3] See C. Bay, *The Structure of Freedom*, p. 77.

CHAPTER I

India 1843–1857

THE SYSTEM of double government used by Great Britain to administer India after 1784 was one of the most complicated and unwieldy instruments ever devised by one country to rule another. Its critics were harsh. Speaking in 1858 just before its demise, John Bright ridiculed it by saying, 'I believe everything the East India Company has said of the Board of Control—to its discredit; and I believe that everything the Board of Control has said to the discredit of the East India Company is perfectly true.'[1] Both the originator and the defenders of double government had cogent reasons, however, for upholding the system. When Pitt set up the Board of Control in 1784 to supervise Indian affairs, he left patronage in the hands of the East India Company because it was feared that extra patronage under the control of the Crown would endanger the balance of the constitution by giving the executive added control over M.P.s.[2] As time went on, the system of double government appealed to mid-Victorian whiggism because it seemed to match the 'mixed' form of the British constitution.[3]

The East India Company consisted of the Proprietors (owners of Company stock) and twenty-four Directors, elected by the Proprietors. The main strength of the Company came from commercial interests in the City and from returning Anglo-Indians who, by purchasing East India stock, hoped to gain power and a voice in patronage. There was little democratic spirit to be observed in the election of Directors; when a Director died, the newcomer used the prospect of patronage

[1] Hansard, vol. 151, 331.
[2] C. H. Philips, *The East India Company 1784–1834*, p. 14.
[3] R. J. Moore, *Sir Charles Wood's Indian Policy 1853–66*, p. 30.

as a bribe by which to attract votes. Nepotism in the appointment of Company servants in India was practised until 1853.

Of the several committees within the Court of Directors, the most important was the Secret Committee. Its legal status dated from 1784, though it had existed before that time. It consisted of the Chairman, Deputy Chairman and Senior Director of the Court of Directors, all of whom enjoyed easy access to the President of the Board of Control. The Committee, contrary to the original intention, sent secret despatches to India and in this way exercised considerable influence, particularly in commercial matters.

Members of the Company who had seats in the House of Commons also helped to safeguard its interests. Between 1784 and 1834 the 'East India' members numbered between 45 and 103.[1] Bright often referred to the Company influence in Parliament. In 1853 he opposed legislation that allowed an East India Director to sit in Parliament because it would add to the influence of the President of the Board of Control.[2]

The renewal of the Company's charter in 1853 involved few changes in the system of Indian government. For the first time, no date was set for the new charter's termination. The Court of Directors was reduced in number from twenty-four to eighteen, of whom six were to be appointed by the Crown. Lastly, the new charter revoked the system of patronage, instituting open competition in its place.[3]

The task of governing India in India rested in the Governor-General in Council. Before 1853 this council consisted of four men, one of whom was not a Company servant, and who exercised his role only for legislative purposes. By the 1853 Act, this council was increased for legislative purposes to twelve members. The power of the Governor-General was extensive, and included the right to make any law or regulation. The executives of this power were the members of the Indian civil or covenanted service, who filled the superior posts. Below this level was the uncovenanted service, in which positions were usually filled by Indians. Only rarely was it

[1] Philips, op. cit., p. 299.
[2] Hansard, vol. 129, 78–9.
[3] Sir C. Ilbert, *The Government of India*, pp. 90–3.

possible to rise from the lower service to the higher one.[1]

There was a wide range of opinion within Britain concerning the principles upon which the Indian Empire should be governed. Edmund Burke had counselled against any attempt by Britain to impose alien values upon India.[2] But increasingly, various reformist groups such as the Utilitarians, the Evangelicals and the Liberals put forward their own programmes for the regeneration of India.[3] In addition, Lancashire cotton interests were beginning to focus their attention upon India's economic situation because of their over-dependence on the United States for supplies of raw cotton.[4] It would be expecting too much to think that the Indian government could satisfy the diversified demands made upon it.

Despite economic improvements initiated particularly while Lord Dalhousie was Governor-General,[5] there was a great deal that a contemporary observer could find to criticize about conditions in India. Communications were slow and unsatisfactory. By 1855 there were fewer than 300 miles of railway in India. Canal building had proceeded at a faster rate, but the great potential had not been realized.[6] There was serious difficulty in the Indian army, where the rank and file were becoming increasingly restive. There were further defects. The first Lieutenant-Governor of Bengal believed that Indian opinion regarded the administration of criminal justice as 'little below that of a lottery'.[7] In Madras the use of torture was proven by a Torture Commission in 1855. A witness from India before a parliamentary committee in 1848 testified that

[1] Sir H. Verney Lovett, *The Cambridge History of India*, vi, 357–61.

[2] E. Stokes, *The English Utilitarians and India*, p. xvi.

[3] For the Utilitarians see Stokes, op. cit. For the Liberals see G. D. Bearce, *British Attitudes Towards India 1784–1858*. Both authors discuss the Evangelicals and their relationship to India.

[4] For a description of the earliest attempts by Lancashire manufacturers to supplement the supply of American cotton see A. Redford, *Manchester Merchants and Foreign Trade 1794–1858*, pp. 217–23. From 1851 until 1860 the United States supplied nearly 75 per cent of imported raw cotton. See Sir John Clapham, *An Economic History of Modern Britain. Free Trade and Steel 1850–1886*, pp. 220–8.

[5] See Bearce, op. cit., pp. 220–5; Moore, op. cit., pp. 133–4; A. W. Silver, *Manchester Men and Indian Cotton 1847–1872*, pp. 51–7.

[6] R. Dutt, *The Economic History of India. 1837 to the Twentieth Century*, pp. 166–78.

[7] Sir H. Verney Lovett, *The Cambridge History of India*, vi, 27.

most Indians were in a state of grinding poverty.[1] One writer summed up his impression of Bengal by commenting: 'There were almost no roads or bridges or schools, and there was no proper protection to life and property.'[2]

II

John Bright first became interested in India because of its potential as a source of cotton. Even though Bright did not become a Member for Manchester until 1847, he had, while a Member for Durham, made himself a spokesman for Lancashire concern about cotton supplies.[3] One of the principal objects of the agitation to repeal the corn laws had been to lower the price of food and thus enable consumers to purchase greater quantities of manufactured goods. In the case of cotton manufacturers, the new-found freedom did not mean much if supplies of raw materials were not forthcoming. Conditions were made difficult for cotton manufacturers by rises in the price of raw cotton, which by Bright's estimate amounted to 40 per cent during seven months in 1846.[4] If Bright may be taken as a typical case, the existing shortage of cotton threatened losses to him of nearly £10,000.[5]

Because of Bright's concern with Britain's dependence on American slave-grown cotton, he determined in January 1847, to move for a select committee to inquire into the obstacles to the growth of cotton in India.[6] It is quite likely too that he wished to enhance his chances of being elected for Manchester, going so far as to admit this to Sir J. C. Hobhouse in an interview with the President of the Board of Control in February 1847. Bright stressed also that he bore no ill will against the government; two days later the cabinet decided to allow the committee.[7] Addressing the House in May, he posited this question: 'first, can India grow a sufficient quantity of cotton

[1] Dutt, op. cit., pp. 136–7. [2] Sir John Strachey, *India*, p. 459.

[3] See Hansard, vol. 78, 937.

[4] Bright Papers, Add. MSS. 43,383. Bright to Cobden, 29 November 1846, f. 175.

[5] Smith Papers, MS. 923.2, S.344 (5). Bright to J. B. Smith, 19 October 1847.

[6] Ibid., MS. 923.2, S.344 (2). Bright to J. B. Smith, 19 January 1847.

[7] Diary of Lord Broughton, Add. MSS. 43,749. 11 and 13 Feb. 1847, ff. 103, 107.

to supply our manufactories? and if she can, what are the obstacles which prevent her doing so?'[1] Despite the £100,000 spent by the East India Company in an attempt to develop the growth of cotton, it was his opinion that Indian cotton had not increased in either quality or quantity since 1820. He stressed, too, the idea that Britain had a responsibility to develop India's prosperity.[2]

Bright's select committee began its sittings in February 1848, under his chairmanship. Twenty witnesses were called; many of them had never been to India, some were merchants, others were employees of the East India Company. The report of the committee emphasized that most witnesses with a record of service in India thought that Indian cotton could compete with cotton from the United States. Their recommendation was that European capitalists should communicate directly with the cultivators, whose position could be greatly improved by a more moderate and long-term land assessment. Many witnesses described communications as inadequate, and spoke of the need for the building of roads or railways.[3] Though Bright was not at all convinced that the report was censorious enough,[4] it was a remarkable condemnation of Company rule, considering the number of members of the East India Company who either sat on the committee or acted as witnesses.

1849 was another grim year for cotton manufacturers, faced as they were with soaring prices for raw cotton. Bright, working in conjunction with the directors of the Manchester Chamber of Commerce, renewed the question of the cotton supply in the House in 1850 by requesting that a Royal Commission be sent to India.[5] In support of this he stated that the committee of 1848 had suffered from certain limitations such as an inability to compare the condition of cultivators in areas

[1] Hansard, vol. 92, 479. [2] Ibid., 478–82.

[3] Parliamentary Papers, No. 511 (IX). *Reports from Committees. Growth of Cotton in India, 1847–48*, pp. iii–x.

[4] Silver, op. cit., p. 24.

[5] Hansard, vol. 112, 10. There is some doubt concerning the initiator of the idea for a Royal Commission. Professor Silver writes that the Manchester Chamber of Commerce 'accepted his [Bright's] lead'. (Silver, op. cit., p. 60.) However, a year later Henry Ashworth spoke of the Chamber as the body 'who had prompted Mr. Bright to bring forward his motion in parliament'. (*Manchester Examiner and Times*, 12 Feb. 1851, p. 3, col. f.)

of differing land assessments.[1] Success, however, did not attend Bright's efforts. In 1847 he had avoided direct criticism of the East India Company. Though professing to do likewise in 1850, he widened his attack so that a definite impression was created of a frontal assault on Company rule. *The Times* noticed this, and wrote, '...it is very evident...that the particular intervention prayed for by Mr. BRIGHT was *not* calculated to promote the ostensible object of the agitation. A Royal Commission might be represented as casting practical imputations on the Government of India'.[2] Perhaps for this very reason the Manchester Commercial Association, a more moderate body than the Chamber, refused to support him for fear that it might upset 'existing operations'. When Sir J. C. Hobhouse revealed this fact to the House,[3] Bright was considerably embarrassed because it made his role as Manchester's spokesman seem rather presumptuous.[4]

The transition in Bright's thinking to the realization that Company rule was the real obstacle to increased production of Indian cotton was fully made by 1851. In that year he attacked for the first time the lack of responsibility of the Indian government to Parliament.[5] By 1853 it was his solemn purpose '*to overthrow the East India Compy*, & to establish a Govt. here responsible to Parlt. & to public opinion'.[6] When in 1853 the charter of the Company was renewed along the lines desired by the Aberdeen government, he continued to attack what he regarded as the anomalies and shortcomings of the double government.[7]

[1] Hansard, vol. 112, 28.

[2] *The Times*, 28 June 1850, p. 5, col. c.

[3] Hansard, vol. 112, 47–8.

[4] Two theses demonstrate that Bright was never so well entrenched in Manchester as is often considered: J. A. Williams, *Manchester and the Manchester School 1830–57*, M.A. Leeds, 1966; J. Skinner, *John Bright and the Representation of Manchester in the House of Commons 1847–57*, M.A. Wales, 1965. See also: N. McCord, 'Cobden and Bright in Politics, 1846–1857', *Ideas and Institutions of Victorian Britain*, ed. R. Robson, pp. 99–101. While the degree of opposition to Bright may be somewhat exaggerated, the stubborn defiance of the Whig grandees, resentful of the oligarchic propensities of Newall's Buildings (the headquarters of the League), is well illustrated. The *Manchester Guardian* became the organ of these dissidents.

[5] Hansard, vol. 115, 1002.

[6] Sturge Papers, Add. MSS. 43,723. Bright to J. Sturge, 27 March, 1853, f. 14. (Bright's emphasis.)

[7] Hansard, vol. 139, 1988–99.

How did Bright view the Indian situation? He started with the assumption that India was potentially a wealthy country,[1] and that it could grow more cotton to supply British needs. That India was not wealthy and was not producing the amount of cotton he believed it should, he blamed on the system of Indian government.[2] He thought the root of administrative difficulty was the double government by the East India Company and the Board of Control. He considered the neglect of transportation facilities and the uncoordinated actions of the Board of Control and the Court of Directors had effectively curtailed the economic development of India, especially in respect of the cultivation of cotton. He alleged that the only interest the Court of Directors had in India was their patronage; the Court of Proprietors had less interest in India than a group of share-holders in a joint stock company, because their dividends did not even depend on the proper management of affairs.[3] The most damaging feature of the double government was its irresponsibility. Bright claimed that the Court of Proprietors had no control over the Court of Directors, and this body exercised no effectual check on the activities of the Secret Committee, which lay helpless at the feet of the President of the Board of Control. The press could do nothing, and Parliament was 'deluded and baffled' whenever it attempted to check anything in regard to India.[4] He further claimed that the double government provided a screen behind which the absolute authority of the President of the Board of Control could be exercised.[5] Thus, as he said, '...this question of divided responsibility, of concealed responsibility, and of no responsibility whatever; that was the real pith of the matter'.[6] *The Times* commented, 'it is notorious that Indian people have made a standing joke of Mr. BRIGHT and his attempt to thread the labyrinth of Indian government and get at its secrets'.[7]

[1] This sentiment pervades many of Bright's speeches. One reference is afforded in Hansard, vol. 152, 1367.

[2] Ibid., vol. 112, 18.

[3] Ibid., vol 115, 1000.

[4] Ibid., vol. 128, 883.

[5] Ibid., vol. 115, 999. In his diary Sir J. C. Hobhouse referred to 'The Secret Committee c'est moi.' (Diary of Lord Broughton, Add. MSS. 43, 753, 21 Dec. 1848, f. 70).

[6] Hansard, vol. 127, 1176.

[7] *The Times*, 24 March 1853, p. 4, col. c.

Bright's plan to remedy the situation was to establish an Indian Secretary of State with a permanent council of five men who would be responsible to Parliament.[1] During the committee stage of the Government of India Bill in 1853, he spoke in favour of a council of seven members chosen from among able men who would have the power to record their disagreements with the Board of Control.[2] Though specific recommendations might vary, the *sine qua non* of Indian reform was to democratize the entire Indian governmental apparatus. Public opinion must be allowed to exert its influence in this area, as in domestic matters. India should not be a private preserve, but a public concern. This stood in stark contrast to Sir Charles Wood's earnest hope, as President of the Board of Control, that in Indian matters M.P.s would not be diverted by any appeal to popular opinion.[3]

When attempts to eradicate the double government failed, Bright tried to modify, during the committee stage of the India Bill, what he considered its worst features. He preferred to see the Directors chosen for a long period and ineligible for re-election, as this would increase their independence.[4] He approved of the idea that six of the Directors were in future to be nominated by the Crown, but wondered why the government should mingle these six good appointments with twelve directors to be chosen by the Court of Proprietors.[5] He objected to the fact that members of the Court of Directors would be eligible to sit in Parliament, because this would render them less effective in both bodies.[6] When Sir Charles Wood proposed to raise the salaries of Directors to £1000 a year, Bright dissented because he felt they did not perform duties commensurate with such salaries.[7] He charged that it was widely known that East Indian appointments were bought and sold, and urged the removal of patronage from the control of the Court of Directors.[8]

[1] Sturge Papers, Add. MSS. 43,723. Bright to J. Sturge, 27 March 1853, f. 15.

[2] Hansard, vol. 128, 1460–1.

[3] Ibid., 1022.

[4] Ibid., vol. 129, 78. The term of office for Directors was four years. See A. B. Keith, *A Constitutional History of India 1600–1935*, p. 71.

[5] Hansard, vol. 127, 1191.

[6] Ibid., vol. 129, 314–15.

[7] Ibid., 1038.

[8] Ibid., 578–9.

Bright treated with scorn the inefficiency of having two administrative offices—the Court of Directors (Leadenhall Street) and the Board of Control (Cannon Row)—so widely separated in London. He proposed a new building in Downing Street to accommodate both agencies.[1] Sir Erskine Perry[2] had suggested this to Bright as an indirect mode of establishing the undivided form of government which they thought preferable.[3] *The Times* considered it an excellent suggestion,[4] but the government, perhaps fearing that this would give some symbolic reflection of unity, rejected the measure

Generally, Bright thought that there were two chief complaints against the Indian system of government. The unsatisfactory condition of the people was one.[5] The other was the generally impecunious state of Indian finances. He thought that: 'In India, probably more than any other country, the question of finance lay at the foundation of all prosperity and progress, and the House might rely upon it that if they were wrong with regard to Indian finance they would be wrong with regard to almost every other question that affected India.'[6] He thought the poor financial condition was partly explained by the expenditure connected with the Indian wars. He felt that high military costs prevented the adoption of desirable reforms such as the abolition of the salt tax.[7]

Faced with high expenditure, the Indian government could hardly expect to raise more money because, as Bright pointed out, the tax collectors in many areas were already too rapacious.[8] He alleged that in certain areas such as Gujarat taxation amounted to from 60 to 90 per cent of the gross product of the soil, and this took place in a country with no mechanical contrivances.[9] In addition, he complained of the tardy method of the East India Company in presenting its accounts.[10]

[1] Ibid., 818–20.

[2] PERRY, SIR THOMAS ERSKINE (1806–82). Became a lawyer; lost fortune in 1840; appointed judge of supreme court in Bombay; knighted in 1841; became Chief Justice in 1847; exceedingly popular with Indians; retired in 1852; M.P. Devonport, 1854; appointed member of Council of India in August 1859.

[3] Bright Papers, Add. MSS. 43,389. Perry to Bright, 6 June 1853, f. 44.

[4] *The Times*, 27 July 1853, p. 5, col. b.

[5] Hansard, vol. 112, 16.

[6] Ibid., vol. 139, 1989.

[7] Ibid., 1996–7.

[8] Ibid., vol. 112, 23–6.

[9] Ibid., vol. 127, 1189.

[10] Ibid., vol. 132, 784–5.

Bright's solution would involve either a much reduced assessment system on land or the institution of the open market system, whereby rents in India would find their proper level.[1] If the condition of the cultivator were improved by such a measure, then perhaps British financiers would be more willing to invest their money. To reduce military expenditure Bright would have liked to make it a rule that any Governor-General who did not add any territory to British India would be greatly honoured.[2] In addition, he wanted the financial accounts to be presented so that Members could check the preceding year's expenditure.[3] Finally, he thought that a country like India with £30,000,000 of revenue and £50,000,000 of debt (in 1855) should have its own Chancellor of the Exchequer who would be responsible for finances.[4]

Bright received some satisfaction in 1855 when the House adopted two of his resolutions. One provided that a complete statement of finances, with an estimate for the current year, should be drawn up and completed to the thirtieth of April of the preceding year. The other demanded that these statements be presented to the House early in the session so that they could receive the attention which their importance deserved.[5]

Bright's desire for financial reform was closely allied with his concern for the condition of Indians, and their attitude to British rule. It was his hope that '... the idea—which he [Bright] believed prevailed very extensively—that we held India more with the object of extorting taxation than of benefiting the people, would speedily be removed'.[6] He wished to see the wider employment of Indians in the civil service, and argued that the 1853 Act would not improve their chances, since the covenanted service was to be retained. He believed that the Company had never shown any inclination towards making Indians fit for service, and, indeed, he supplied evidence to the effect that they had even prevented the establishment of a university at Calcutta.[7] He warned that he would hate to be a

[1] Hansard, vol. 112, 23–4.
[2] Ibid., vol. 127, 1190–1.
[3] Ibid., vol. 132, 784–5.
[4] Ibid., vol. 139, 1995.
[5] Ibid., 2014.
[6] Ibid., vol. 127, 1189.
[7] Ibid., 1171, 1184–5.

party to a treatment of the Indians which might lead them to insurrection.[1]

Bright wished to see an equality not only of opportunity but also of treatment for Indians. He pointed out that Indian judges did twice as much work as the British judges, for one-seventh the salary. He thought that the districts of collectors and magistrates were much too large, and suggested that they should be halved, with the additional places created going to Indians.[2]

Of course, such alleged practices as torture were an abhorrence to Bright. When Danby Seymour[3] went to India and returned in 1854 with the claim that Indians were on occasion tortured to extract taxes, Bright declared that he believed Seymour's accusations were true.[4] He went on to say: 'It was perfectly natural that the hon. Baronet [Sir J. Hogg] should censure the hon. member for Poole for stating unpalatable truths. It was a part of the system of the Government to which the hon. Baronet belonged to suppress all such impertinent exposures by dogmatic assertion and arrogant abuse.'[5] In 1855, reinforced with the report of the Torture Commission, Bright scathingly criticized[6] Sir J. W. Hogg (M.P. for Honiton) and R. Mangles (M.P. for Guildford), the latter of whom a year previously had denied the existence of torture.[7]

Bright's readiness to befriend the cause of Indians and to set up punctilious standards of behaviour towards them was well illustrated by an occurrence in 1851. At that time, he met Rungor Bapojee, the Vakeel of the late Raja of Sattara, who complained of the treatment of the Raja's family. Immediately Bright went to see Lord Broughton (President of the Board of Control) and, as he said, 'urged that generosity would make more friends than cruelty'.[8]

His support of extensive public works arose both from his concern for the welfare of Indians and from a desire to increase facilities for the transportation of cotton. While realizing from

[1] Ibid., 1193.

[2] Ibid., vol. 129, 779,781.

[3] SEYMOUR, HENRY DANBY (1820–77). Educated at Eton and Oxford; M.P. for Poole, 1850–68; Joint Secretary to Board of Control, 1855–8.

[4] Hansard, vol. 135, 79–80.

[5] Ibid., 80.

[6] Ibid., vol. 139, 1997–8.

[7] Ibid., vol. 135, 66–9, 88.

[8] Walling, p. 126.

the example of Ireland that relatively good roads did not ensure prosperity, he cited authorities who thought that costs were raised as much as 200 per cent by lack of proper transportation facilities.[1] He felt it was impossible to estimate the wealth that could be unlocked by extended irrigation. During one debate he charged that Manchester, with a population of 400,000, had spent more on public works between 1834 and 1848 than had the Company for the whole of India.[2] The one road of which he felt the Company was so proud, from Calcutta to Benares, was, in Bright's opinion, built for military purposes.[3]

Although Bright foresaw that one way of extending public works was for European capitalists to invest in Indian projects, he believed the primary impetus would have to come from the government. Then, 'if the Indian government would endeavour to improve the condition of the people by attending to economic principles, by establishing better means of communication, by promoting irrigation, and by affording facilities for education, the Indian population would...be convinced that there was a feeling of sympathy entertained towards them'.[4] At Manchester he presented a resolution which condemned the government for not spending an adequate portion of the revenues on internal improvements in India.[5] At a meeting of the Manchester Chamber of Commerce he was asked to support a resolution to be presented by T. Milner Gibson[6] that at least 10 per cent of the revenue should be allocated to public works.[7]

The state of the Indian judiciary and education system was also unsatisfactory to Bright. He said he was sure that Indians and British alike were forced to constant perjury by the corruption of the Company courts.[8] This was one of the reasons why so few Europeans willing to invest capital lived in the interior

[1] Hansard, vol. 112, 21–3.
[2] Ibid., vol. 125, 45.
[3] Ibid., vol. 128, 877.
[4] Ibid., vol. 127, 1188–9.
[5] *Manchester Examiner and Times*, 22 June 1853, p. 6, col. f.
[6] GIBSON, THOMAS MILNER (1806–84). Elected to Parliament in 1837 as a Conservative; resigned in 1839 and became a liberal; entered struggle to repeal corn laws; became M.P. for Manchester in 1841; defeated in 1857; re-elected for Ashton-under-Lyne in December 1857; president of the Board of Trade from July 1859, to July 1866; retired from politics in 1868.
[7] *Manchester Examiner and Times*, 23 March 1853, p. 5, cols. e–f.
[8] Hansard, vol. 128, 877.

of India.[1] His only contribution to improvement was a suggestion in the House in 1853 that the laws should be consolidated.[2] As for education, he thought that the Company had overthrown vernacular education and in its stead spent only £66,000 on European education. He thought the Company had failed in its duty to educate the Indians[3] so that they could hope to raise their status.

III

What support did Bright receive in this campaign? One of his strongest supporters in the earliest years of his concern with India was the Manchester Chamber of Commerce, although this liaison became of less importance as 1857 approached. The common bond of interest was the desire to develop India as a cotton growing area. When Bright's request to Parliament in 1850 for a Royal Commission was refused, he and Thomas Bazley,[4] President of the Manchester Chamber of Commerce, set about organizing a fund to finance an individual commissioner to tour India.[5] Alexander Mackay, a barrister-at-law, contracted to go to India, but unfortunately he died there, though not before his reports were sufficient to be edited into a volume called *Western India*.[6]

In 1853, when the efforts of Bright were directed towards the abolition of the East India Company, he received some valuable aid from the Manchester Chamber of Commerce; several meetings were called and petitions drawn up.[7] He himself introduced a deputation to Sir Charles Wood in April 1853, from the mercantile associations of Manchester and Liverpool.[8] But even by this time (1853) Bright was beginning to be critical of the attitude adopted by the Chamber. In its annual report

[1] Ibid., vol. 127, 1181–2.
[2] Ibid., vol. 128, 1436–8.
[3] Ibid., vol. 127, 1185–6.
[4] BAZLEY, SIR THOMAS (1797–1885). Became manager of cotton mills in Manchester; one of the founders of the Anti-Corn Law League; chairman of Manchester Chamber of Commerce from 1845 to 1859; M.P. for Manchester, 1858–80; baronet in 1869.
[5] Bright Papers, Add. MSS. 43,383. Bright to Cobden, 12 Oct. 1850, ff. 201–2.
[6] A. Mackay, *Western India*, ed. J. Robertson.
[7] *Manchester Examiner and Times*, 23 March 1853, p. 5, cols. e–f; p. 8, cols. a–e.
[8] Ibid., 20 April 1853, p. 8, cols. a–b.

of activities and policies for the year 1853 it had affirmed its intention not to interfere with the political form of the government of India.[1] Bright criticized its willingness to view India as an economic rather than a political problem.[2] He also thought that the reliance of the Chamber on deputations to the President of the Board of Control was less than useless.[3]

As greater points of difference arose between Bright and the Chamber, he began to place more and more reliance on a body formed in London early in 1853. This was the India Reform Society, which held its first meeting on 12 March 1853. The founders of the society were Danby Seymour and J. F. B. Blackett (M.P. for Newcastle upon Tyne), who had noticed the writings of John Dickinson[4] on India and had conceived with him the idea of a reform committee.[5] But by Dickinson's own admission, it was Bright who 'was the backbone of our Committee, and he brought with him into our ranks about thirty M.P.s'.[6] The first meeting, which was chaired by Seymour assisted by Dickinson as honorary secretary, attracted twelve M.P.s.[7]

At this first meeting the committee drew up a five-point programme which included the assertion that the character of alterations in the East India Company's Charter Act, which was to terminate on 30 April 1854, was a question which demanded serious consideration. It protested against the late appointment of committees of both Houses which were to investigate the nature and results of Indian administration. It also protested that the inquiry then being carried on by these committees would be unsatisfactory unless reference were made to the petitions and wishes of educated Indians. In addition the committee felt that it was their duty to insist upon a temporary act so that time would be given for a full deliberation

[1] *Manchester Examiner and Times*, 16 February 1853, p. 3, col. c.

[2] Ibid., 23 March 1853, p. 8, col. e. [3] Ibid., 22 June 1853, p. 6, col. e.

[4] DICKINSON, JOHN (1815–76). Son of wealthy paper manufacturer; spent much time on continent in support of various liberal parties; his uncle, General Thomas Dickinson, an engineer in India, directed him towards Indian reform; wrote series of letters in *The Times* in 1850 and 1851 on cotton production in India; published numerous pamphlets including (1) 'India, its Government under Bureaucracy' (London 1852), and (2) 'Dhar not restored' (1864).

[5] Bell, p. 14. [6] B.M. 08023, aa 14 (8), *Speech of Mr. Dickinson*, p. 8.

[7] *Daily News*, 15 March 1853, p. 1, col. c.

on the permanent administration of the Indian Empire.[1]

The formation of the Society was largely unnoticed by the daily press, unless the notice of a meeting were advertised in a particular paper. The weekly *Nonconformist* welcomed the 'association of influential gentlemen'.[2] The *Spectator* thought the association had 'an exclusive if not personal look about it'.[3] In May *The Times* reported one of the India Reform meetings. One point that stands clear from this account is the readiness of the Society to work in conjunction with and in support of Indians. Letters written by Indians of Bombay and Madras were read, though nothing of their contents was revealed in *The Times* report. The Society had received a letter from a prominent lawyer saying that conditions of justice were equally as bad in Bombay as in southern India.[4]

The first headquarters of the Society were in Charing Cross Road,[5] but they were soon changed to 12, Haymarket.[6] Membership cost one guinea, which would entitle the holder to a list of Society publications.[7] The chief financial help was to come from India, and by May a considerable amount had been contributed by Indians to the Society.[8] Bright approached H. Ashworth and T. Bazley and at a 'trade and commerce' meeting in Manchester commended the Society to the city's financial help through subscriptions.[9]

From its opening meeting of twenty-two members and twelve M.P.s, the Society soon expanded. An advertisement in the *Daily News* on 17 March showed an increase of four M.P.s.[10] Before the end of March, Bright estimated thirty such public men belonged to the Society,[11] while later in May, H. A. Bruce calculated that the number had risen to forty.[12] One advertisement of the Society that probably shows the membership at its

[1] Ibid.

[2] *Nonconformist*, 16 March 1853, p. 219. [3] *Spectator*, 26 March 1853, p. 294.

[4] *The Times*, 10 May 1853, p. 4, col. d.

[5] *Daily News*, 15 March 1853, p. 1, col. c.

[6] Ibid., 17 March 1853, p. 1, col. d.

[7] *Nonconformist*, 6 April 1853, p. 1, col. a.

[8] *The Times*, 10 May 1853, p. 4, col. d.

[9] *Manchester Examiner and Times*, 22 June 1853, p. 6, col. f.

[10] *Daily News*, 17 March 1853, p. 1, col. d.

[11] *Manchester Examiner and Times*, 23 March 1853, p. 8, col. e.

[12] *Letters of the Rt. Hon. Henry Austin Bruce*, i, 122.

apogee listed thirty-nine M.P.s.[1] Included in this list were Viscount Goderich (later Lord Ripon), T. Milner Gibson and E. Miall.[2] There was a strong representation of Irish, including T. Kennedy (M.P. for Louth), G. H. Moore (M.P. for Mayo Co.) and F. Lucas (M.P. for Meath).

The India Reform Society served a number of purposes. Primarily it provided an information centre for M.P.s. It was also a propaganda agency whose meetings and pamphlets, it was hoped, would stimulate interest in India. It provided an organization in London with whom associations of Indians or Britons in India could correspond. Dickinson became a correspondent with many people, both Indian and British, in every part of India. His biographer makes the claim that 'hardly any Indian nobleman or gentleman who has risen to distinction in any capacity...within the last twenty years [1877] has not at some time been on the file of Mr. Dickinson' correspondents'.[3] Finally the Society served as a crucible for the formulation of concepts and ideas regarding the government of India.

One development in 1855 shows this capacity of the Society; it also demonstrates why Bright began to rely more on the Society than on the Manchester Chamber of Commerce for practical help. Because of his association with both bodies,[4] Bright had perceived the possibility of combining the potential capital of the Chamber with the contacts and ideas of the Society. After consulting several times in 1854 with Colonel A. Cotton,[5] an eminent engineer who had spent thirty years in

[1] India Office Library, India Reform Public Works, Tr. 565, No. 8, preface. For a full list of members see Appendix I.

[2] MIALL, EDWARD (1809–81). Minister of an Independent Congregation, 1831; started weekly, *Nonconformist*, 1841; opposed established church from editor's chair; attempted to bring Chartists and Anti-Corn Law League into closer harmony; M.P. for Rochdale, 1852–7; M.P. for Bedford, 1868–74.

[3] Bell, p. 21.

[4] In 1855 Bright said he considered himself to be an *ex officio* member of the Chamber. (*Manchester Examiner and Times*, 10 Feb. 1855, p. 11, col. c.)

[5] COTTON, SIR ARTHUR THOMAS (1803–99). Attended East India Company's military college at Addiscombe, obtained commission in Madras engineers in 1819; most famous irrigation projects concerned work on the Cavery and Caleroon rivers, the Godavery, and the Krishna rivers; knighted in 1861; retired from government service in 1862; retained active interest in India, especially irrigation and cheap water communication.

India, he became fired with Cotton's idea of opening up the Godavery river to navigation. In the *Indian News* of 17 January 1855, appeared a letter from Col. Cotton to Bright giving his opinion of the scheme. He thought that such a plan could succeed, and listed the advantages that would result. The export of cotton from Madras would be greatly increased; so also would the imports of British manufactured goods, particularly Lancashire products. It would provide an example of capitalists working without government aid for the advantage of both India and Britain.[1]

After informing Sir Charles Wood of his intentions, Bright made plans to bring his case before the Manchester cotton spinners. Bright had elicited a promise from Wood that as long as their plan was practicable and they asked for no government guarantees, he would support any plan devised by Manchester. Thus on 18 January, Bright, with Dickinson, Seymour and Milner Gibson, went to Manchester to meet Bazley and his associates. Col. Cotton was there with Captain Fenwick, the only man to have navigated the Godavery in its entirety. So prepared was Bright that another engineer in favour of the project, Bourne of Glasgow, had constructed a model steamboat and other accessories to show how Cotton's plans could be developed. After Cotton had expounded the facts in the mayor's office, the meeting was thrown open to questions. Bright himself asked questions that clarified certain points on harbour facilities and fuelling capabilities. He then suggested that a committee should be formed of Bazley, H. Ashworth, J. A. Turner (elected M.P. for Manchester in 1857) and several others which would report on the advisability of setting up a joint stock company with £100,000 capital: eventually £250,000 would be needed.[2]

The reaction of the India Reform Society was hopeful.[3] Bright followed up his request by addressing the Manchester Chamber in February 1855, again giving his approval of the Godavery plans. He thought investors would receive a worthy margin of profit as well as the satisfaction of having done

[1] *Indian News*, 17 Jan. 1855, pp. 14–15.
[2] *Manchester Daily Times*, 19 Jan. 1855, pp. 2–3.
[3] Bell, p. 19.

something for India.[1] But much to the disappointment of the Society, the Manchester Chamber did not endorse the Godavery plans. Dickinson attributed the failure to the fact that the Manchester men looked upon the supply of American cotton as too reliable and satisfactory to gamble on developing the cotton fields in India.[2] Manchester cotton interests, it seemed, could only be stirred to action by a crisis. 'Spending money to get cheap cotton seemed self-defeating.'[3] From the point of view of the Society, the only satisfying element of the episode was the continuing collaboration of Captain Fenwick. He went back to India and entered the service of the Maharaja Holkar, Prince of Indore. His letters to Dickinson were 'habitually communicated' to Bright.[4]

The short-term effects of the Society—that is, its influence on the India Bill of 1853—were not fruitful. However, it may have altered the tactics of the government. It was the opinion of H. A. Bruce that the 'firm tone of our Society' caused the government at least to consider its position carefully before proceeding to legislate without the committee of the House of Commons having completed its work. Eventually, evidence was allowed as to the form of government, which Bruce thought would not have happened but for the Society.[5] Certainly it was the members of the Society such as J. F. B. Blackett and Bright who offered criticism of the government Bill. But even here their efforts were largely unavailing from the point of view of effect on immediate legislation.

Nevertheless, the efforts of Bright and other Indian reformers had put extreme pressure upon Sir Charles Wood, who felt it necessary to placate Radical opinion by promising to expedite the building of railways in India. Wood feared for the stability of Lord Aberdeen's coalition government, and pressed Lord Dalhousie in India to select appropriate public works schemes which might be financed out of the surplus funds.[6] Thus, as a result of Radical pressure, considerable capital was invested in India by the British government.

[1] *Manchester Examiner and Times*, 10 Feb. 1855, p. 11, col. c.

[2] Bell, p. 19.

[3] Bearce, op. cit., p. 224.

[4] Bell, p. 20.

[5] *Letters of the Rt. Hon. Henry Austin Bruce*, i, 122.

[6] Moore, op. cit., pp. 127–32.

An impression was created too in India. Indian newspapers, unless they were completely under the spell of the government, gave much more extensive coverage of the Society than did their British counterparts.[1] The Bombay Association, formed in 1852 by leading Indians, distributed Society tracts as well as collecting a sizeable donation to be sent to Britain.[2] Perhaps the most telling effect was created by the visit of Danby Seymour in 1853–4 which, because of various controversies surrounding his investigations, tended to polarize opinion between reformers and the upholders of the *status quo*.[3]

As 1857 approached, however, the vitality of the India Reform Society was sapped. There were two main reasons for this. One was the lack of funds. In 1855 they had taken over the publication of the *Indian News*, but it had to be relinquished for lack of money. Four hundred pounds would have kept it in operation. With Bright's approval, the Society's expenses were cut to a minimum, but even this cost friends, as people who might have lent their services for lectures or reports would not do so without fee. From India came much gratitude but few rupees. There were no yearly fees and few English subscribers.[4] The other cause was that many of the members looked upon the Society as an *ad hoc* association set up with the specific aim of influencing the 1853 bill.[5] Interest subsided when that bill was passed.

There were other reasons. Bright's accession to the chairmanship of the Society in April 1855,[6] although a credit to his reputation as an Indian reformer, did nothing to enhance the popularity of the Society because of his critical attitude to the Crimean War. This latter event in itself diverted attention from Indian subjects. Then, J. F. B. Blackett had died in 1856; Danby Seymour had to give up his connexion with the Society when he consented in 1855 to be one of Palmerston's Joint

[1] See *The Bombay Times, and Journal of Commerce*, 8 April 1853, 20 May 1853, etc.; *The Spectator* (Madras), 9 May, 1853, etc.

[2] *The Bombay Times, and Journal of Commerce*, 11 Nov. 1853.

[3] *The Spectator* (Madras), numerous articles in February and March 1854.

[4] Bell, pp. 23–5.

[5] This is quite evident from Bruce's description of the aims of the Society. (*Letters of the Rt. Hon. Henry Austin Bruce*, i, 122.)

[6] Bright Papers, U.C. Bright to his wife, 23 April 1855. Bell incorrectly stated that this occurred in 1856. (Bell, p. 21.)

Secretaries to the Board of Control. More and more of the work fell upon Dickinson, as the original thirty M.P.s whom Bright had enlisted became complaisant.[1]

When Bright needed personal assistance, it was Dickinson upon whom he chiefly relied. Cobden called Dickinson '...a single-minded devotee who labours like a galley-slave from the purest impulse of benevolence'.[2] In many cases it was Dickinson's knowledge and guidance upon which Bright depended in preparation for an Indian speech.[3] Another worthwhile ally was John Benjamin Smith (M.P. for Stockport). The son of a cotton merchant, Smith retained a hand in the business until 1836 when he retired to take a more active part in politics. Having been at one time the President of the Manchester Chamber of Commerce and Chairman of the Anti-Corn Law League, he had an interest in the development of Lancashire and free trade.[4] Cobden considered Smith to know more on the subject of cotton than any other M.P.[5] Before the India Reform Society was formed, Bright had had dinner with Smith several times,[6] and from such discussions ideas regarding the scope of the new organization must have emanated.

There were other men who supported Bright's Indian work. T. Milner Gibson, though he did not involve himself with the Manchester Chamber of Commerce as fully as did Bright, lent some valuable aid. In March 1853, Bright wrote: 'To-night I am to dine with J. B. Smith—after that to go with Gibson to St Albans Coffee-House—Haymarket—to see a few persons on Indian affairs. It is proposed to form a Com[tee] to promote Indian reform.'[7] Sir Erskine Perry was an admirer of Bright, and praised his speech of 3 June 1853, as the 'most powerful improvisation I have met with in our times'.[8] Perry played a very important role in the parliamentary scene from 1854 to

[1] Bell, pp. 21–4.

[2] J. A. Hobson, *Richard Cobden*, p. 102.

[3] In 1855 Bright wrote: '...Dickinson came in to help me to prepare a speech... on the Indian budget.' (Bright Papers, U.C. Bright to his wife, 4 Aug. 1855.) See also letters of 29 April 1858; 6 June 1858.

[4] There is a short biographical sketch of Smith in: Joseph Thompson, *The Owens College: its Foundation and Growth*, pp. 101–12.

[5] Smith Papers, M.S. 923.2. S.345 (57). Cobden to J. B. Smith, 19 May 1857.

[6] Bright Papers, U.C. Bright to his wife, 9 and 10 March 1853.

[7] Ibid., 9 March 1853.

[8] Bright Papers, Add. MSS. 43,389. Perry to Bright, 6 June 1853, f. 43.

1857, adding a great deal of lustre to the Radical cause. He associated himself with the India Reform Society,[1] but regretted Bright's absence from Parliament in 1856 because his presence was needed 'to head the movement'.[2]

In Lord Aberdeen's cabinet there was one man who agreed with Bright's Indian policies. This was Sir William Molesworth,[3] first Commissioner of Works, who, after he had heard Bright's explanation of his views, assured him that they coincided with his own, and that he would convey them to the cabinet.[4] Bright in 1853 had also tried to influence Lord John Russell, but with less success. Bright wrote: 'Walked with him [Russell] thro' Westminster Hall, speaking on India, and advising him not to go wrong by hasty legislation, but he did not say anything decisive.'[5]

Since both the Indian Reformers and the Tories were opposed to Wood's India Bill, there arose the opportunity for co-operation between them. After arranging to meet with Disraeli,[6] Bright learned that Lord Stanley (the eldest son of Lord Derby, the Conservative leader) might introduce resolutions against proceeding with the Bill.[7] Rather ineffectual opposition was eventually extended, but to no avail. The Radical–Tory alliance was hampered by Lord Derby's influence. He surmised that many of the rank and file of the party were convinced that there were too many good Tories in the East India Company to justify an attack.[8] But the Radicals too were not united. Some maintained their allegiance to the Whigs. The episode caused the *Manchester Examiner and Times* to remark upon the curious split in the free trade party.[9] But actually this 'split' was quite easily explained by the fact

[1] Bell, p. 23.

[2] Bright Papers, Add. MSS. 43,389. Perry to Bright, 7 April 1856, f. 69.

[3] MOLESWORTH, SIR WILLIAM (1810–55). Career at Cambridge ended by duel with tutor; travelled widely before becoming M.P. in 1832; was a Utilitarian; his special interest was colonial policy; favoured policies of Edward Gibbon Wakefield; supported colonial self-government; Colonial Secretary in 1855.

[4] Walling, p. 140.

[5] Ibid., p. 139.

[6] Bright Papers, Add. MSS. 43,389. Disraeli to Bright, 5 June 1853, f. 42.

[7] Walling, pp. 146–7.

[8] W. D. Jones, *Lord Derby and Victorian Conservatism*, pp. 194–5.

[9] *Manchester Examiner and Times*, 9 July 1853, Supplement, p. 1, col. a.

that twenty-four members of the India Reform Society sided with the Tories.[1]

Bright received help for Indian reform from some anti-slavery agitators in Britain. He would not associate with any movement of this kind except in so far as its members would attempt to end slavery by the use of free-labour cotton from India.[2] He explained his views to J. Sturge: 'Further, I am not quite prepared to join in proceedings in this country with regard to a great evil existing in another country, out of which may grow political hostilities leading to great mischiefs.'[3] When Bright referred in a speech to 'over-zealous people' trying to interfere with the United States,[4] the *Anti-Slavery Advocate* severely criticized his attitude.[5] But he did get support from George Thompson,[6] who headed an organization known as the 'North of England Anti-Slavery and India Reform League'. One of its supporters concluded: 'Now, *we can destroy this monopoly* [the U.S. cotton monopoly], *simply by doing justice to India*;— a momentous truth, to which the mission of Mr. Mackay shews that you are already generally alive in Manchester.'[7] Bright himself commended their efforts and the tone of the resolutions which were to be submitted to the Conference.[8]

What support did Bright get from the press? The attitude of *The Times* as the most influential paper was important. In 1847 it approved of Bright's inquiry by select committee.[9] In 1850, commenting on Bright's request for a Royal Commission, it agreed with him that India could be expected to supply a large portion of the cotton for Manchester, but added that it

[1] Hansard, vol. 128, 1074–7.

[2] *Manchester Examiner and Times*, 22 June 1853, p. 6, col. d.

[3] Sturge Papers, Add. MSS. 43,723. Bright to J. Sturge, 18 April 1853, f. 18.

[4] *Manchester Examiner and Times*, 8 Jan. 1853, p. 5, col. e.

[5] *Anti-Slavery Advocate*, Feb. 1853, p. 36, col. b.

[6] THOMPSON, GEORGE (1804–78). Widely known as advocate of abolition of slavery in British colonies and throughout the world; member of Anti-Corn Law League; member of British India Society; M.P. for Tower Hamlets 1847–52.

[7] *Manchester Examiner and Times*, 2 Aug. 1854, p. 9, col. a.

[8] The resolutions acclaimed the use of free-labour cotton. (*Manchester Examiner and Times*, 5 Aug. 1854, p. 11, col. e.) The advantages of free-labour produce were also the prime motives for Joseph Sturge's wish to help in the Indian question. (Bright Papers, Add. MSS. 43,383. Bright to Cobden, 28 Nov. 1853, f. 285.)

[9] *The Times*, 12 May 1847, p. 4, cols. d–e.

was only proper that Manchester should by its capital and enterprise do more for itself than it was doing.[1] In 1853, after initially coming out on 1 March in favour of the double government of India,[2] it switched opinion, and within a fortnight condemned the results of the double government.[3] From this vantage point it was able to support Bright's view. In March it wrote, 'What can be more forcible or more just than Mr. BRIGHT's account of our existing apparatus for the misgovernment of India?'[4] Though suspicious of Bright for what they regarded as his 'vested interest'[5] in India and afraid that, if the India bill passed as the Whigs wished it, India, 'like the Corn Laws, will be a standing dish in the seasonal bill of fare, and Mr. BRIGHT will be made the greatest man of his day',[6] it could not help but feel that Bright had 'ably exposed' the existing government.[7] When the second reading passed, *The Times* expressed an oblique hope that much of it would be changed in committee,[8] and regretted that more of Bright's changes had not been taken up in this stage of the Bill.[9] *The Times* even gave support to Bright's views on cotton. It wrote, 'The defence in the matter of cotton is a retort on the Manchester people, as if it rested with them.'[10] Even with *The Times* and Bright in accord, not so much was achieved as might have been expected from such a combination.

In Manchester Bright had the support of the *Manchester Examiner and Times*. It was edited by Alexander Ireland[11] and appealed to business interests Bright occasionally wrote for the paper,[12] and gave Ireland advice on affairs.[13] In 1853 it emphasized the need to deliver the Indian people from war

[1] Ibid., 20 June 1850, p. 5, cols. b–c.
[2] Ibid., 1 March 1853, p. 5, col. a.
[3] Ibid., 10 March 1853, p. 5, cols. a–b; 14 March 1853, p. 4, cols. b–c; see also 25 March 1853, p. 4, cols. b–c.
[4] Ibid., 24 March 1853, p. 4, cols. b–c.
[5] Ibid., col. b.
[6] Ibid., 10 June 1853, p. 4, col. e.
[7] Ibid., 29 June 1853, p. 4, col. d.
[8] Ibid., 2 July 1853, p. 4, cols. e–f.
[9] Ibid., 13 July 1853, p. 5, col. e.
[10] Ibid., 7 June 1853, p. 4, col. e.
[11] IRELAND, ALEXANDER (1810–94). Journalist and man of letters; became publisher and business manager of the *Manchester Examiner* (shortly to be the *Manchester Examiner and Times*) in 1846; paper set up as organ of the independent liberals; Ireland was friendly with Carlyle and Leigh Hunt.
[12] Walling, pp. 113–14.
[13] B.M. Add MSS. 44,877. Bright to Ireland, 22 Sept. 1850, f. 142.

and famine, as well as the need for social and moral improvement.[1] In June the paper called for mercantile support for Bright's arguments.[2] Although it is quite possible that a meeting was at that point already projected, a group of merchants did congregate within a fortnight, with Bazley in the chair and Bright as one of the speakers.[3] The attitude of the paper on India was that: 'Manchester has taken the lead, and she must keep it. This question of the future government of British India is her question.'[4] For this purpose—giving leadership to Manchester opinion—the paper was invaluable, but, of course, its influence extended little beyond the confines of Lancashire.

Some help came from other sources. Bright and Cobden partially remedied the lack of a London paper which expressed their views on matters of foreign, domestic and imperial policy by having a hand in the policy-making of the *Morning Star*, set up in 1856.[5] Perhaps because of Miall's connexion with the *Nonconformist*, that paper gave its support to the cause of Indian reform. It commended the work of Bright and his associates: 'The Indian reformers, or, as they are nicknamed, the "Young Indians", fought to the last with great gallantry, but with no very considerable present success.'[6]

IV

An evaluation of Bright's motives in regard to India is a difficult task. Professor Briggs comments that Bright lacks the 'attractive simplicity' of Abraham Lincoln 'because he was too enmeshed in the economic philosophy of the English manufacturing interest'.[7] Thus does the absence of a liberal consensus impose a different set of criteria. Granted, Bright could be faulted for some of his reasons for interest in India. In June 1853

[1] *Manchester Examiner and Times*, 20 April 1853, p. 4, cols. c–d.
[2] Ibid., 11 June 1853, p. 4, cols. d–e.
[3] Ibid., 22 June 1853, p. 6.
[4] Ibid., 18 June 1853, p. 4, col. d.
[5] J. Morley, *Life of Richard Cobden*, p. 637, n. 8.
[6] *Nonconformist*, 3 Aug. 1853, p. 619, col. a.
[7] Briggs, *Victorian People*, p. 210.

he continued to stress the point that Manchester's special interest in India was due to its potential as a source of cotton.[1] He even admitted on one occasion that he advocated employment of Indians because it would be cheaper.[2]

These examples to the contrary, however, it is apparent that by 1853, at least, Bright had begun to devote himself to Indian affairs because he felt the tremendous duty placed on Britain's shoulders when she took control of most of the country. This contention is borne out by the increase in cotton supplies in 1851. He wrote: 'I think however we are approaching more satisfactory times even in Cotton—for the supplies are promising better, & in America & even in India more land is being cultivated with cotton.'[3] Yet this prospect did not cause any slackening of interest in India. The transition from cotton lobbyist to Indian reformer was gradually taking place. In 1853 he said that he took an interest in India because 'the population was so great, the interests were so vast, and the wrong done so great, that he could not but feel the deepest interest in the subject.... He felt deeply the responsibility that pressed on us as the governors of so many millions of people, and he felt that responsibility increased by the cruelty, the rapine, and the guilt that had too often marked our career in the East'.[4]

What Bright regarded as the unsatisfactory condition of the people of India affected him in the same way as Ireland did. Comparing the two countries, he said, 'We have had bad government in Ireland; it had often been said, and with some show of truth, that India is about 20 Irelands put together.'[5] His concern for the proper treatment of all residents of India led him to support the idea of an equity tribunal to which claims could be brought.[6]

The annexations of territory in Asia led Bright to take a close interest in the subject. His Quaker views could not condone the actions taken, and at Manchester in 1853 he

[1] *Manchester Examiner and Times*, 22 June 1853, p. 6, col. d.
[2] Hansard, vol. 129, 781.
[3] Bright Papers, U.C. Bright to his wife, 12 April 1851.
[4] Hansard, vol. 139, 1998–9.
[5] *Manchester Examiner and Times*, 23 March 1853, p. 8, col. d.
[6] Hansard, vol. 129, 812–13.

declaimed: 'We have now thousands of men engaged in a war in India, in an attack on the Burmese empire, of which I will only say, that of all the atrocious and unjustifiable wars which have been carried on by this country in India, I believe that there is not one of a blacker character.'[1]

Bright was interested in India because he believed that through the efforts of its Members, Parliament could effect a change for the good of India. He took the view that, having conquered India, it was Britain's duty to govern her well. He also thought that Parliament's success in modifying colonial policy[2] was reason enough to believe that the House of Commons could effect changes if the double government were removed. He stated that: 'The population of India is helpless unless Parliament comes forward to its relief.'[3] India, he thought, '...should be governed in the manner most consistent with the true dignity of this country and with the true interests of India herself'.[4]

Bright contended that there were two ways of retaining India—either by the sword, or by doing justice to the people by providing a 'wise and judicious administration, which would convince the educated Natives of India, that although there was some humiliation in being governed by a foreign country, yet that under the circumstances in which India was placed, she derived enormous advantages from her connexion with this Empire, where Government was based upon experience, civilization, and justice'. He added a warning that with a free press and an increasing study of English in India, Members could not expect that enlightened Indians would not complain of being governed by a foreign power unless justice were done to their demands.[5]

Bright had thus disturbed the smooth surface of Indian politics. By playing his part in the India Reform Society, which brought into play the sentiments of the Indians themselves, and by stirring the lethargy of public and parliamentary opinion in Britain, he almost succeeded in dealing a death blow to the East India Company, and certainly helped to put

[1] *Manchester Examiner and Times*, 2 Feb. 1853, p. 6, col. c.

[2] Hansard, vol. 128, 887.

[3] Ibid., vol. 112, 33.

[4] Ibid., vol. 135, 81.

[5] Ibid., vol. 129, 781–2.

its continued existence after 1857 out of the question. He had formulated plans for responsible governmental control over Indian administration, and further developed the ideals, advanced by earlier thinkers and administrators, upon which that government should be based.

As a student of the Indian situation, he characteristically assumed his own pre-eminence. He claimed in the House in 1853 that no one out of office had paid more attention to the subject of Indian government than he had.[1] However, he was not confident about the possibility of achieving reform in India. He wrote: 'I am reading India [sic] history but the subject is almost too vast, & the chance of doing anything so small that I often fear I am but wasting my time.'[2] Unfortunately, as Bright widened the scope of his Indian activities, the greater was the likelihood of such melancholy reflection.

[1] Ibid., vol. 125, 48.
[2] Bright Papers, Add. MSS. 43,383. Bright to Cobden, 12 Oct. 1850, f. 202.

CHAPTER II

India 1857–1889

BRIGHT's first illness, which forced him to withdraw from politics in 1856 and 1857, 'marks not merely an interval but a natural division and fresh starting point in his life'.[1] Bright was regaining his health in Italy when he heard news of his defeat at Manchester in March 1857. This election, which saw not only Bright but Cobden and Milner Gibson go down to defeat, was a magnificent victory for Lord Palmerston, who had capitalized on the jingo spirit in Britain resulting from the Chinese war.

Cobden had made a pledge to stay out of politics for an undetermined time, but Milner Gibson and Bright soon found their way back to the House. Milner Gibson was re-elected for Ashton-under-Lyne. Bright received an invitation from Birmingham to represent that city on condition that he be willing to support the repression of the Indian mutiny which had broken out in May 1857. Bright's answer was an assurance that he would support repressive measures because it was 'mercy to India to suppress it'.[2]

Such was the unsettled state of parties at this time, with Tories, Peelites, Russell-Whigs and Radicals all manœuvring as distinct groups, that despite Lord Palmerston's overwhelming success in 1857, he suffered the humiliation of defeat in the House in 1858 on an amendment which criticized the ministry's handling of the Conspiracy to Murder Bill. Bright and Milner Gibson had the satisfaction of being the tellers in the division.

The result of Lord Palmerston's defeat was a return to the Derby–Disraeli team which retained control of the government until March 1859, when Disraeli's Reform Bill had the unintended effect of uniting the diverse opposition groups. In

[1] Trevelyan, *The Life of John Bright*, p. 254.

[2] Ibid., p. 261.

the election that followed, the Conservatives gained a few seats, but not enough to control the government if the Whigs and Radicals were to unite. In May 1858, more than 100 members of what were termed the 'Independent Liberals' had met together and determined to have their own whips and party.[1] But in June 1859, the Liberals and Whigs patched their differences and decided to co-operate. This decision was partly due to promises made by Russell to Bright regarding non-intervention in the Italian liberation struggles.[2] It also arose from the nature of the experiment of the 'Independent Liberal' party which the *Star* concluded had been unsatisfactory.[3] From this point Lord Palmerston was able to maintain control until his death in 1865.

Meanwhile in India a momentous event had been occurring. A group of mutinous soldiers escaped from Meerut on 10 May 1857, and went to Delhi where they incited the populace to rebel. The outbreak spread, but the British were fortunate in that only in Oudh did it enlarge into a total revolt. But in the North-Western provinces and some sections of central India, there was opposition enough to be menacing to British rule. By December 1857, the greatest danger had passed, but it was not until the following year that armed opposition was put down.[4]

The causes of the mutiny were varied. The most immediate was the sepoy belief that cartridges greased with the fat of cows or pigs were being used in offence to their religious beliefs.[5] However, there were deeper-lying causes. One was the annexation policy of Lord Dalhousie, which caused unrest especially in Oudh. The sense of social superiority entertained by British administrators did nothing to ingratiate them with the Indians. The absence of any Indians in the legislative council of the Governor-General meant that there was no adequate way of

[1] *Morning Star*, 8 May 1858, p. 3, col. b.

[2] Trevelyan, op. cit., p. 281.

[3] *Morning Star*, 24 May 1858, p. 2, cols. d–e.

[4] Though the outbreak at Meerut was likely planned, there is not sufficient evidence to conclude that there was collusion with soldiers at Delhi. (J. A. B. Palmer, *The Mutiny Outbreak at Meerut in 1857*, pp. 129–32.) R. C. Majumdar argues that the revolt of the sepoys was not a part of any general conspiracy. (R. C. Majumdar, *The Sepoy Mutiny and the Revolt of 1857*, p. 391.)

[5] M. Maclagan, *'Clemency' Canning*, pp. 70–4.

ascertaining Indian feeling. The sepoys were in a state of unrest because the officers would not consider any reforms.[1]

The mutiny so adversely affected the prestige of the Company that its continued existence was not feasible. Nonetheless the Company proceeded to petition Parliament in February 1858, for an Indian council that would provide the minister of the Crown responsible for India with qualified assistants who would act as 'a check and not a screen'.[2] This petition had some influence on subsequent legislation, especially in regard to the Indian council. However, the abolition of the Company was a virtual certainty as it became, in part, the scapegoat for the mutiny.[3] Bright commented in September 1857, that nearly all observers agreed that its expiry was imminent.[4]

Lord Palmerston was the first to attempt new legislation for the future government of India. In February 1858, he brought forward a bill whose aim was to transfer the government of India to the Crown. By this scheme the home administration was to be controlled by a president with the help of a council of eight persons nominated by the Crown. Eligibility to be a councillor would depend on whether one had been a Director in the Company or had spent enough time in India to qualify. The tenure of office was eight years.[5]

When Palmerston was defeated on the Conspiracy to Murder Bill, Lord Ellenborough, President of the Board of Control in the Derby government, dropped the Whig proposals and drew up a new bill. This measure was unwieldy because of its proposed provisions for entrance to the council. Some councillors were to be Crown nominees and others were to be elected by the inhabitants of cities that traded with India, such as Manchester, and by the holders of East India Company stock.[6] Councillors, who were to be eighteen in number, would have a term of six years and would not be eligible to sit in the House. Ellenborough also allowed for a 'secret committee' to be set up. When the Bill met with little but ridicule, Disraeli gladly

[1] T. R. Holmes, *The Cambridge History of India*, vi, 168–71.
[2] Sir H. Verney Lovett, *The Cambridge History of India*, vi, 206–7.
[3] Moore, *Sir Charles Wood's Indian Policy 1853–66*, p. 33.
[4] Bright Papers, Add. MSS. 43,384. Bright to Cobden, 19 Sept. 1857, f. 110.
[5] Ilbert, *The Government of India*, p. 94.
[6] Keith, *A Constitutional History of India 1600–1935*, p. 165.

accepted a proposal of Lord John Russell that the House should go into committee to discuss resolutions which Russell suggested should be drawn up by the government.[1] Ellenborough resigned shortly afterwards because of the publication of his despatch disapproving of Canning's proclamation declaring the British government's assumption of property rights in Oudh.[2]

Ellenborough's successor was Lord Stanley, who secured the assent of the House to resolutions which formed the basis for the eventual legislation. His Bill provided that a Secretary of State would take the place of the Board of Control and the Court of Directors. The Secretary would have a seat in the Cabinet and be individually responsible for the government of India. He would be assisted by a council of India consisting of fifteen men, eight of whom would be appointed by the Crown, while the other seven would be elected by the former Court of Directors. At least nine of these councillors had to have served in India for at least ten years. As the elected members died, they would be replaced by nominees of the council. Councillors could not sit in Parliament, and were to hold office 'on good behaviour'. They did not have the initiative of legislation as had the Court, but they could record their dissent if over-ruled by the Secretary of State. Their function was to exercise moral control over the Secretary of State, and their only effective check was over expenditure, proposals for which required majority consent. The Crown was to appoint the Governor-General and the Governors of the presidencies, while the Secretary of State appointed members of the councils in India. Each year there was to be a financial statement presented to Parliament for approval.[3]

II

Bright professed to be less surprised by the outbreak of the mutiny than other British observers. He had always suspected that the system of double government would lead to chaos.[4]

[1] Hansard, vol. 149, 860, 863–4. [2] Maclagan, op. cit., pp. 183–5, 201.
[3] Sir H. Verney Lovett, *The Cambridge History of India*, vi, 208–10.
[4] Layard Papers, Add. MSS. 38,985. Bright to Layard, 22 Aug. 1857, f. 291.

Though he was critical too of the means by which Britain had acquired control of India, he felt it was necessary in the interests of both Britain and India to suppress the revolt.[1] He did not think it was reasonable to expect that the government should stand idly by while hundreds of Englishmen were murdered.[2]

As far as Bright was concerned, the mutiny had created an entirely new situation where his previously self-professed knowledge of India[3] was now largely inapplicable.[4] This induced him to vow that he would advise nothing on the matter until February 1858.[5] He ended the written address to his electors with the words: 'I will say no more.'[6] His sense of the perplexities of the new situation, including the problems of finance and the hostility between the races, confounded his efforts to suggest a remedy. He was thankful that he was not able to step on the public platform, because, apart from pointing out the dangers, it would be impossible for him to know what to say.[7] When requested by Joseph Sturge to state his views on Indian government, he refused to do so.[8] He kept his pledge and uttered nothing in Parliament concerning India until March 1858. Until this time he offered no blueprint for Indian government that he wished to see implemented. He had, however, given certain indications in his letters about the development of his thoughts on the subject. In November 1857, he assumed that Palmerston would institute a minister for India with a council to aid him. But now he considered a council less desirable than he had thought previously,[9] because it would lessen the responsibility of the minister to Parliament.[10] His new opinion in regard to the Indian council led him to denounce Ellenborough's provisions for a council as 'clap-trap'. He told the House in March 1858, that a council of eight would give more responsibility to Parliament than a council of

[1] *The Times*, 10 Aug. 1857, p. 10, col. b.
[2] Sturge Papers, Add. MSS. 43,723. Bright to J. Sturge, 24 Sept. 1857, f. 85.
[3] *The Times*, 4 Dec. 1857, p. 10, col. b.
[4] Sturge Papers, Add. MSS. 43,845. Bright to J. Sturge, 19 Oct. 1857, f. 55.
[5] Layard Papers, Add. MSS. 38,985. Bright to Layard, 22 Aug. 1857, f. 290.
[6] *The Times*, 10 Aug. 1857, p. 10, col. b.
[7] Bright Papers, Add. MSS. 43,384. Bright to Cobden, 19 Sept. 1857, f. 110.
[8] Sturge Papers, Add. MSS. 43,845. Bright to J. Sturge, 19 Oct. 1857, f. 56.
[9] See p. 20.
[10] Bright Papers, Add. MSS. 43,384. Bright to Cobden, 24 Nov. 1857, f. 117.

eighteen. He himself would support the lowest figure proposed.[1] He thought, too, that some comprehensive act was needed to give the people ownership in the land and security in its possession. Besides legislation, the greatest need was to improve the treatment of Indians by British officials and residents.[2]

Though he was ready to assert his opinions early in 1858, he was not unaware of the great difficulties facing those who had the responsibility for drawing up a bill.[3] He was also cognisant of the problems in India that militated against future concord between British and Indians. One was the fact that a government system had to be built from a foundation of conquest that had been made worse by the mutiny.[4] Another difficulty was the size of the Indian empire. He felt that it had overextended itself and was too vast for management.[5] In addition, he thought the Indian question was so complex that it was almost too much for any one man to solve.[6] Later in 1858 he wrote: '...the whole Indian question is a swamp to which there seems neither bottom nor firm shore—England cannot govern distant nations—our statesmen have no time and no principles...How then can they direct the govt. of 20 nations in India? the thing is a dream. Nevertheless we may try to do something.'[7]

Accordingly, Bright did, on 24 June 1858, put forward his formula for the future government of India. He presented it during the second reading of the third India Bill. While he did not oppose the passing of the Bill, he thought there were many defects in it. Firstly, he thought that it was too much of a replica of Company rule. He felt that if the East India Company had never existed no such arrangement as Lord Stanley favoured would have been put forward. He thought there were two indictments against the past administration of India. One was the condition of the cultivators in India, which he continued to think unsatisfactory. The other was financial. According to him, there was a deficit of £60,000,000 that had slight chance of

[1] Hansard, vol. 149, 843–5.
[2] Layard Papers, Add. MSS. 38,985. Bright to Layard 17 Oct. 1857, ff. 328–9.
[3] Sturge Papers, Add. MSS. 43,845. Bright to J. Sturge, 19 Oct. 1857, ff. 58–9.
[4] Hansard, vol. 151, 348.
[5] Ibid., 339. [6] Ibid., 347.
[7] Sturge Papers, Add. MSS. 43,723. Bright to J. Sturge, 16 Aug. 1858, f. 109.

being reduced because the Indian government could not survive on its revenue and was, in addition, a poor credit risk.[1]

Bright then offered his solutions. He proposed to abolish the office of Governor-General because, as ruler of one-sixth of the world, no man could adequately fill this post. He thought that the Indian empire, composed of diverse nations speaking a variety of languages, was too vast for management by one man. Although he saw little chance of abolishing the office in 1858, he hoped that 1863 would see such a transformation. To replace the old system he proposed five independent presidencies in India which would be equal in rank; he suggested Calcutta, Madras, Agra, Bombay and Lahore as capitals. In each presidency he would institute a Governor and council who would confine their duties to their own area. The Governor would control taxation, justice, public works and the army. Only in an emergency would the presidency armies need to be united. Each governor would then communicate directly with the Secretary of State in Britain without having to have recourse to a Governor-General.[2] In London there should be a Secretary of State with direct responsibility to Parliament for Indian affairs. He would be assisted by secretaries or, if necessary, a board whose size and duties would be limited to prevent any blurring of responsibility.[3]

In the presidencies the Governor would be assisted by an 'open' council, by which Bright meant the inclusion of non-official members, thus helping to break down the influence exerted by the civil service.[4] When that was done, he said: '...you would have begun to unite the Government with the governed; and unless you do that, no Government will be safe.'[5] He gave the example of Ceylon, where he thought that Cingalese in the Governor's council[6] had added to the effectiveness of the government. He thought there were many persons in India who were qualified to take any position the government wished to give them.[7] A decentralized and more representative system would, in Bright's opinion, curtail further annexations and encourage a 'constant rivalry for good'.[8]

[1] Hansard, vol. 151, 330–8. [2] Ibid., 339–44. [3] Ibid., 333.
[4] Ibid., 343–4. [5] Ibid., 345. [6] S. D. Baily, *Ceylon*, p. 100.
[7] Hansard, vol. 151, 344. [8] Ibid., 345.

Furthermore, Bright thought that in future the Secretary of State for India should be the best man available for cabinet duty. This office should not be a reward to 'party' men, but should go to a man who was both capable and informed in Indian matters. Lastly, he recommended a general amnesty by the Queen offering security of property, the right of adoption (to allow a family to continue its inheritance), freedom of religion, a court of law to settle cases between the subjects and the government of India, and a Commission to look into finances.[1]

Bright's plans for the economic development of India were revealed most fully during the two debates on Indian finance in 1859. He said he thought the finances of a country determined public order, and that their condition provided a moral criterion. Though India had £80,000,000 of debt and a diminishing revenue,[2] he thought there was a chance for improvement. It would not come, however, from an imperial guarantee, as this would only increase the temptation to indulge in greater expenses.[3] He would reduce the expenses of governing India by lowering the emolument for the Indian civil service. The excuses of health risks and distance from England did not suffice for Ceylon, where salaries were half those in India. Reductions would result in greater savings, and perhaps better salaries could be paid to Indian officials. Even more urgent was the need for severe pruning of the military outlay. He found it difficult to square the British tendency to extol itself as a Christian nation with the expenditure of £36,000,000 on the army in India, especially when most experts were agreed that the population was not uncompliant. He thought it would be better for the honour of Britain to withdraw if they had to maintain their power at great cost.[4] The least that could be done would be to relieve the Indian taxpayer of the expenses of the Afghan war, which the British taxpayer should bear.[5]

[1] Ibid., 347–52.

[2] Ibid., vol. 152, 1360.

[3] Ibid., vol. 155, 802–4.

[4] Ibid., vol. 152, 1366–7. Bright argued later in the session that it had been agreed that the large Indian soldiery had been one of the causes of the mutiny and yet it appeared that that force was again being built up, which in turn necessitated a greater European garrison to keep watch. (Hansard, vol. 155, 807.)

[5] Ibid., vol. 155, 804

The great need was to introduce elasticity into the financial system. Bright thought this could be done by reforms that would give clear ownership of land or security of tenure, followed by good linking roads and proper irrigation; this would provide India, as it would any country, with the means to develop industry and greater prosperity.[1] He was convinced too that if Indians sat on the Governor-General's council they might be more willing to consent to a tax on the propertied class than if they were excluded from any position of trust.[2] He thought a better system of bookkeeping and an up-to-date financial account given early in the session to Parliament would improve the situation.[3]

Aside from these specific proposals, Bright had laid his general economic principles before the House in the same speech as his decentralization plans. He had said then that: 'You may govern India, if you like, for the good of England, but the good of England must come through the channel of the good of India.'[4] No country could profit in trade with India unless the latter were first made prosperous by the honest administration of justice and by security for life and property.[5]

Bright also made recommendations for the social improvement of India. He thought that the attitude of British officials towards the indigenous population was as important as the economic and political changes he desired. One of the reasons why he opposed an increase in military strength in India was that he thought the British treatment of Indians deteriorated when a strong military force was present.[6] He protested against the lowering of the age limit for eligibility to write the civil service examinations which had prevented a young Indian of Bright's acquaintance[7] from taking the examinations after

[1] Hansard, vol. 152, 1361–8.

[2] Ibid., 1369.

[3] Ibid., vol. 155, 815–16. Bright had asked the Secretary of State three times in July 1859, when the financial statement for that year would be ready. (Hansard vol. 154, 586, 1202; vol. 155, 29.)

[4] Ibid., vol. 151, 346.

[5] Ibid., 347.

[6] Ibid., vol. 155, 809.

[7] The young Indian's name was Rustamji Hirjibhai Wadia. Dadabhai Naoroji had interested himself in the case, and consulted Sir Erskine Perry about it. Perry, in turn, came to Bright for assistance. (R. P. Masani, *Dadabhai Naoroji*, pp. 81–2.) Masani gives the incorrect impression that Bright never raised the subject in Parliament.

making the trip to England.[1] He was also concerned that families such as the ex-royal family of Tanjore whose territories had been taken over by the British government should be well provided for. In general, he thought that a liberal policy towards Indians would be the wisest and most economical for Britain to follow.[2]

What were the reasons behind the assumption of these theories held by Bright? His decentralization plan, he believed, was closer historically to the traditional government of India than the existing system. It was based on the idea that Britain would one day leave the country and that India would then suffer chaos unless an attempt were made to fashion five compact presidencies in the interval. He thought it was possible that in fifty years the presidency of Madras could become an independent 'state' with its own interests and pride.[3] In addition, the plan would fulfil to the greatest extent his new dictum that India should be ruled in India.[4] He realized by 1858 the difficulties involved in the ruling of 'a people by a people'.[5] That is, it was becoming increasingly evident that the 1853 situation, in which the parties were so evenly balanced, could not be counted upon as a permanent factor in the political market place. Therefore the Radical aspiration of ruling an empire by a democracy was dimmed by the realization that this goal was not shared in enough influential quarters. Moreover, if the *hubris* connected with mere size could be curtailed by decentralization, then India could safely be ruled in that country. The proposal was predicated less upon administrative efficiency than the certainty of the inevitable tendency of power to corrupt.

As for the origin of the plan, it seems to have been devised by Dickinson, Smith and Bright. Before his speech on 24 June 1858, Bright planned to meet both Dickinson and Smith.[6] Dickinson had already given him help for a proposed speech in April.[7] In a speech to the Manchester Chamber of Commerce in 1866, Dickinson said, '...in 1858 I persuaded Mr. Bright to

[1] Hansard, vol. 155, 820–1.
[2] Ibid., vol. 161, 2095–6.
[3] Ibid., vol. 151, 345–6.
[4] Ibid., vol. 150, 1979.
[5] C. S. Parker, *Life and Letters of Sir James Graham 1792–1861*, ii, 340–1.
[6] Bright Papers, U.C. Bright to his wife, 6 June 1858.
[7] Ibid., 29 April 1858.

propose to the House of Commons the separation of the Presidencies of India'.[1] In a letter to Smith, Bright referred to 'our scheme of dividing the Presidencies'.[2] The proposition of abandoning the office of Governor-General was his own. Dickinson did not agree with it.[3]

Bright's recommendation of the use of Indians in the government was a part of his political philosophy that those who were expected to contribute towards the wealth of a country should enjoy some political rights. His pleas for better treatment of the Indians and his suggestion for a general amnesty after the mutiny flowed easily from his Quaker religion. His desire for retrenchment and stringency in the Indian economy was consistent with his traditional views on government spending.

Bright had opportunities of applying his principles to events and legislation. One such instance centred largely around the appointment of James Wilson[4] by Sir Charles Wood to help straighten out the financial difficulties of the Indian government. Wilson set out to remedy the situation by reducing expenditures and raising government income by such measures as an income tax.[5] Wilson's plan for increasing the revenue by direct taxation met with strong opposition from Sir Charles Trevelyan,[6] who, as Governor of Madras, was not in favour of such a move. On 26 March 1860, Trevelyan stated his opinion in writing and in public that he disagreed with Wilson. Lord Canning, the Governor-General, felt that criticism of taxes one day might lead to criticism of the army the next, and Trevelyan's action resulted in dismissal.[7]

Bright had already partially committed himself to the side of Trevelyan by his parliamentary commendation of the

[1] B.M. 08023 aa 14 (8). *Speech of Mr. Dickinson*, p. 8.

[2] Smith Papers, MS. 923.2. S. 344. (42). Bright to J. B. Smith, 26 Jan. 1861.

[3] Bell, p. 31.

[4] WILSON, JAMES (1805–60). Founder of the *Economist*; M.P., 1847–59; Financial Secretary to the Treasury, 1853–8; Vice-President of Board of Trade, 1859; financial member of Governor-General's council, 1859–60; died in Calcutta.

[5] H. R. C. Hailey, *The Cambridge History of India*, vi, 315.

[6] TREVELYAN, SIR CHARLES EDWARD (1807–86). Entered Bengal civil service, 1827; Assistant-Secretary to Treasury (in London), 1849–59; K.C.B., 1848; Governor of Madras, 1859–60; recalled in 1860; financial member of council in Calcutta, 1862–5.

[7] Lord Edmond Fitzmaurice, *The Life of Lord Granville*, i, 375–7.

appointment.[1] In May 1860, Danby Seymour raised a debate on Trevelyan's dismissal in the House of Commons, during which Bright defended the latter's point of view in regard to new taxation. Bright himself thought that Wilson was approaching the question in the wrong way when he attempted to raise revenue rather than concentrating on cutting expenditure. He could not agree that a tax applicable in some parts of India should have to be levied on other localities where it would be unrealistic to do so.

Bright drew a moral from this episode. To him the incident demonstrated the desirability of decentralized government, in which case the laws passed for each presidency could coincide with the conditions and wants of that particular area.[2] Bright was not alone in seeing the issue in this light. The *Bombay Times and Standard* viewed the conflict between Wilson and Trevelyan as symbolic of the rift between exponents of centralization and decentralization respectively.[3] For Bright, the work of Trevelyan bore out not only his economic and political ideas, but also his social policy. He praised the fact that Trevelyan had conciliated the Indians by removing certain ceremonial distinctions and by showing courtesy towards them.[4]

Another important application of Bright's theories occurred in 1861 during the debates on the East India Council Bill. Lord Canning had become very dissatisfied with the system of business used by his own executive council. Consultation among Canning, Sir Charles Wood and Sir Bartle Frere[5] resulted in legislation not only to improve the administration of the Governor-General's Council, but also to restore the legislative councils in the presidencies, which had been abolished by the 1833 Charter Act. The Governor-General's executive council was increased to five ordinary members with the additional power of calling in from six to twelve members for

[1] Hansard, vol. 152, 113.
[2] Ibid., vol. 158, 1146–50.
[3] *Morning Star*, 22 May 1860, p. 2, col. b.
[4] Hansard, vol. 155, 812–13.
[5] FRERE, SIR HENRY BARTLE EDWARD (1815–84). Entered Bombay civil service, 1834; Chief Commissioner of Sind, 1850–9; K.C.B., 1859; Member of council—the first civilian from outside Bengal—1859–62; Governor of Bombay, 1862–7; Member of council of India, 1867–77; Governor of the Cape of Good Hope, 1877–80; baronet, 1876.

purposes of legislation. In the presidencies the legislative councils were restored, although no legislation could be passed or approved without the Governor-General's consent. The Act provided that legislative councils could be extended to the North-Western provinces and the Punjab in the future.[1] Although the measure in no way broke down the centralized power of the Governor-General to the extent that Bright would have wished, this did not prevent at least one Member, A. Dunlop (M.P. for Greenock), from crediting Bright with originating the plan.[2] Another Member, A. S. Ayrton (M.P. for Tower Hamlets) thought that 'the first question which stared them in the face was the one which had been raised with so much ability by the hon. Member for Birmingham'.[3]

During the debate Bright helped to secure an extension of the duration of tenure of unofficial members of the Governor-General's council from one to two years. He thought it was absurd to expect men to come from all over India to take up an appointment for such a short time.[4] He did not agree with an amendment of Danby Seymour's that cast some doubt upon the need for a financial member within the Governor-General's council. Bright thought there was such a need for a Chancellor of the Exchequer,[5] and Seymour complied with Bright's request to drop the amendment.[6] Bright tried without success to give the right of making rules to govern the Governor-General's council to that body rather than to the Governor-General.[7]

A. H. Layard[8] raised the question of the admission of Indians to the Governor-General's council. He proposed that not less than one-quarter of the council should be Indians.[9]

[1] Sir H. Verney Lovett, *The Cambridge History of India*, vi, 226–36.

[2] Hansard, vol. 163, 647.

[3] Ibid., 1330.

[4] Ibid., 1355–61.

[5] Bright had urged the need for such an appointment in 1855. See p. 22.

[6] Hansard, vol. 163, 1342–6.

[7] Ibid., 1362–3.

[8] LAYARD, SIR AUSTIN HENRY (1817–94). Became protégé of Stratford Canning in Constantinople; travelled widely throughout East; attaché at Constantinople in 1849; became M.P. in 1852; travelled to India in 1857–8; Under-Secretary for foreign affairs, 1861–6; upheld Lord Beaconsfield's policies as ambassador at Constantinople, 1877–80.

[9] Hansard, vol. 163, 1350–1.

Sir Charles Wood objected, thinking it undesirable to make a 'statutory distinction'.[1] Bright agreed with Wood, and proposed instead that the Secretary of State should inform the government of India as to the need to employ Indians in this capacity. Such a step would establish a precedent for the future. Wood accepted this compromise.[2]

Bright estimated that the 1858 legislation had not changed the essential form of the Indian government. He could not see any indication that Britain had learned anything from the Indian revolt. He looked with alarm in 1861 on the £121,000,000 joint budget of Great Britain and India, and feared that never again would it be possible to keep Indian finances separate from the British exchequer. He felt that Wood as Secretary of State and Canning as Governor-General were poor statesmen who would not be able to overcome the old traditions and strength of the civil service.[3]

From this he drew two important conclusions. One was that the only hope for improvement lay in a further reform of the Indian government more in accordance with his 1858 views.[4] The best way to achieve this, he thought, was by enfranchising the British people who would then deal with this question more satisfactorily.[5] Despite the modification of his previous views on this subject, he still believed that the fundamental principles of Indian government should be democratically determined.[6] The less hoped-for possibility was another revolt that would force a further change in government.[7]

The other deduction was in regard to the cotton supply, and it was a corollary of his first conclusion. He felt that if India was not producing cotton with all her advantages, anyone

[1] Sir H. Verney Lovett, *The Cambridge History of India*, vi, 236.

[2] Hansard, vol. 163, 1352–3.

[3] Gladstone Papers, Add. MSS. 44,112. Bright to Gladstone, 9 Jan. 1861, f. 33.

[4] B.M. Add. MSS. 33,963. Bright to Col. Rathbone, 23 Jan. 1861, ff. 57–8.

[5] *The Times*, 9 Sept. 1859, p. 7, col. e. Bright had written in a letter to Gladstone that the people of Britain would not tolerate the expense of Indian government '& some day the People will say so, & will act upon that opinion'. (Gladstone Papers, Add. MSS. 44,112. Bright to Gladstone, 9 Jan. 1861, f. 34.)

[6] See editorial, *Morning Star*, 31 May 1858, p. 2, col. e.

[7] *The Times*, 9 Sept. 1859, p. 7, col. e.

should be able to see that some legal or governmental obstacle stood in the way. But such was the 'obtuseness or the cowardice of Lancashire capitalists' that they could not look at the question in that way. He felt that they knew next to nothing about politics. There was no point in Lancashire carrying complaints to the Secretary of State for India; instead they would serve their interests better if they took vigorous steps to change the whole structure of Indian government. He felt that he could not co-operate with them as long as they did not seek a root-and-branch change in the existing system. As far as he was concerned, the only feasible plan was his decentralization scheme, which would allow each presidency to attend to its own political economy.[1]

Bright applied this attitude in several matters relating to India. J. B. Smith informed Bright in the autumn of 1859 of his plan to back financially and politically a renewed project for the improvement of navigation on the Godavery river.[2] Smith introduced his scheme to Parliament in February 1860, stressing the amount of cheap cotton that could be transported if it were adopted.[3] In contrast to his interest during 1854–5, Bright declined to take part in the venture, saying that he had little faith in the advance of any project in connexion with the Indian government. He felt that there was a lack of any clear definition of probable relations between the promoters and the government.[4] But even more important was his objection to the composition of the Board, largely made up of Manchester capitalists.

By January 1861, Smith was still pursuing what he referred to as his 'pet scheme'.[5] He was preparing to meet Bazley, and felt that Wood was disposed to approve the Godavery scheme on favourable terms. He thought, however, that Bright's name was needed if they were to succeed.[6]

Bright was pushed into giving a definitive answer when Smith asked him to attend a meeting in Manchester to support

[1] B.M. Add. MSS. 33,963. Bright to Col. Rathbone, 23 Jan. 1861, ff. 56–8.
[2] Bright Papers, Add. MSS. 43,388. J. B. Smith to Bright, 30 Sept. 1859, f. 198.
[3] Hansard, vol. 156, 526–30.
[4] Smith Papers, MS. 923.2, S.344. (40). Bright to J. B. Smith, 6 Dec. 1860.
[5] Hansard, vol. 163, 502.
[6] Bright Papers, Add. MSS. 43,388. J. B. Smith to Bright, 15 Jan. 1861, f. 201.

the plan. There were two main reasons for his refusal. One was a distaste for the people in Manchester who were supporting the project—'full of flunkeyism' and lacking in manhood. His other reason he put this way: 'The whole question is *political*—& must be treated as such, & I shall have nothing to do with it under any other character.... I shall only act as far as I can to promote a full reconstruction of the Indian Govt.'[1] When Smith renewed his attempt at persuading Bright, urging the importance of common opinion in the Manchester School,[2] Bright deplored the fact that Manchester rejoiced in being represented by J. A. Turner 'who trusted in the East India Compy & crawled on his belly in the dust before them, rather than help me to get the Commission for which I moved in 1850'.[3]

The crisis in Lancashire due to a shortage in cotton caused by the American Civil War seemed to Bright to be proof of the past and present misgovernment on India. He did not think that any sudden increase in the supply could be expected from India.[4] Nor did he think the quality of Indian cotton would be sufficiently good, because it was even more adulterated than it had been in previous years.[5] He stressed the fact that Indian cotton production could be increased only by degrees.[6] He believed that the only certain way to ensure a speedy resumption of the supply was through the victory of the North in the American Civil War.[7]

From a combination of sulkiness at Manchester waywardness and conviction that no remedy was possible for the lack of cotton, he was silent on the subject in Parliament until 1863. He then stated that there were only two ways to increase the

[1] Smith Papers, MS. 923.2, S.344. (42). Bright to J. B. Smith, 26 Jan., 1861. (Bright's emphasis.)

[2] Bright Papers, Add., MSS. 43,388. J. B. Smith to Bright, 11 Jan. 1862, f. 204.

[3] Smith Papers, MS. 923.2, S.344. (43). Bright to J. B. Smith, 13 Jan. 1862. Turner had been President of the Manchester Commercial Association at that time. See p. 18.

[4] *The Times*, 6 Feb. 1862, p. 7, cols. a–b.

[5] Smith Papers, MS. 923.2 S.344. (47). Bright to J. B. Smith, 24 Dec. 1863. Indian cotton had always been dirtier than American because of land haulage and deliberate attempts to increase the weight by adding foreign matter.

[6] *The Times*, 6 Feb. 1862, p. 7, cols. a–b.

[7] P.M.H.S. Bright to Sumner, 6 Sept. 1861, vol. 46, p. 95.

supply from India. One was by giving security of tenure to the cultivators. The other was by introducing his decentralization plan, which he felt would result in an increase of from 5 to 10 per cent in investment in the presidencies.[1]

Outside Parliament Bright put forward another remedy. He suggested that the Indian government make a public declaration that any land concerned in cotton production would be exempt from the land tax for five years. Short of this, he could see no hope for the restoration of prosperity in Lancashire.[2] He had acquired this idea from F. C. Brown, a gentleman whose family had lived sixty years in India. He had submitted to Bright in manuscript form a series of letters from India which he eventually published and dedicated to him.[3] The plan to exempt cotton-growing land from tax was criticized in *The Times*. It accused Bright of regarding India as merely 'a plantation to grow cotton for Lancashire'.[4] Sir Charles Wood, addressing his constituents at Halifax, opposed the proposal because he said half the revenue of India was derived from the land tax.[5] Bright did not raise the subject again.

III

While still dealing with the period 1857–70, this section will endeavour to reveal the texture rather than the substance of Bright's work in relation to India. It will attempt to answer such questions as: how important was the problem of India to Bright? how much support did he get for his views on India? to what extent were his views taken into consideration by leading politicians, and what were his contacts with India?

Despite their differences on India, Bright seems to have relied most on Cobden during the mutiny period. Both were clearly very much disturbed by the affair, and early in September 1857 Bright expressed a desire to see Cobden about it.[6]

[1] Hansard, vol. 172, 224–8.
[2] *The Times*, 19 Dec. 1862, p. 9, col. d.
[3] B.M. 08226 h 56 (8). F. C. Brown, *The Supply of Cotton from India*, pp. v–vi.
[4] *The Times*, 20 Dec. 1862, p. 8, col. d.
[5] *Morning Star*, 14 Jan. 1863, p. 2, col. e.
[6] Bright Papers, Add. MSS. 43,384. Bright to Cobden, 19 Sept. 1857, ff. 109–10.

They were agreed on the need to put down the mutiny.[1] Their short-term views on India were similar; Bright wrote: 'I incline to think that his [Cobden's] views & mine on what can be done *now* are not far apart.'[2] But on the long-term policy to India their views diverged. Cobden did not believe that India could ever be ruled for the sake of Indians, and called this 'a self-complacent piece of cant'.[3] To his mind, the solution was to give up all territorial aggrandisement (a point on which Bright would agree) and to make a case from a free trade point of view[4] that would involve the withdrawal of British rule from India. Bright, on the other hand, felt that it was impossible to expect any country to give up its Empire and colonies.[5] Nevertheless, there is no doubt that Cobden was the man to whom Bright extended his confidences on India in late 1857.

However, when the time came to deal with the three India Bills in 1858, Cobden, since he was not in Parliament and was perhaps uninterested in the issue, withdrew to the background. At this juncture, Bright co-operated most fully with T. Milner Gibson, J. B. Smith and J. Dickinson. In March 1858, when the first two India Bills were before Parliament and Bright was in Rochdale, it was Smith who sent him copies of the Bills with his comments.[6] In London, Smith was in close consultation with Milner Gibson and S. Lucas (editor of the *Star*).[7] Dickinson had acquired such a position with Bright and the *Star* that he was able to write to that paper advising it to oppose Ellenborough's Bill.[8]

Discussion on Ellenborough's Bill was made more complicated by the fact that none of these men wished to see the return of Lord Palmerston. Milner Gibson, in particular, did not like the idea of turning Ellenborough's Bill into a political triumph for Palmerston. He thought that it would be better

[1] Cobden Papers, Add. MSS. 43,650. Cobden to Bright, 22 Sept. 1857, f. 265.

[2] Sturge Papers, Add. MSS. 43,845. Bright to J. Sturge, 19 Oct. 1857, f. 57. (Bright's emphasis.)

[3] Smith Papers, MS. 923.2, S. 345. (59). Cobden to J. B. Smith, 8 Aug. 1857.

[4] Sturge Papers, Add. MSS. 43,722. Cobden to J. Sturge, 5 July 1857, f. 253.

[5] Ibid., Add. MSS. 43,723. Bright to J. Sturge, 24 Sept. 1857, f. 86.

[6] Bright Papers, Add. MSS. 43,388. J. B. Smith to Bright, 31 March 1858, ff. 178–9.

[7] Ibid., 1 April 1858, f. 181.

[8] Ibid., 31 March 1858, f. 178.

if the House were to consider resolutions that would embody the principles upon which a good India bill might be built.[1] He thought that such a course would have a greater chance of success if Lord John Russell were to propose it.[2] In fact, this was the procedure adopted,[3] and it is not out of the question that it might have been arranged by Milner Gibson, since it was the complicity of Lord John Russell with Milner Gibson that had turned out Lord Palmerston earlier in the year.[4] The reason that Milner Gibson felt inclined in June 1859, to take a cabinet position with the Palmerston government was his debt to Lord John Russell.[5] It is significant that Bright, on 9 April, was planning a talk with Milner Gibson[6] three days before Lord John Russell's suggestion was put to the House.

This incident, if the documents record it correctly, indicates not only the Members of Parliament with whom Bright was working, but also the influential position he and some of his friends had acquired on Indian matters. There are other instances of their influence. It was Bright's opinion that C. P. Villiers had been sent to see him in late 1857 to gather ideas on India for his brother, Lord Clarendon, because possibly 'they think my views about India may have some following'.[7] The Derby government had gone to greater lengths to accommodate Bright's views. Smith was told that the government had inserted a clause in the second India Bill providing for the election of five members of the Indian council as a conciliatory measure towards Bright; and he wrote: 'The govt. are anxious a [sic] far as they possibly can to get the support of the friends of India, & are not insensitive of your influence with this party.'[8]

[1] Bright Papers, Add. MSS. 43,388. Milner Gibson to Bright, 1 April 1858, ff. 75–6.

[2] Ibid, J. B. Smith to Bright, 4 April 1858, f. 77.

[3] See pp. 42–3.

[4] According to Bright's diary, Bright, Milner Gibson, Lord John Russell and Sir James Graham agreed to an amendment to the Conspiracy to Murder Bill. (Walling, p. 233.) On 19 Feb. 1858, Milner Gibson presented the amendment to Parliament. The voting went against Lord Palmerston by 234 votes to 215. (Hansard, vol. 148, 1758, 1844–7.) Lord Palmerston blamed the defeat on the '... work of Lord John Russell and Sir James Graham in the interest of the Radicals.' (*The Letters of Queen Victoria*, eds. A. C. Benson and Viscount Esher, iii, 338.)

[5] Walling, p. 243.

[6] Bright Papers, Add. MSS. 43,384. Bright to Cobden, 9 April 1858, f. 127.

[7] Ibid, 24 Nov. 1857, f. 117.

[8] Ibid., Add. MSS. 43,388. J. B. Smith to Bright, 31 March 1858, f. 179.

While the Derby government was wrestling with the second India Bill, Bright received a hint[1] that they would like him to make certain proposals to change the Bill in return for help over the second reading. Bright, in reply, criticized the elective feature in the Indian council and urged them to reduce it to twelve members to be nominated by the Crown. He also suggested a commission to inquire into land tenures and the means of promoting industry in India. Although, as is known, this was not the course followed, it shows the extent to which his influence had to be taken into account.

There were several reasons why Bright's opinions on India carried weight. One was his connexion with the *Morning Star*. Although he had neither a pecuniary interest in the paper nor a day-to-day control over it,[2] he took a keen interest in its fortunes, and kept its welfare in view by attempting to procure competent writers, especially on the subject of India. When A. H. Layard planned a six-month tour of India in October 1857, Bright tried to gain his correspondence for the *Star*.[3] He thought the writing of the *Star* on India had improved with the acquisition of the former editor of the *Friend of India*, H. Mead,[4] whom J. B. Smith had first recommended.[5] Another writer on the paper, John Hamilton, was complimented by Bright in 1857 for a 'fine article' he had written on Lord Canning. Bright suggested to Hamilton that it would be a good plan to acquire by each mail a newsworthy letter from Calcutta, Bombay and Madras.[6] By April 1858, Bright himself was writing articles on India for the *Star*.[7]

[1] It was not a letter, and no name is mentioned. All the information in this paragraph is taken from Bright Papers, Add. MSS. 43,384. Bright to Cobden, 31 March 1858, ff. 121–2.

[2] Scottish National Library, MS. Acc. 1993. Bright to E. Ellice, 16 Dec. 1859. The circulation of the *Star* in 1857 was 30,000 copies daily. (Bright Papers, Add. MSS. 43,384. 24 Nov. 1857. f. 118.) This figure, however, declined in succeeding years. (Read, *Cobden and Bright*, p. 186.)

[3] Layard Papers, Add. MSS. 38,985. Bright to Layard, 17 Oct. 1857, f. 329.

[4] Ibid. Bright, though not naming Mead directly, is clearly referring to him.

[5] Bright Papers, Add. MSS. 43,388. J. B. Smith to Bright, 5 Oct. 1857, f. 172.

[6] National Library of Ireland, MS. Autograph A.L.S. (Photostat). Bright to John Hamilton, 23 Nov. 1857.

[7] Bright Papers, Add. MSS. 43,384. Bright to Cobden, 9 April 1858, f. 126.

The *Star*, of course, gave its support to Bright's decentralization scheme.[1] In fact, careful readers could have discerned the germ of Bright's thoughts on India from an editorial in January 1858. It proposed six or seven local governments in India free of interference by an 'obstructive Supreme Government'.[2] In May 1858, the paper denied the value of an Indian council, claiming that Parliament was the 'legitimate Home Council for India'.[3] Another editorial condemned the revenue system of India as inelastic.[4] The editors of the *Star* thought that it was hopeless to struggle for reform of matters of detail in Indian government without an organic change that would start with abolition of the Indian council and centralized government. Like Bright, the *Star* expressed the opinion that the eventual salvation of India lay in the reform of the British House of Commons.[5] In general, then, the *Star* gave almost unqualified support to the '...wisdom of the views propounded by Mr. BRIGHT'.[6]

The support of the India Reform Society was another reason why Bright's views were influential, though the Society was not without difficulties. By Bright's own admission, the Society was still suffering in 1858 from its two chief defects: a lack of funds and the fact that a half-dozen Members of Parliament had to shoulder the principal work. Even so, he had known no other political organization to do as much work with so little money.[7]

The mutiny had the temporary effect of re-invigorating the India Reform Society. In 1857 several meetings were held; Bright, being ill, did not attend all of them. These meetings were held in the hope of attracting men of diverse political views who would lend their support for the specific object of abolishing Company rule. For instance, one meeting attracted both the Marquis of Clanricarde and Ernest Jones, the Chartist leader.[8] This caused the chairman of the next meeting, Viscount Bury, to remark that some criticism had been raised concerning the previous meeting because 'the men who took part in it were of such different politics and opinions that the

[1] *Morning Star*, 28 June 1858, p. 2, cols. c–e.
[2] Ibid., 27 Jan. 1858, p. 2, col. d.
[3] Ibid., 31 May 1858, p. 2, col. e.
[4] Ibid., 18 Feb. 1859, p. 4, col. c.
[5] Ibid. 7 March 1859, p. 4, cols. d–e.
[6] Ibid., 12 May 1860, p. 4, col. d.
[7] Ibid., 28 May 1858, p.2, col. b.
[8] Ibid., 10 Dec. 1857, p. 2, cols. b–d.

agitation must subside'.[1] Prominent among those who took part in the meetings, besides those already mentioned, were J. A. Roebuck, H. Mead, E. Miall, C. Gilpin (M.P. for Northampton), and W. H. Schneider (M.P. for Norwich). A petition adopted at the first meeting vigorously denounced the administration of the East India Company.[2] Ernest Jones agreed with Bright's opinion that help for India would come only through extended enfranchisement of the British people.[3]

The most successful meeting arranged by the Society was one which met to hear a speech by A. H. Layard on his return from India in 1858. At least thirty M.P.s or ex-M.P.s crowded St James's Hall, Piccadilly, to hear Layard's verdict on the mutiny. Cobden, Milner Gibson, J. B. Smith, J. Caird,[4] Sir E. Perry and Sir J. Graham were among those present. Bright was there, but would not yield to the noisy clamour at the conclusion of the meeting for him to speak because, as Milner Gibson explained, he did not yet feel able to address public meetings.[5]

More representative of the typical Society meeting held after the excitement of the mutiny had diminished was the one which met in May 1858. It was a private meeting held at the committee rooms with Bright in the chair. Those who spoke included J. B. Smith and A. J. Otway (formerly M.P. for Stafford). Bright called for professionally trained judges to be sent to the interior of India to set an example of treating the Indians with respect, as well as to give them legal training. He reaffirmed the aims of the Society in regard to promoting the appointment of non-official members to the Legislative council, and procuring the right of Indians to admission to offices for which they were qualified.[6]

One of the chief advantages of the Society as far as Bright was concerned lay in the contacts it established with various

[1] Ibid., 18 Dec. 1857, p. 2, col. a. [2] Ibid., 10 Dec. 1857, p. 2, cols. b–d.

[3] Ibid., col. c.

[4] CAIRD, SIR JAMES (1816–92). An agricultural expert who supported free trade; visited Canada and the United States, 1858; M.P., 1857–65; during Lancashire cotton famine became interested in Indian cotton; visited Ireland in 1869; appointed to Indian famine commission, 1878–9; K.C.B., 1882; close friend of Bright.

[5] *Morning Star*, 12 May 1858, p. 3, cols. c–e.

[6] Ibid., 28 May 1858, p. 2, col. b.

sources of opinion and groups in India. This is well brought out in a comment of his in Parliament referring to the effects of the 1858 legislation: '...I know it from private correspondence which comes by every mail to an association in this city with which I have been many years connected—correspondence both from Europeans and Natives, that not even a shadow of change has been brought about in India.'[1]

The relationship of the Society with India was a two-way affair. Copies of speeches, petitions and minutes of meetings were exchanged between Great Britain and India.[2] Dickinson advised sending the copies of a speech by Smith in 1864 to 'Govt. & Members of Council at Calcutta, Madras & Bombay, to a few personal friends, & to the leading journals'.[3] Newspapers in India were aware of the Society; the *Hindoo Patriot* commented that the 'agent' of this association was guiding the editorial policy of the *Star*.[4] An instance of the value of Dickinson's information from India occurred in 1858 when he informed Bright about Canning's intended proclamation[5] which soon led to Ellenborough's resignation.

Despite such work of the Society, its fortunes languished after 1858. Dickinson's marriage in 1859 may have prevented him from giving his attention so completely to India.[6] His father had never favoured his son's activities on behalf of India, and only allowed them because of Bright's and Smith's connexion with the Society. He would not, however, allow the young Dickinson to enter Parliament. The subscribers to the Society were so few that funds barely kept the committee rooms open. Then in 1861 the Society was badly weakened when Bright resigned as chairman because the demands on his time were so heavy. Dickinson took over as chairman,[7] but by 1863 he had little hope of effecting any good for India and began to study law.[8] It is likely that the Society expired in

[1] Hansard, vol. 152, 1370.

[2] See Leech, p. 179; *Morning Star*, 28 May 1858, p. 2, col. b.

[3] Smith Papers, MS. 923.2, S.347. J. Dickinson to J. B. Smith, 27 July 1864.

[4] *Hindoo Patriot*, 10 Dec. 1857, p. 194, col. c.

[5] Hansard, vol. 150, 945. But see Blake, *Disraeli*, p. 382.

[6] Bell, p. 31; Smith Papers, MS. 923.2, S.344 (37). Bright to J. B. Smith, 6 Oct. 1859.

[7] Bell, pp. 31–2.

[8] Bright Papers, U.C. Bright to his wife, 5 June 1863.

1868. From 1866 Dickinson began to pay more attention to the affairs of the Native States, and from 1870 onwards his health and private affairs prevented him from taking up any new Indian question.[1] The demise of the Society reflected the failure of its founders to make India a matter of constant public attention. Only some calamity such as the mutiny could do this. India was, and remained, an affair for experts.[2]

The support that Bright received for his decentralization scheme indicates why his views on India were influential. According to the Indian correspondent of the *Star*, who himself did not favour Bright's plan, decentralization would be popular among officials in India because so much of their work was stifled by a 'presumptuous remote authority'.[3] According to Bright, the British-Indian Association of Calcutta favoured decentralization because the distinguishing characteristic of India was its variety, not its uniformity.[4] Sir Bartle Frere, who was on the Governor-General's council in 1859, blamed the interference of the central government for most of the 'evils of the present situation' in India. He agreed with Bright's proposals for decentralization as long as the central government were retained to look after matters 'of general & imperial interest'.[5] He thought that every ruler of a presidency should govern as best he could, subject only to the limitation of finances.[6] When Bright met Frere in 1875, the latter encouraged him not to abandon the subject, but rather to elaborate upon it.[7]

Among leading men in Britain Bright's scheme met with much favourable reaction. R. V. Smith, who had been President of the Board of Control from 1855 to February 1858, agreed that India should be divided into an increased number of presidencies.[8] Lord John Russell was much in sympathy with Bright's views. He thought Bright's speech of 24 June 1858 was 'one of the most remarkable ever delivered in this House'. Although not agreeing that it would be possible to abolish the

[1] Bell, pp. 53–5. [2] A. P. Thornton, *The Imperial Idea and its Enemies*, p. 40.

[3] *Morning Star*, 16 Sept. 1858, p. 2, col. a.

[4] Hansard, vol. 152, 1368.

[5] Ripon Papers, Add. MSS. 43,617. Frere to Lord Goderich, 4 Jan. 1859, ff. 20–1.

[6] Ibid., 5 Sept. 1859, ff. 26–7.

[7] Walling, p. 369. [8] Hansard, vol. 151, 361.

office of Governor-General, he thought that in decentralization Bright had discovered the only method of improving the government of India. Bright's ideas were 'the true principles upon which the Government of India ought in future to be conducted'.[1] Sir Stafford Northcote, when he was Secretary of State for India in 1867, seriously considered the practicability of decentralization.[2] Bright himself, writing about his decentralization plan, commented: 'I believe in no projects of reform which do not begin here, & when I have advised this in Parlt, I find all the leading men agreeing with me—but unhappily there is no hand strong enough to undertake the work.'[3]

Among less prominent M.P.s Bright's ideas also received support. W. J. Fox (M.P. for Oldham) endorsed the general principles laid down by Bright in his speech of 24 June.[4] Danby Seymour said in Parliament that some measure of decentralization was called for along the lines which Bright had suggested.[5] William Ewart (M.P. for Dumfries) thought that centralization had been carried too far, although he tended to favour decentralization in the form of municipalities.[6] A. H. Layard welcomed the East India Council Bill because it was a step in the direction favoured by Bright, although he did not think the time had yet come for full decentralization.[7] James Caird agreed with Bright's proposals.[8]

It is difficult to determine the amount of support that Bright could count on in the House of Commons. The *Star* estimated in 1861 during the debate on the East India Council Bill that there were about twenty-five Members who strove to prevent ministerial responsibility to Parliament for Indian affairs from becoming fictitious.[9] Because the only division taken during this debate secured sixty Members on the side for which Bright voted,[10] this might be taken as some indication of those

[1] Hansard, vol. 151, 1095.
[2] A. Lang, *Life, Letters and Diaries of Sir Stafford Northcote*, p. 173.
[3] B.M. Add. MSS. 33,963. Bright to Col. Rathbone, 23 Jan. 1861, f. 58.
[4] *Morning Star*, 6 Aug. 1858, p. 2, col. b.
[5] Hansard, vol. 155, 831–2.
[6] Ibid., vol. 152, 1381–2.
[7] Ibid., vol. 163, 1015–16.
[8] Walling, p. 424.
[9] *Morning Star*, 21 June 1861, p. 4, col. d.
[10] House of Commons *Division Lists 1861*, pp. 225–6.

Members who were either committed to support Bright's ideas or very greatly concerned about India. Among his supporters were those who would follow him on any question. Lord Fermoy (M.P. for Marylebone) mentioned that 'The hon. Gentleman [Bright] was followed by a number of Gentlemen who placed implicit confidence in him.'[1] Then there were those who supported Bright on specific questions. E. S. Cayley (M.P. for Yorkshire North Riding) remarked in 1861 that he usually followed Bright on Indian questions.[2] It seems that those who constantly supported Bright were not very numerous. Cobden, writing to Bright about India, referred to 'your handful of earnest men'.[3] But there was, of course, always the possibility that a speech of Bright's could sway a larger following on any occasion.

Yet decentralization was not successfully carried in one single measure in the House of Commons. There was the weight of opinion in Calcutta to contend with. During Sir Stafford Northcote's tenure as Secretary of State for India, Sir John Lawrence opposed decentralization because, as A. Lang wrote, 'a man who is at the centre is always likely to oppose it.'[4] Then again, many observers preferred to regard Bright's plans as visionary.[5] Finally, the slow progress towards decentralization begun in 1861 may have been more in harmony with the 'spirit of gradualism' that has always affected British politics.

Support from Manchester during the years 1857 to 1870 was of little significance. Bright's departure from that city in 1857 and his views on how to enlarge the cotton supply increased the tendency of the Indian reformers, whom he led, to differ even more with the Manchester cotton interests over India. One example of this was the disagreement between the reformers and the Manchester Chamber of Commerce over the form of an Indian council. In 1858 the Chamber drew up a petition to Parliament for an India board consisting of four or more permanent secretaries to assist the Secretary of State. The secretaries would be chosen by the House of Commons from among

[1] Hansard, vol. 160, 1127.

[2] Ibid., vol. 163, 1359–60.

[3] Cobden Papers, Add. MSS. 43,650. Cobden to Bright, 14 April 1858, f. 287.

[4] Lang, op. cit., p. 174.

[5] See *The Times*, 26 June 1858, p. 8, col. f, p. 9, col. a.

'experienced Indian officials'.[1] The *Star* made the erroneous statement that the views presented by the Manchester Chamber to Parliament on a proposed India council were similar to those of the 'Indian Reform party'.[2] Dickinson, to correct this impression, wrote to the *Star* denying that they were the views of the India Reform Society 'led by Mr. Bright in the House of Commons'. Dickinson thought that the Secretary of State should be able to choose his own subordinates as this would sharpen his responsibility to Parliament. In addition, he did not think that an India board composed of 'experienced Indian officials' was the best kind of assistance for the Secretary of State for India. He preferred 'fresh, local, Indian experience' to the 'Leadenhall experience' to which the Manchester petition pointed.[3]

In addition, Bright did not aid the endeavours of the Cotton Supply Association formed in 1858 in Manchester. Although it contained some of his past and present associates, such as Bazley, Seymour and Otway,[4] he did not become a member. One need only register fully the implication of their motto—'Cotton knows no politics'—to realize why he would remain dissociated from it. J. B. Smith objected to it because the Association intended to spend sums of money in all parts of the world to develop the growth of cotton. He thought the money would be better spent in India, which showed every indication of being able to compete with the United States if 'European capital and agency were made available'.[5]

How important was the question of India at this time to Bright? During 1857–9, according to his own testimony, it was the most important question facing Britain. In 1859 he said: 'If this matter of India were settled so that we could feel satisfied about it, it would afford me greater pleasure than any change connected with the institutions of the Government of England which could take place.'[6] This feeling was displaced in the ensuing years because of the importance that he attached

[1] *Morning Star*, 10 April 1858, p. 3, col. b.
[2] Ibid., p. 2, col. d.
[3] Ibid., 12 April 1858, p. 2, col. b.
[4] *Manchester Examiner and Times*, 10 April 1858, p. 6, cols. a–b.
[5] *Morning Star*, 10 Feb. 1859, p. 2, col. f.
[6] Hansard, vol. 155, 49–50.

to the American Civil War[1] and the Irish situation, especially with the outbreak of Fenianism. As a result some of his associates lost touch with him. Smith wrote in 1865, 'It is so long since I heard of you or from you that I have determined to enquire where you are.'[2] Bright's resignation from the chairmanship of the India Reform Society in 1861 and his silence in Parliament marked his recognition of the difficulties of the Indian situation, and an awareness that his own views would find obstacles in being adopted in an unreformed Parliament. He was pragmatic enough not to pursue a line of political agitation which was not likely to yield results: 'I oppose evil when I see a prospect of doing any good',[3] he wrote on one occasion. There were signs, such as the East India Council Bill, that progress towards decentralization in India would be gradual rather than sudden. The plea of overwork offered by Bright as reason for withdrawing as chairman of the India Reform Society[4] cannot be gainsaid. As a cabinet minister he gave his full attention to the Irish church and land questions, which left little time for India. Then again, it was not easy to arouse either the House of Commons or the British public on the Indian question. With the improvement in the condition of India,[5] the increasing difficulties in Ireland, and the importance he attached to the reform question as a solution to both British and Indian problems, he seems to have made a practical decision, tinged with a note of disappointment, that the question of India could not demand as much of his time as it had previously.

Thus it was a unique tribute to Bright's reputation that Gladstone offered him the Indian Secretaryship in December 1868. Bright was finally obliged to take the Board of Trade, refusing the Indian position because, for one reason, he feared the labour connected with such an important office.[6] In

[1] Bright wrote in 1863: 'Till America is disposed of, I cannot feel deeply about English or European subjects.' (Bright Papers, U.C. Bright to his wife, 22 June 1863.)

[2] Bright Papers, Add. MSS. 43,388. J. B. Smith to Bright, 23 Aug. 1865, f. 218.

[3] Sturge Papers, Add. MSS. 43,723. Bright to J. Sturge, 24 Sept. 1857, f. 85.

[4] Bell, p. 32.

[5] Bright admitted that there had been progress made in communications and security of tenure for cultivators. (P.M.H.S., Bright to J. Lyman, 13 Jan. 1862, vol. 46, p. 102.)

[6] Bright Papers, U.C. Bright to Mrs Leatham, 6 Dec. 1868.

addition, he still believed that one day the soundness of his plans for decentralization would be realized. He did not feel, however, that public opinion was yet ready for such a step. He would thus have been in office without being able to carry into effect the principles which he believed to be right for the Indian government.[1] Finally, and very much to the point, he felt that he could not take part in the duties of that office connected with military affairs.[2] What a tragedy that the Quakerism that had partly enabled him to see the wrongs in India was one reason which prevented him from assuming the position to rectify them!

IV

Bright's interest in India remained throughout his career, but though he attained great prominence among Indian reformers in the years 1870 to 1889, he never again provided such forthright leadership. His support for Indian reformers in many cases was solicited rather than offered. His advocacy was eagerly sought, however, by a new generation of Indian reformers, and his name was exalted by Indians as a man who understood their aspirations.

Bright's work during this time must be seen against a background of change in India. The meeting of the first Indian National Congress at Bombay in December 1885, marked a new stage in the development of Indian national consciousness. Though its inception was in some part due to Europeans such as A. O. Hume[3] and Sir William Wedderburn,[4] its chief strength was the strong support given by Indians such as Sir Pherozeshah Mehta and Dadabhai Naoroji.[5] There had been

[1] *The Times*, 22 Dec. 1868, p. 4, col. e.

[2] Bright Papers, U.C. Bright to Mrs Leatham, 6 Dec. 1868.

[3] HUME, ALLAN OCTAVIAN (1829–1912). Son of Joseph Hume, M.P.; educated at Haileybury; entered Bengal civil service, 1849; retired in 1882; took a prominent part in organizing and supporting the National Congress and in criticizing the Government of India.

[4] WEDDERBURN, SIR WILLIAM (1838–1918). Entered Bombay civil service, 1860; rose steadily to position of Chief Secretary to Bombay Government; retired in 1887; M.P. 1893–1900; President of Indian National Congress in 1889; author of pamphlets, and papers relating to condition of Indians.

[5] Sir W. Wedderburn, *Allan Octavian Hume*, p. 69.

beginnings before this of an Indian tendency to associate politically. An all-Indian association, called the British Indian Association, had been formed in 1851 to promote greater government efficiency. This was followed by the formation of a similar organization in Bombay in the next year.[1] Surendranath Banerjea helped to form an Indian Association in 1876 to represent middle-class opinion.[2] In 1885 the first meeting of the Bombay Presidency Association was held.[3] Symptomatic of the heightened interest of educated Indians in politics was the sending of Lalmohun Ghose to London in 1879 as representative of the Indian Association.

These organizations were both a sign and a cause of increasing Indian nationalism. Various events prior to the holding of the first Indian National Congress hastened the development of Indian political maturity. The Vernacular Press Act of 1878, passed in an attempt to muzzle the Indian press, alarmed Indians. The controversy over the Ilbert Bill in 1883 'helped to intensify the growing feeling of unity among the Indian people'.[4] Sir Surendranath Banerjea credits the administration of Lord Ripon, because of its fair-minded policy, with having much to do with the 'beginnings of a united national life'.[5] Much credit must also go to A. O. Hume, who in a letter to the graduates of Calcutta University in 1883 appealed to them to unite for a national cause.

Bright's effectiveness within the years 1870 to 1873 was severely limited by a recurrence of the illness which had affected him in 1856–7. He was forced to resign his cabinet post in 1870. Although he agreed to return to Gladstone's cabinet as the Chancellor of the Duchy of Lancaster in 1873, the after-effects of this breakdown probably still limited his powers.

[1] I. M. Cumpston, 'Some Early Indian Nationalists and Their Allies in the British Parliament 1851–1906', *Eng. Hist. Rev.*, lxxvi, no. 299 (April, 1961), 279.

[2] Sir Surendranath Banerjea, *A Nation in Making*, p. 41.

[3] H. P. Mody, *Sir Pherozeshah Mehta*, i, 167.

[4] Banerjea, op. cit., p. 85. The Ilbert Bill was a measure designed to withdraw the privilege of Europeans in the provinces of being judged in court by Europeans only. It was eventually amended so that half of the jury had to be British subjects. (Sir Francis Du Pré Oldfield, *The Cambridge History of India*, vi, 387.)

[5] Banerjea, op. cit. p. 88.

Between 1870 and 1889 Bright still saw a great deal that was wrong with India. In 1877 he charged that the government in India extracted £50,000,000 a year from a population which 'has no voice; it is dumb before the Power that has subjected it'.[1] On another occasion he said, 'Our Indian Empire...is governed by a despotism—that is, a government which has no representative institutions.'[2] He felt remorse that, after so many years of British rule in India, famines such as that of 1877 were possible.[3] Cutting through what he regarded as the cynicism of British rule in India, he wrote regarding the abolition of the opium duties: 'To save the amount in reduced estimates & expenditures might be possible, but as England holds India for what she can get out of it in places salaries & pensions there is no use in recommending that method.'[4] However, he rebutted suggestions that the logical end of his arguments was the abandonment of India, although it would be necessary for Britain to become 'a little bit rational about it'.[5]

What did 'becoming rational' in India involve? The first important changes must be made in financial policy. Bright still started from the position that India was essentially 'in great and abject poverty'.[6] The most obvious but at the same time the most difficult reduction in expenses could be effected by reducing the military budget. He pointed out that £30,000,000 more had been spent in military costs by Conservatives from 1874 to 1880 than by the Liberals from 1868 to 1874. Were it not for this fact, reductions in the salt tax or measures to ward off famine could have been initiated.[7]

After the famine of 1877 Bright, on the same platform in Manchester as Sir Arthur Cotton, pledged his belief in the value of irrigation schemes in India. He did not, as he had done in 1854–5, recommend any particular canal, but rather asked that the government deal with the question.[8] In Parliament he recommended that an inquiry into possible irrigation

[1] *The Times*, 12 Dec. 1877, p. 6, col. f. [2] Ibid., 17 April 1879, p. 11, col. c.
[3] Hansard, vol. 237, 343.
[4] Sturge Papers, Add. MSS. 43,723. Bright to J. Sturge, 10 Oct. 1876, f. 140.
[5] *The Times*, 17 April 1879, p. 11, col. d.
[6] Ibid., 12 Dec. 1877, p. 6, col. f.
[7] Ibid., 4 Jan. 1882, p. 6, col. a. [8] Ibid., 12 Dec. 1877, p. 7, col. b.

schemes be carried out in India.[1] In 1883 he recommended the plan of land banks for India as devised by Wedderburn to help overcome the high rates of interest charged to Indian cultivators.[2]

Bright still regarded it as impossible for one man, the Governor-General, to rule India,[3] and continued to advocate his decentralization scheme.[4] His ideas on this matter received some kind of sanction by the Liberal party when a pamphlet, written by William Digby,[5] was published by the National Liberal Federation in 1881. Digby quoted extensively from Bright's 1858 speech in Parliament, and thought his proposals were the answer to India's difficulties. He called for vigorous measures to help realize Bright's programme.[6]

It is evident, however, that Bright was shifting the emphasis in his speeches from decentralization to the wisdom of allowing self-government to India. In 1876 he said, '...I trust it is not very remote, when there may be some kind of free institutions established in that country'.[7] His belief grew more demanding with time. In 1885 he said, 'Wisdom suggests and urges a policy that will conciliate millions, and arrangements that will enable India to enter tranquilly on the path of self-government and independence.'[8] Hand in hand with this, Britain should learn that 'her absolute rule in her Asiatic Empire is temporary'.[9]

The possession of India, in Bright's view, also meant that friendship with Russia was of utmost importance. In 1873 he thought that the sooner there was a conterminous frontier between Russia and Great Britain in northern India, the better.

[1] Hansard, vol. 237, 344–8.

[2] *The Times*, 5 July 1883, p. 11, col. d.

[3] Gladstone Papers, Add. MSS. 44,113. Bright to Gladstone, 20 Feb. 1872, f. 12.

[4] *The Times*, 12 Dec. 1877, p. 7, col. b.

[5] DIGBY, WILLIAM (1849–1904). Educated at British schools in India; became editor of *Madras Times* in 1877; returned to England in 1879 to become a newspaper editor; active in Liberal causes; directed Indian political agency which distributed Indian news in Britain.

[6] W. Digby, *Indian Problems for English Consideration*, pp. 58–63.

[7] *The Times*, 5 Dec. 1876, p. 4, col. d.

[8] Ibid., 8 Dec. 1885, p. 7, col. d.

[9] Ibid., Bright thought that the decision to educate the Indians had practically resolved the future course to self-government. (*The Times*, 8 Dec. 1885, p. 7, col. c.)

He wrote, 'Two great nations & two civilized & honourable Govts with a defined frontier, will be a far better security for peace than a debateable land between two frontiers.'[1] But this did not imply that Britain should take over Afghanistan. In 1879 he condemned the attempts of the Disraeli government to do so.[2] By 1882 he was content without the conterminous border. He asked, 'if it is not better that we should have upon our Indian frontier a people independent and friendly rather than hostile people in subjection to us?'[3] In the constant preaching of the danger of Russia to the Indian empire, he felt that there was another danger as well: 'You persuade the people of India by writings in the Press and by the speeches of public men in this country that we run great hazard from the advances of Russia, and if you have enemies in India, of course you feed their enmity by this language, and if they wish to escape from the Government of England you make them turn naturally and inevitably to Russia as the power that can help them.'[4]

Bright continued to advocate the better treatment of the Indian population by British officials. In 1875 in Parliament he recalled his advice in 1858 in this regard,[5] and he thought there was yet room for improvement. He expressed his hope that the proposed visit of the Prince of Wales in 1876 would set a worthy example of the correct attitude to be taken towards Indians.[6]

Finally, Bright set Britain the task of ruling India above considerations of economic advantage. He said, 'Our right to India and the rule of it at present must depend upon the services which we render to the millions of her people. It cannot depend permanently on our imports from India of rice, jute, tea, cotton, and wheat, or exports of calico from the mills of Lancashire.'[7] India must be persuaded that she was not being governed 'for mere selfish objects'.[8] In 1878 he had advised that irrigation schemes could not be built by the govern-

[1] Granville Papers P.R.O. 30/29/52. Bright to Granville, 2 Jan. 1873.

[2] *The Times*, 17 April 1879, p. 11, col. c.

[3] Ibid., 4 Jan. 1882, p. 6, col. a.

[4] Ibid., 14 Jan. 1878, p. 10, col. b.

[5] See Hansard, vol. 151, 347–9.

[6] Ibid., vol. 225, 1519–20.

[7] *The Times*, 9 July 1887, p. 9, col. d.

[8] Ibid., 23 Nov. 1885, p. 10, col. f.

ment solely on economic grounds. Some would fail to pay a profit, but they might save lives. He did not agree with the Secretary of State for India, Lord George Hamilton, who talked of it as a business matter.[1] It was Bright's opinion that 'India was not committed to our control to be held as a field for English ambition and for English greed.'[2]

Bright's contribution to parliamentary debates on India was slight between 1870 and 1889. His chief medium for raising Indian topics was the public platform in Birmingham or London. His interest in India was at its lowest point in the 1870s, when Goldwin Smith wrote of him: 'But time and perhaps social influences have mellowed the Great Tribune...in Parliament he has been silent and apparently apathetic.'[3] Bright himself wrote, 'Tonight we are to have India & some considerable debate—but I do not think I shall take part in it. If others will say what is wanted, I let them say it, & do not interfere. I seem to have no desire to talk in the House.'[4] Though his interest showed some signs of resuscitation in 1877, it was again curtailed when he became a cabinet minister in 1880. When he resigned as Chancellor of the Duchy of Lancaster in July 1882, he once again became active in the support of Indian causes. Both Indians and Europeans who came from India to seek supporters in Britain realized that his eminent position could count powerfully on their side.

One reason for his declining interest in the 1870s was that he lacked the intimate contacts of which he had had the advantage in the 1850s. It is significant that at the time of the Indian famine in 1877 it was still the same J. B. Smith with whom he had conferred in 1847 to whom he turned for information and advice.[5] In 1878 he wrote to his wife, '...I have no one to consult with who knows anything of India, or cares about it'.[6] He was sixty-seven in 1878, and this may have been another factor. He wrote to Smith, 'If you & I were younger

[1] Hansard, vol. 237, 347.
[2] *The Times*, 2 Aug. 1883, p. 6, col. b.
[3] M. E. Wallace, *Goldwin Smith*, p. 82.
[4] Bright Papers, U.C. Bright to his wife, 22 Jan. 1878.
[5] Smith Papers, MS. 923.2, S.344 (59). Bright to J. B. Smith, 30 Aug. 1877.
[6] Bright Papers, U.C. Bright to his wife, 20 Jan. 1878.

perhaps we might have been able to do something in this matter [famine].'[1]

With the accession of Lord Ripon to the Governor-Generalship of India in 1880 and his own resignation from the cabinet in 1882, Bright began to play a greater part in Indian affairs again. He looked with hope to Lord Ripon for the implementation of his proposed policies in India. Indeed, he may have had some influence in Gladstone's choice of Ripon.[2] Dr S. Gopal in his book has criticized the lack of support given in Britain to Lord Ripon while he was in India.[3] It would be unfair to include Bright in this general condemnation, for after he had resigned he took up Lord Ripon's cause with enthusiasm. And little wonder, for Dr Gopal remarks, 'He [Ripon] represented in India the doctrines of Bright and Gladstone, and shared their idealism and their belief that religious and ethical principles should guide nations as well as men.'[4]

Lord Ripon was anxious to secure Bright's help. He wrote, '...I need not say what a great advantage it would be to the cause which I have at heart, if you would say a few words in support of my proceedings...in the House of Commons'.[5] Bright did not say anything in the House, but he did take the chair at a meeting in Willis's Rooms on 1 August 1883, in company with W. E. Forster (M.P. for Bradford), H. Richard (M.P. for Merthyr Tydfil), T. B. Potter (M.P. for Rochdale), and other supporters of Lord Ripon. He gave his unqualified approval to the work in which Lord Ripon was engaged, including the Ilbert Bill and Ripon's scheme for extending municipal government. He also welcomed Ripon's encouragement of private enterprise, which he thought was an improvement over the system of government administration of business.[6] He praised Ripon's policy as '...not based on suspicion or on ancient prejudices, or on a spirit of monopoly, but based on

[1] Smith Papers, MS. 923.2, S.344 (61). Bright to J. B. Smith, 8 Sept. 1877.

[2] Bright wrote that he and Gladstone discussed the claims of various men to that position. (Walling, p. 437.)

[3] S. Gopal, *The Viceroyalty of Lord Ripon 1880–84*, p. 215.

[4] Ibid., p. 221.

[5] Bright Papers, Add. MSS. 43,389. Ripon to Bright, 30 Dec. 1882, f. 348.

[6] *The Times*, 2 Aug. 1883, p. 6, cols. a–b.

what is just and generous, and on broad views of statesmanship'.[1]

Ripon was grateful for such support, and wrote, '...I shall persist firmly in that policy in spite of the vehement opposition which it has encountered from the Anglo-Indian jingoes'.[2] On another of the several occasions that Bright spoke on India, he branded the Anglo-Indians as the greatest impediment to the generous treatment of Indians.[3] This opinion contrasts with his earlier view when he, like Dickinson,[4] had regarded the presence of an English population in India as a nucleus of progressivism. Disputes, such as occurred with the Bengal indigo planters in the 1860s, revealed the futility of this hope.

Another policy of Lord Ripon's that Bright undoubtedly agreed with but said little about was the abolition of Indian customs duties in 1882.[5] Many Indians were dissatisfied with Lancashire's expressed desire to repeal them.[6] But in a curious way they dissociated Bright from their distaste despite his free trade views. Ripon, in explaining to the people of India his reasons for withdrawing the duties, was careful to point out that he did so not because of Manchester pressure, but rather because he was a confirmed free-trader. He did not think that anyone who had stood beside Bright and Cobden during the Anti-Corn Law League agitation would find it possible to accuse them of any selfish aims.[7] The *Hindoo Patriot*, though it conducted a vigorous campaign against repeal,[8] had welcomed Bright's re-election to Parliament in 1874 because of his 'grand services'.[9]

There were several reasons why Bright was not associated with the disgust felt by many Indians for those who wished to institute free trade in India. For one thing, he had conducted no campaign, nor had he ever spoken in Parliament on the

[1] Ibid., col. b.

[2] Bright Papers, Add. MSS. 43,389. Ripon to Bright, 27 Aug. 1883, f. 349.

[3] *The Times*, 8 Dec. 1885, p. 7, col. c.

[4] Bell, p. 32.

[5] Bright spoke of the abolition of the cotton duties in 1882 as a desirable measure. (*The Times*, 4 Jan. 1882, p. 6, col. a.)

[6] G. D. Birks, 'Industrialization in India', *The Annals of the American Academy of Political and Social Science*, ccxxxiii (May, 1944), 121–2.

[7] *Speeches of the Marquis of Ripon*, ed. Kali Prasanna Sen Gupta, pp. 246–7.

[8] *Hindoo Patriot*, 31 Aug. 1874, p. 413, col. a.

[9] Ibid., 16 Feb. 1874, p. 77, col. a.

subject. Though there could be no mistaking his views on the issue, he was fair-minded, and criticized publicly the Manchester Chamber of Commerce because in 1877 some of its members were advocating the imposition of a 5 per cent excise duty on Indian manufactured goods.[1] Since Manchester sponsored this proposal, Bright refused to attend a meeting there because he felt he could not speak from their platform.[2] In 1877 Bright felt that only through greater economy in the public expenditure, by increased public revenue, or by a new tax could the cotton duties be repealed.[3]

One reason for Bright's resurgence of interest in India from 1877 to 1887 (except the years 1880 to 1882) was the Indian famine of 1877. He hoped that, as the mutiny had destroyed the East India Company, the famine would allow the introduction of irrigation measures as recommended by Sir Arthur Cotton.[4] Another cause was the influence of Indians who sought his aid. One with whom he was particularly well acquainted was Lalmohun Ghose,[5] who had planned with Bright the meeting held at Willis's Rooms in 1883.[6] For his part, Bright gave his support to the proposed parliamentary candidature of Ghose in 1884 at Greenwich.[7] Bright also met Dadabhai Naoroji in 1886, and promised to help him get a candidacy for Parliament.[8] On at least two occasions in the 1885 election campaign (21 November and 6 December) Bright had delegates from India on his platform.[9]

Lalmohun Ghose had been sent to Britain by the Indian Association,[10] and it is some indication of Bright's prestige that he was sought out.[11] There are other examples of his importance to those interested in India. When Sir William Wedderburn formed a parliamentary committee on India in 1883, it seemed

[1] Leech, pp. 180–1.
[2] Smith Papers, MS. 923.2 S.344. (59). Bright to J. B. Smith, 30 Aug. 1877.
[3] Leech, p. 180.
[4] Smith Papers, MS. 923.2, S.344. (60). Bright to J. B. Smith, 7 Sept. 1877.
[5] B.M. 10606 a 36, By one who knows him, *Lalmohun Ghose*, p. 17.
[6] Walling, pp. 503–4.
[7] *The Times*, 25 Nov. 1884, p. 10, col. d.
[8] Masani, op. cit., p. 231.
[9] *The Times*, 23 Nov. 1885, p. 10; and 8 Dec. 1885, p. 7. The three delegates were M. Ghose (Bengal), N. Chandavarkar (Bombay), and S. Ramasawny Mudaliyer (Madras).
[10] See p. 69.
[11] Walling, p. 424.

necessary to him to approach Bright to act as chairman.[1] In a memorandum printed in *India* in 1890, Wedderburn wrote that Bright had approved the organization of an Indian committee of about fifty Members, and had consented to be the chairman of a small working committee. Wedderburn believed that the scheme commended itself to Bright because it was reminiscent of the India Reform Society of 1853.[2] According to Wedderburn, there were over fifty M.P.s who were members of the committee. In 1885 this committee supported the motion of J. Slagg (M.P. for Manchester) for an inquiry into the 1858 Government of India Act. A change in government prevented the motion from proceeding.[3]

Another example of the esteem with which Bright was held by Indian reformers is afforded by the visit of A. O. Hume in 1885. The first man he contacted was Bright, who at that time was in company with Sir James Caird in Scotland.[4] One of the points they agreed upon was that information on Indian affairs for English newspapers would be provided by an association in India.[5] Hume's discussion with Bright and others, including R. T. Reid (M.P. for Hereford), led to the conclusion that it was not yet time to put the 1883 committee on a permanent basis. As a result, the committee fell into abeyance and was not revived until after Bright's death.[6]

Bright's sympathetic attitude evoked much appreciative response in India. An admirer wrote, '...we in Bombay are not wanting in any degree in appreciation of what you have done in past times...which entitles you to the high consideration and gratitude of the population of this vast Indian Empire'.[7] Reverence for him among Indians continued long after his death. Gandhi invoked the magnanimity of Bright's spirit during his struggles in South Africa.[8]

Though Bright's work in Parliament between 1870 and 1889

[1] Ripon Papers, Add. MSS. 43,618. Sir W. Wedderburn to Ripon, 4 March 1889, f. 2.

[2] *India*, 5 Dec. 1890, p. 295.

[3] Wedderburn, op. cit., p. 93.

[4] Ibid., p. 54.

[5] Walling, pp. 530–1.

[6] Wedderburn, op. cit., pp. 57, 93.

[7] Bright Papers, Add. MSS. 43,389. J. Ratnogan (?) to Bright, 25 Feb. 1878, ff. 228–9.

[8] *The Collected Works of Mahatma Gandhi*, i, 161.

was negligible, he had made admirable use of the public platform to set an ideal of service and good government for India. His support of Lord Ripon was extended at a critical time. His emphasis upon the need to set India on the path to self-government was all the more timely since the British government in this period 'had no sense of direction, no definite conception of the goal towards which the Government of India was to travel'.[1]

[1] S. R. Mehrotra, *India and the Commonwealth 1885–1929*, p. 26.

CHAPTER III

The Colonies 1843–1870

SPEAKING in 1828 on the question of relinquishing Canada, William Huskisson declared: 'I may be allowed to say, that England cannot afford to be little. She must be what she is, or nothing.'[1] Huskisson could well have been throwing down the glove here for a clash of opinion about the Empire, the echoes of which continued to ring in twentieth-century politics.[2] Of the anti-imperialists, Radicals showed greater hostility to the Empire because basically they saw it as leading to obfuscating emotionalism, class self-interest, and unwarranted expense. But even the harshest critics, the Utilitarians, leave some considerable doubt whether the rigour of their denunciations should be interpreted as recommendation for dissolution.[3]

When the colonial critic surveyed Britain's Empire as it was after 1815, he was confronted by a world-wide group of possessions, the size and variety of which were not unduly impaired by the loss of the Thirteen Colonies. British control extended over a large part of North America, including Upper and Lower Canada, the Maritime colonies of Newfoundland, Prince Edward Island, Nova Scotia and New Brunswick. The British West Indies comprised numerous colonies. In West Africa Britain had only trading sites, with the exception of Sierra Leone, which had been set up in 1787 as a settlement for liberated slaves. The importance of safeguarding a sea-route to India had necessitated the retention of Ceylon, Mauritius and the Cape of Good Hope in 1814. The founding of New

[1] Quoted in K. Knorr, *British Colonial Theories, 1570–1850*, p. 362.

[2] See the verdict of O. Macdonagh in: O. Macdonagh, 'The Anti-Imperialism of Free Trade', *Econ. Hist. Rev.*, xiv, no. 3 (1962), 500–1.

[3] Knorr, op. cit., pp. 266–8.

South Wales in 1788 as a penal establishment was soon followed by the colonization of other parts of Australia. In 1840, New Zealand was brought under the British Crown.

At the time Bright entered Parliament in 1843, the spokesman for colonial affairs was the Secretary of State for War and the Colonies. Implementing his policies was the Colonial Office, which attracted men who were young, energetic and generally very capable.[1] One of the most important figures connected with the Colonial Office in the first half of the nineteenth century was James Stephen, who held the office of Permanent Under-Secretary of State for the Colonies from 1836 to 1847. Stephen did not think of the colonies as a source of profit, but rather as an onerous responsibility. He thought such territories as Canada and Australia would eventually become independent, but that in the meantime they should be governed in the best interests of their inhabitants.[2] During his term in the Colonial Office, Stephen became a spokesman for evangelical tendencies, then so pervasive in British society. However, some cabinet ministers were formidable enough to put their own stamp on the department; one might cite the example of the third Earl Grey, who was Colonial Secretary from 1846 to 1852. It was he who first notified the government of Canada in 1851 that it was official policy henceforth to insist upon greater colonial responsibility for the cost of military protection.[3] He also insisted (in accordance with Wakefield's ideas) on the imperial retention of the control of land in Australia despite the unpopularity of such a system.[4]

Following the American Revolution, there had been some disillusionment in Britain regarding the value of settlement colonies. This arose not so much from pessimism as from the realization that profits in trade with countries such as the United States did not depend on sovereignty.[5] This sentiment

[1] See D. M. Young, *The Colonial Office in the Early Nineteenth Century*, pp. 68–71, 120–3.

[2] Sir L. Woodward, *The Age of Reform 1815–1870*, pp. 367–8.

[3] C. P. Stacey, *Canada and the British Army 1846–1871*, pp. 79–81. This book, recently republished, traces the ramifications of this announcement.

[4] D. Southgate, *The Passing of the Whigs 1832–1886*, p. 167.

[5] H. T. Manning, *British Colonial Government after the American Revolution 1782–1820*, p. 5.

was further strengthened by the 'Swing to the East' in the trading pattern of British merchants during the latter half of the eighteenth century.[1] In settlement colonies the general tendency of the British government was to strengthen as much as possible the ties with the mother country, and the constitutions granted to them were designed to reproduce the conditions of the more stratified British society.

The attempt to re-create 'the social and political features of 18th Century England' in the colonies was impracticable.[2] This is well brought out in the case of Upper and Lower Canada. Here a system of government that attempted to combine a representative assembly with a nominated executive was running into difficulties. In the early decades of the nineteenth century, radicals in both Canadas were dissatisfied with the rate of reform, and resented the control of the oligarchic 'Family Compact' in Upper Canada and the 'Château Clique' in Lower Canada. Soon resentment grew less moderate, and extremists like W. L. Mackenzie in Upper Canada and L. J. Papineau in Lower Canada took matters into their own hands. In 1837 an insignificant brawl in Montreal turned into a minor revolt; the rebellion in Upper Canada scarcely deserved the name, but such incidents seemed to prove to Radicals in Britain that colonial policy had been misguided.

To assess the situation the British government sent Lord Durham to Canada. In his famous report 'that still stands as one of the greatest state papers in the history of the British Empire',[3] he proposed local self-government as the solution to difficulties. That events had led to insurrection was not by any means entirely the fault of British statesmen. As a matter of fact, opinion in favour of granting responsible government to the settlement colonies had been current in Britain since the late eighteenth century.[4] Before Durham's mission the Whig ministers were ready to concede local self-government, and were handicapped as much by lack of agreement within colonial assemblies as to what they wanted as by any disinclination on

[1] V. T. Harlow, *The Founding of the Second British Empire*, i, 62. But see also G. S. Graham, *The Politics of Naval Supremacy*, pp. 101–2.

[2] Harlow, op. cit., i, 10.

[3] D. G. Creighton, *Dominion of the North*, p. 246.

[4] See P. Knaplund, *Cambridge History of the British Empire*, ii, 298–9.

their own part to grant responsible government.[1] Even before the difficulties with Upper and Lower Canada had arisen, Parliament had displayed a new awareness of colonial problems, particularly because of the endeavours of Joseph Hume.[2] Bright took his seat at a time when the solution of responsible government had been proposed, but it had not yet been put into practice in the newly united colony of Canada.

Nor were conditions much improved in the first few years of Bright's membership in the House. It was Gladstone's judgment in 1849 that the authority of the Crown, because of such riotous incidents as accompanied the signing of the Rebellion Losses Bill in Canada, was suffering blows equal in precedent only to the tea-riots in Boston.[3] The Constitutional Act of 1791 in Canada had provided that an amount of land equal to one-seventh of all land granted was to be given to the Protestant church,[4] and this provision remained a source of dissension among Protestant churches and those who supported secularization until 1853. The Australian Colonies Government Bill in 1850, though granting partially elected councils, made no mention of responsible government, and was met with hostility in New South Wales.

In Ceylon, Lord Torrington had arrived in 1847 to face a financial crisis, and had instituted a series of new taxes to relieve the situation. In July 1848, an insurrection broke out in the province of Kandy because of dissatisfaction with the taxes and British rule generally. The revolt was put down, but martial law was continued so long that criticism forced the Governor to resign in 1850. Until 1852 the transportation of criminals to such places as Van Diemen's Land and the Cape Colony caused unrest within the colonies concerned. In 1849 Sir William Molesworth thought conditions were so deplorable that he moved for a Royal Commission to investigate the administration of the colonies.[5]

[1] H. T. Manning, 'The Colonial Policy of the Whig Ministers 1830–37', *Can. Hist. Rev.*, xxxiii, no. 3 (September, 1952), 203.

[2] H. T. Manning, *British Colonial Government After the American Revolution 1782–1820*, p. 525.

[3] W. S. Childe-Pemberton, *Life of Lord Norton*, p. 76.

[4] V. Harlow and F. Madden, *British Colonial Developments 1774–1834*, pp. 213–14.

[5] *Selected Speeches of Sir William Molesworth*, ed. H. E. Egerton, pp. 216–64.

Bright had displayed an early interest in colonial problems, his attitude undoubtedly shaped principally by Adam Smith. The latter had contended that Britain gained nothing from her possession of a colonial Empire. He had also shown that there was a difference between wealth and power, and that the attempt to create the latter by empire building did not necessarily lead to wealth. He had advocated colonial free trade and independence. But he had also said that no nation had ever given up its provinces, because it would be a blow to its pride.[1] Bright accepted these dicta,[2] and, as Knorr points out, 'Adam Smith's phrases of the "appendage" of the "splendid and showy equipage" of empire will be found an ever recurrent theme in their [Manchester School's] untiring denunciation of their country's "projects of empire".'[3]

In addition, Bright may have been influenced by such Dissenters as Richard Price and Joseph Priestley who had stressed that 'free association' with the colonies was 'the best bond of kinship'.[4] From the colonial reformers, such as Lord Durham, he inherited the passion to free the colonies from strict home supervision so that they could manage their own affairs. Bright was not greatly influenced by the Wakefield School. He did not share their enthusiasm for colonization, and early in his career he had decided that three acres of land for each man in the United Kingdom would enable him to maintain himself at less cost than a voyage to the colonies.[5]

II

The keynote of Bright's thoughts on the colonies was that the United Kingdom's first duty was to prepare the colonies of European settlement for self-government. He thought that if this were done, economic independence should follow logically. As he said in 1850, in reference to supplies for Canada's

[1] Knorr, op. cit., pp. 164-91.

[2] When it is stated that Bright accepted the idea of colonial independence, it is meant to refer to the granting of self-government by the mother country, or to colonial independence achieved by the expressed desires of the colonies.

[3] Knorr, op. cit., p. 195.

[4] Thornton, *The Imperial Idea and its Enemies*, p. 10.

[5] Brougham Papers, U.C. MS. 14,047. Bright to Lord Brougham, 5 July 1842.

ecclesiastical establishments, 'The Canadian government was as free as this Government, and nothing was more scandalous than that we should pay this money, and nothing more degrading to them than that they should receive it.'[1] If Britain fulfilled her duty, as she should, of allowing self-government in the settlement colonies, then he thought it only right and natural that economic obligations on the part of the mother country should lapse.

Rigid economy was needed in Bright's political schema, for if the liberal state were to be instituted, the most that could be done to aid any individual was to make living as cheap as possible. The political counterpart of this doctrine was enfranchisement of the masses. Just as Francis Place imagined that removal of the Combination Laws would cause the disappearance of unions, so Bright thought something approximating manhood suffrage would end working-class politics. His criticisms of the imperial system must be seen in light of the fact that in its unreformed state the Empire represented an excrescence of aristocratic class rule. The Empire in the mid-Victorian period was suspected less for what it was than for what it was connected with.

Bright, rightly, considered himself to have been a colonial reformer, as is to be seen in a letter to Cobden written in 1857 as a summary of the work of the Manchester School, 'Look again at our Colonial policy. Through the labours of Molesworth, Roebuck, & Hume—more recently supported by us & by Gladstone, every article in the creed which directed our Colonial policy has been abandoned, & now men actually abhor the notion of undertaking the government of the Colonies.'[2]

The assumption from which Bright proceeded on colonial affairs was well stated in 1848 when he said, 'It was all very well to talk about "this great Empire"; but for his own part, he could not help thinking that unless the colonies and dependencies which were united to England were inhabited by a free, happy, contented and prosperous population, it would be infinitely better for the English Crown and the English people

[1] Hansard, vol. 112, 1333.

[2] Bright Papers, Add. MSS. 43,384. Bright to Cobden, 16 April 1857, f. 92.

to abandon the thought of dependencies altogether, and to be content with this tight island of their own.'[1] His desire for satisfactory conditions in the colonies led him to ask a question in Parliament in 1849 about the unrest in Canada resulting from the signing of the Rebellion Losses Bill.[2]

This same concern for the inhabitants of Britain's colonies motivated him in 1850 to censure Earl Grey, Secretary for War and the Colonies, for not properly handling the inquiry into Lord Torrington's administration in Ceylon.[3] Torrington had been accused of using unduly severe methods in the suppression of revolt in Ceylon. A motion for a select committee had passed in 1849, but its operations were being hampered by government refusal to allow certain witnesses to report, and by not allowing the publication of evidence.[4] Bright did not think that conditions were so good in the colonies that such charges as those against Lord Torrington could be allowed to pass without a proper inquiry.[5] Later in 1850 he complained again of the methods of inquiry used, and urged that the evidence be placed before the House rather than the government.[6] On 12 August he supported a motion of Hume for printing the evidence. He thought that the private letters responsible for Lord Torrington's dismissal should be printed if it would mean better government for the colony.[7] Hume dropped his motion, however,[8] and it was not until 1851 that a motion was brought up condemning Lord Torrington's measures; it was defeated by eighty votes.[9]

One division during the Ceylon proceedings shows the union of the Manchester School, the colonial reformers and the Conservatives against the Whigs. On 6 February 1850, this combination supported Hume's motion that the select committee on Ceylon be given the power to call certain persons from Ceylon as witnesses. It was narrowly defeated by 109 votes to 100. The Manchester School was represented by Bright, T. Milner Gibson and J. B. Smith, while Molesworth

1 Hansard, vol. 97, 1185.
2 Ibid., vol. 105, 499.
3 Ibid., vol. 108, 450–2.
4 Bailey, *Ceylon*, pp. 108–9.
5 Hansard, vol. 108, 452.
6 Ibid., vol. 113, 346.
7 Ibid., 1051–3.
8 Ibid., 1056.
9 Bailey, op. cit., p. 109. Bright was not present.

and C. B. Adderley (M.P. for Staffordshire West) were among recognized colonial reformers in the division.[1]

In 1850 Bright took a very serious view of the extent of dissatisfaction with the Colonial Office felt in most British colonies. He wanted to know, considering the number of threats to suspend allegiance, why the government of the colonies remained unreformed. Certainly it was not the wish of 'the people' at home, and he expected improvement of colonial administration when a wider franchise was granted in Britain.[2] He amplified these remarks in Manchester in January 1852. He thought that both the colonists and the mother country would benefit if the former were given free institutions and complete control over their finances and military forces. But it was almost impossible, with the existing representative system in Great Britain, to insist on a reform of the Colonial Office. He thought it was absurd to suppose that one man in Downing Street could rule forty or fifty colonies in all parts of the world.[3]

Bright tried by private representations to secure the appointment of prominent colonial reformers to the cabinet. In 1852 he successfully urged the appointment of Sir William Molesworth to the Aberdeen government.[4] When Sidney Herbert retired as Secretary of State for the Colonies in 1855, he pressed his political ally, C. P. Villiers, to seek the office.[5]

In Parliament Bright regularly attacked what he regarded as unsuitable colonial appointments. In 1851, attention was directed to South Africa, where Sir Harry Smith, as Governor of the Cape, was involved in a Kaffir war. Bright criticized Smith for the pursuance of this war. He thought it was an unfortunate aspect of British colonial rule that officials sent out as governors were of two kinds: either military types, or men who had a bad banking account. He declared that if he were a colonist he would demand independence so that he would not be dragged into such 'barbarous' wars. He thought that a policy of 'mercy and justice' extended towards the Africans would result in peace.[6]

[1] Hansard, vol. 108, 458–60. [2] *The Times*, 31 Jan. 1850, p. 5, cols. d–e.
[3] Ibid., 18 Dec., 1851, p. 8, col. b.
[4] Smith Papers, MS. 923.2, S.344 (9). Bright to J. B. Smith, 27 Dec. 1852.
[5] Walling, p. 186. [6] Hansard, vol. 117, 763–6.

In 1854 Bright continued to press for the appointment of better colonial governors. He criticized the selection of Francis Lawley for South Australia, saying, 'I am not one of those who think that colonial appointments of this kind are unimportant; for let the House bear in mind, almost the only tie which connects our Colonies with the mother country is the tie of colonial government, and probably nothing in the whole colonial system is more important than the appointment of the individuals who in those Colonies shall represent the Crown.'[1] He thought that the proper men to appoint to such positions were those whose conduct the whole country had approved, and whom the colonists themselves would have good reason to trust. As it was, he felt that 'vast interests may be jeopardised' and the good will of the colonists lost by unwise appointments.[2]

Perhaps it was because of the reputation Bright had thus acquired that it was he and J. A. Roebuck (M.P. for Sheffield) who accompanied P. F. Little,[3] a representative of Newfoundland, to the Colonial Office in 1855 to protest against the conduct of Baillie Hamilton as Governor of that island.[4] In Parliament, the question was raised by Roebuck, who alleged that the Governor had held back the introduction of responsible government.[5] Palmerston agreed that there had been some delay in its inception, but assured Members that responsible government would shortly be implemented.[6] Bright criticized the tendency to appoint as colonial governors men who had some claim upon a political party. He thought it would be better if the Newfoundland Assembly could appoint the governor of the colony, and he recommended that the government look into the possibility of allowing a number of colonies to do the same. He maintained that representations on behalf of two-thirds of the Newfoundland Assembly had produced so little action that he considered the colonists had good cause to seek independence. In the same speech, he said that he was not satisfied with the way deputations were received at the Colonial

[1] Ibid., vol. 135, 1249. [2] Ibid., 1249–50.

[3] P. F. Little was the leader of the Liberal party in Newfoundland. (D. W. Prowse, *A History of Newfoundland*, pp. 464–5.)

[4] Walling, p. 185. [5] Hansard, vol. 137, 884–5.

[6] Ibid., 886.

Office. Lack of continuity in this office was another fault of imperial administration. Within a few months there had been no less than four Colonial Secretaries.[1]

Bright always upheld the ideal of allowing the colonies full internal self-government. In a letter published in *The Times* in 1858 he reminded Glasgow trade delegates that most of the land in the colonies belonged to the colonists, and that any attempt on the part of the home government to procure the land for immigrants would cause dissension.[2] Even when Canada decided in 1859 to impose semi-protective tariffs, a decision that was odious to him, he defended the right of the Canadian government to do so. Liberty had been granted to such an extent that it was too late to withdraw it.[3] Nor did he favour the suggestion put to him by E. Ellice (M.P. for St Andrews) that the Colonial Secretary should veto acts of the Canadian Parliament. He thought the use of such a veto would bring about great irritation and, perhaps, an early separation.[4]

In Bright's view, one of the advantages of granting self-government to the colonies would be a reduction in wars with native tribes in various colonies. In the 1840s he was concerned about the clashes in New Zealand between white settlers and the Maoris. More responsibility in government, including bearing the cost of their own wars, would, he thought, diminish the chances of such conflicts.[5]

If responsible government and good Crown appointments were one side of the coin, the other was financial retrenchment. Bright's dislike for established churches reinforced this consideration. In 1847 he made a complete study of the expense of supporting ecclesiastical establishments in the colonies, and was only prevented from introducing this subject to the House by his engagement on a parliamentary committee. He found that £46,000 was being expended in this way. He presented this fact in a letter to *The Times*.[6] In 1850 he protested against

[1] Hansard, vol. 137, 886–7.

[2] *The Times*, 8 Sept. 1858, p. 7, col. f.

[3] Ellice Papers, MS. Acc. 1993. Bright to E. Ellice, 16 Dec. 1859.

[4] Ibid. By the Union Act of 1840 the British government retained the right to disallow or reserve any Canadian legislation. (F. Madden, *Imperial Constitutional Documents 1765–1952*, p. 22.)

[5] Hansard, vol. 96, 1077–8.

[6] *The Times*, 9 Dec. 1848, p. 5, col. e.

the allocation of £11,228 for church establishments in Canada.[1] For the same purpose (to curtail expenses) he thought it possible that there could be one governor for three or four adjacent islands in the West Indies.[2]

Bright's concern for economy prompted him to speak in 1853 on the third clause of the Clergy Reserves (Canada) Bill. This clause would have prevented any deficiencies in the clergy reserves being drawn from the Consolidated Fund.[3] Lord John Russell then reversed the stand of the government by asking for the withdrawal of this clause because, he said, a solemn agreement had been made in 1840 that it should not be altered.[4] Bright remonstrated that the people of Britain, who were not so prosperous as the people of Canada, should have to be held responsible for the payment of any sum.[5] He personally advised Lord John Russell not to be so timorous in the face of difficulty.[6]

Concern for economy and the principles of free trade led Bright to uphold repeal of the sugar duties. The abolition of slavery in 1833 and the introduction of beet sugar in Europe had increased existing difficulties for the West Indian planters. But as far as Bright was concerned, the sugar duties were to be bracketed in the same category as the corn laws.[7] It was his opinion that the sugar duties were not only enervating Britain, but that they were also conducive to the use of poor agricultural methods in the colonies.[8]

Bright became very impatient with those who felt that anti-slavery principles should take precedence over the general application of free trade doctrines. J. J. Gurney, taking the usual Quaker view, explained to Bright that while he supported the principle of free trade, he could not extend his approval to the free entry of Brazilian sugar because it was slave produced.[9] Bright suspected Peel of using this fact as an excuse

[1] Hansard, vol. 112, 1331–3.
[2] Ibid., 1336.
[3] Ibid., vol. 125, 481.
[4] Ibid., 484. Bright attributed this turn of events to the 'clamour of the bishops and Mr. Gladstone'. (Walling, p. 139.)
[5] Hansard, vol. 125, 499–501.
[6] Walling, p. 139.
[7] Hansard, vol. 73, 661.
[8] Ibid., vol. 75, 451–2.
[9] *The Journal of the Friends Historical Society*, xxix (1932), 34–5. J. J. Gurney to Bright, 24 Feb. 1844.

to continue protection to West Indian sugar. He thought that men such as Gurney and Joseph Sturge were thus being tricked into upholding protection, and he argued that while the country had increased in population by about five millions since 1824, its imports of sugar since that time had actually decreased.[1]

Even in 1844 Bright's views on the sugar duties were so well recognized that *The Times* carried a short news item conveying the reason for his absence from one important division.[2] He did not speak during 1846, when the duties were repealed, but in 1848 he fought against a successful attempt to postpone to 1854 the change to free trade. Sir L. Woodward considers this to have been a fair request,[3] and certainly there was a great deal of distress in the islands,[4] but Bright moved an amendment upholding the 1846 Act. It was his argument that protection had prevented the introduction of effective agricultural methods in the West Indies. The colonies would have to wait upon increased production for their real security.[5] He was defeated by 302 to thirty-six.[6]

III

In the years 1857 to 1870 Bright further elucidated his views on colonial affairs. Although it was true that he did not want any extension of empire, neither did he favour its dismemberment except under circumstances where a particular colony desired independence. This is fully examined in the case of Canada. His concern with colonial matters did decline in this period, but he could still be aroused to support a colonial cause. This occurred between 1866 and 1870, when Joseph Howe enlisted his aid in opposing Nova Scotia's inclusion in the Canadian confederation.

The chief reason for the decline in Bright's interest in colonial affairs was that Canada, the eastern Australian colonies, and New Zealand had achieved responsible government early

[1] Sturge Papers, Add. MSS. 43,845. Bright to J. Sturge, 1 Sept. 1843, ff. 12–15.
[2] *The Times*, 26 June 1844, p. 6, col. c.
[3] Woodward, op. cit., p. 373.
[4] I. M. Cumpston, *Indians Overseas*, pp. 122–3.
[5] Hansard, vol. 99, 1414–35.
[6] Ibid., 1468–70.

in his parliamentary career. He credited responsible government with having transformed Canada from a rebellious to a very loyal colony.[1] He had also come to realize by 1868 that individual Members of Parliament could no longer hope to control expenditure. He looked to the setting up of a committee for this purpose as the best safeguard for retrenchment.[2]

Nevertheless, Bright remained steadfast in his opposition to all British expenditure for colonial needs. This opposition applied to imperial guarantees on loans for colonial economic schemes such as railways. In 1861 Cobden informed Bright of the presence of emissaries from New Brunswick and Nova Scotia whose purpose was to obtain money from the British government to help build a railway from Halifax to the St Lawrence.[3] Bright was as firmly opposed as was Cobden to such an idea, and considered writing a letter to the *Star* about it.[4]

This attitude to expenditure influenced Bright's view on the defence of the Empire. He protested in Parliament in 1859 against the prevailing system whereby the colonists did not pay, according to him, one farthing towards the naval and military services of their country. He would disagree with British expenditure for their defence except in wartime.[5] In 1865 he affirmed in Parliament that it was the duty of the government of a great empire to defend all its parts.[6] However, in practice, it seems that he was more than reluctant to assent to the use of British troops in self-governing colonies, even during times of possible war, as will be seen in the case of Canada.

Bright had declared in Parliament in 1849 that he considered the Empire was in no way a factor aiding trade. In a debate at that time, he stated that Sir Charles Wood had given the impression that the sums spent on maintaining colonies enabled Britain to acquire greater supplies of raw materials. Bright said he did not see how the presence of soldiers in Australia enabled Britain to get more wool.[7] In 1858, at Birmingham, he

[1] *The Times*, 30 Oct. 1858, p. 9, col. d.
[2] Ibid., 11 Nov. 1868, p. 12, col. c.
[3] Cobden Papers, Add. MSS. 43,651. Cobden to Bright, 7 Dec. 1861, ff. 306–7
[4] Bright Papers, Add. MSS. 43,384. Bright to Cobden, 9 Dec. 1861, f. 281.
[5] Hansard, vol. 152, 1302–3.
[6] Ibid., vol. 178, 165.
[7] Ibid., vol. 102, 1296.

declared that, with the exception of those in Australia, he thought that not one of the colonies, considering what it had cost in wars and defence, could be counted as profitable gain for the mother country.[1] The *Star* supported this argument in an editorial in 1863.[2]

Although Bright claimed that the Empire was of no value to Britain economically, he did not wish Britain, if the Empire were to disintegrate, to be responsible for the breaking-up. He thought it was impossible for Britain to give up her colonies. He wrote, '...give up all the colonies & dependencies of the Empire? Can any Statesmen do this, or can any country do this? I doubt it.'[3] In 1863, commenting favourably on the cession of the Ionian islands by Britain, he mentioned only Gibraltar, ironically enough, as another territory that Britain would be wise to vacate.[4] In specific reference to Canada, he wrote in 1859, 'I have no dread of the separation but I would avoid everything likely to provoke it.'[5]

An article by Professor J. Galbraith has relevance here. He points out that the differences in meaning between the terms 'Colonial Reformer', 'Liberal Imperialist' and 'Little Englander' are so slight that their use frustrates meaning instead of clarifying it. He argues that none of these groups advocated separation no matter how much they may have wanted it privately, and that terms such as 'Little Englander' were always used by opponents rather than by friends.[6] The principal aim both of Bright, as a member of the Manchester School, and of the colonial reformers was colonial self-government and the reduction of imperial expense.

If Bright did not wish Britain to be responsible for the dismemberment of the Empire, he was equally not anxious to see its aggrandizement. In 1858 he promised that he would not uphold one shilling spent in the extension of the Empire,

[1] *The Times*, 30 Oct. 1858, p. 9, col. c.
[2] *Morning Star*, 30 April 1863, p. 4, cols. d–f.
[3] Sturge Papers, Add. MSS. 43,723. Bright to J. Sturge, 24 Sept. 1857, f. 86.
[4] *The Times*, 16 Jan. 1863, p. 7, col. e.
[5] Ellice Papers, MS. Acc. 1993. Bright to E. Ellice, 16 Dec. 1859.
[6] J. Galbraith, 'Myths of the "Little England" Era', *Am. Hist. Rev.*, lxvii, no. 1 (Oct., 1961), 35–42. I have, however, used the term 'colonial reformer' for want of a better phrase.

which he felt was already large enough to satisfy anyone's ambition.[1] In 1859, when Lord John Russell hinted in the House that the possibility of acquiring cotton from the Fiji Islands was one of the reasons favouring the acceptance of their sovereignty by Britain, Bright countered by saying that although it was true that he was very interested in the growth of cotton, it was not to be assumed from this that he favoured taking control of those islands.[2]

On the other hand, if a colony wished to withdraw from the Empire, Bright would not object. This principle was to have special application to Canada, particularly between 1858 and 1870. He became convinced that the eventual destiny of Canada would be as part of the United States. He first decided this in 1859 when Canada had inaugurated a protective tariff.[3] He repeated the opinion in 1861 when he voiced his hope that one day the American continent would be a vast 'federation' of states without great armies or trade barriers.[4]

The association of the North American colonies with Britain had tended to magnify the difficulties of Canadian–American relations. After the estrangement of the American Revolution, the war of 1812 had broadened the 'schism' between Americans and Canadians.[5] There had been numerous border disputes between the United States and the provinces of British North America which threatened to bring on catastrophe. One dangerous source of conflict, the Maine–New Brunswick border, had been saved only by the wise concessions of the Webster–Ashburton treaty in 1842.[6] The 'manifest destiny' spirit in the United States caused apprehension among Canadians over the danger of possible American expansion. The rise of the Fenian movement in the United States also caused anxiety. For their part, the Americans were annoyed by ineffective measures to prevent Southern raiders from finding shelter in Canada before proceeding on an attack, as in the St Albans case. As tensions rose towards the end of the Civil War, Britain sent Colonel Jervois, a defence expert, to invest-

[1] *The Times*, 30 Oct. 1858, p. 9, col. e.
[2] Hansard, vol. 154, 1053.
[3] *The Times*, 30 Jan. 1885, p. 6, col. c.
[4] Ibid., 6 Dec. 1861, p. 6, col. b.
[5] H. L. Keenleyside and G. S. Brown, *Canada and the United States*, p. 79.
[6] A. B. Corey, *The Crisis of 1830–42 in Canadian–American Relations*, pp. 181–2.

igate Canadian defences. His report in 1864 emphasized that Canada could not be held by the regular and militia without extra fortifications.[1]

In 1865 Bright supported an amendment that would have cancelled a proposed expenditure of £50,000 on the fortifications of Quebec. One of the chief reasons for this was his unfailing opposition to imperial outlay for colonial purposes. Alluding to the proposed confederation of Canada that was, according to the Governor-General, to call into existence a 'new nationality', he said he would oppose any vote of taxes to defend a nationality not his own.[2]

Another powerful reason for Bright's opposition to a vote for Quebec fortifications was the fear that an increase in British garrisons in Canada would endanger peace with America. When he had first learned in 1861 that reinforcements were being sent to Canada,[3] he had been puzzled as to the reason.[4] He was worried that such a move could mean that the British government was preparing for war on the pretext that cotton could then be acquired.[5] He tried to soothe possible misunderstanding on the part of Charles Sumner,[6] with whom he regularly corresponded.[7] In Parliament on 17 February 1862, he made the point that the despatch of troops to Canada would be interpreted by the United States as an unfriendly act.[8] He wrote to Milner Gibson warning him that peace was being endangered, and that if he stayed in the cabinet and so became involved in such decisions, it would be impossible to resign later.[9]

By 1865 Bright was convinced that war would not break out,

[1] R. W. Winks, *Canada and the United States. The Civil War Years*, pp. 351–2.

[2] Hansard, vol. 177, 1614.

[3] Cobden Papers, Add. MSS. 43,651. Cobden to Bright, 3 Sept. 1861, f. 251.

[4] P.M.H.S., vol. 46, p. 94. Bright to Sumner, 6 Sept. 1861.

[5] Ibid., vol. 45, p. 154, 14 Dec. 1861.

[6] SUMNER, CHARLES (1811–74). American statesman; elected to U.S. Senate, in 1851; firm opponent of slavery; chairman of committee on foreign relations 1861; his influence declined after Civil War and was demoted from chairmanship.

[7] P.M.H.S., vol. 45, p. 156. Bright to Sumner, 21 Dec. 1861. Trevelyan states that Bright's letters were made available to President Lincoln. (*The Life of John Bright*, p. 310.)

[8] *The Times*, 18 Feb. 1862, p. 6, col. f.

[9] Bright Papers, Add. MSS. 43,388. Bright to Milner Gibson, 7 Dec. 1861, ff. 92–3.

but thought that if it did, Britain would be responsible, not the United States or Canada.[1] He emphasized in the House that fortification of Quebec would not frighten the United States, but would be an overt sign of distrust.[2] Correspondents had told him of the effects of the conduct of the British press and politicians on Canadian–American relations.[3] Sumner had written, 'If England were right, there would be little trouble here, & our war would soon be at an end.'[4] W. Whiting, of the United States War Department, had written to Bright assuring him of his government's pacific intentions.[5] Sumner thought that feelings in the United States against Canada had subsided in the latter part of 1864, and that peace was likely.[6] Bright's conclusion was that to avoid hostilities, Britain should refrain from obvious preparations for war.

Bright also objected to the Quebec fortifications because he thought that Canada would have to pay double any sum spent by Britain only because she was connected with Britain, not because there were any insoluble differences between Canada and the United States. He estimated that Canada would not tolerate such expense, and that if separation resulted, the whole blame would be placed on Great Britain. Future relations would be severely damaged by such a course.[7]

Finally, Bright did not think that Canada could be defended. To defend a frontier of over 1500 miles at a distance of 3000 or 4000 miles was, he thought, to any sane man impossible.[8]

What should be done if there were war? He said in Parliament in 1865 that in this case the only 'extrication' from it was 'in the neutrality or in the independence of Canada'.[9] He went on to say, 'I suspect from what has been stated by official Gentlemen in this Government and in previous

[1] Hansard, vol. 178, 165–6. Bright mentioned that the House of Lords, the City and the press were responsible for the war fever. (Hansard, vol. 177, 1618–19.)

[2] Ibid., vol. 178, 166.

[3] Bright Papers, Add. MSS. 43,391. Donald Ross to Bright, 6 Jan. 1862, ff. 76–7.

[4] Ibid., Add. MSS. 43,390. Sumner to Bright, 1 Jan. 1865, ff. 187–8. Sumner mentioned the speeches of Lord John Russell as one exacerbating factor.

[5] Bright Papers, Add. MSS. 43,391. W. Whiting to Bright, 27 Feb. 1865, f. 246.

[6] Ibid., Add. MSS. 43,390. Sumner to Bright, 1 Jan. 1865, f. 187.

[7] Hansard, vol. 178, 166–70.

[8] Ibid., 165.

[9] Ibid.

Governments that there is no objection to the independence of Canada whenever the Canadians shall wish it.'[1] He said he welcomed the expression of such opinions as it '...marked an extraordinary progress in sound opinions in this country'.[2]

Bright was not alone in his feeling that Canada could not be defended in case of war, and that it would be safer for her to be an independent nation in such circumstances. Major A. H. A. Anson (M.P. for Lichfield) gave as his opinion that it was impossible to defend Canada.[3] Seymour Fitzgerald (M.P. for Horsham), who raised the debate, believed that Canada would run no risk if she were an independent nation.[4] W. E. Forster (M.P. for Bradford) thought that Canada's best defence was neutrality.[5] C. B. Adderley thought it should be made clear to Canadians that Britain was not attempting to defend the whole frontier, but only her own troops in Quebec. He added that 'Canada had been trusting to a broken reed in relying for her defence upon England'.[6] Robert Lowe (M.P. for Colne) thought that it should be made plain to Canada that she had a perfect right to become independent or a part of the United States if she wished.[7] Disraeli commented, 'I do not grudge Canada its independence.'[8]

One advantage of Canadian independence from Bright's view was that it would save Canada from the ravages of war. Moreover, it would reduce Canada's defence expenditure and this might allow a lowering of import duties.[9] It would decrease the dangers represented by the Fenians. In 1866 he wrote, 'If I were a Canadian I should consider if it were not better to escape these injuries by separating from England.'[10] It would also, of course, relieve Britain of the responsibility for Canada's defences.

Another powerful factor in forming Bright's attitude to the question of independence for Canada was connected with his vision of a North American federation. He was concerned

[1] Hansard vol. 178, 168. Palmerston confirmed this opinion in the next speech. (Ibid., 173–4.)

[2] Ibid., 168.

[3] Ibid., vol. 178, 117.

[4] Ibid., vol. 177, 1546.

[5] Ibid., 1565.

[6] Ibid., vol. 178, 120.

[7] Ibid., 153–4.

[8] Ibid., 159.

[9] Ibid., 167–8.

[10] P.M.H.S., vol. 46, p. 152. Bright to Sumner, 14 Dec. 1866.

about the dangers to trade between Canada and the United States resulting from strained Anglo-American relations. He deplored the abrogation of the reciprocity treaty.[1] To a member of the commercial convention about to meet in Detroit in 1865, he expressed the hope that trade relations would be renewed between Canada and the United States. He thought it would be unfortunate if resumption were made impossible by Canada's connexion with Britain.[2] In April 1865, Bright thought that Canada would favour annexation to the United States rather than suffer increased taxes to fight, not a Canadian, but an imperial war. This idea grew out of his suspicion that the confederation scheme of the British North American colonies would never succeed.[3]

This opinion made it logical for Bright to aid the anti-confederate cause. However, before this struggle began, he became involved as one of the protagonists in the Governor Eyre case. His attention was drawn to it by the ugly situation in Jamaica resulting from the suppression of a disturbance by Eyre in 1865. He branded Eyre as the murderer of a negro preacher in the Jamaican assembly, and demanded that he stand trial for this act.[4] Despite assurances from Milner Gibson, then President of the Board of Trade, that a full inquiry would take place,[5] Bright, in the opening days of the 1866 session, repeated his conviction.[6] His reasons for taking an interest in this issue were undoubtedly humanitarian, but in his speech he gave another: 'Why, Sir, if such transactions as these could take place in the island of Jamaica, and there was no man to point a finger at them in this country, what might happen in all our other colonies and all the other dependencies of this wide Empire?'[7]

Meanwhile in British North America, confederation was finally moving forward, as the threat of Fenian invasions in 1866 seemed to render the arguments for union more convincing. The confederation of the provinces of British North

[1] Ibid., p. 134. Bright to Sumner, 19 Feb. 1865.

[2] Leech, p. 169.

[3] Smith Papers, MS. 923.2, S.344. (49). Bright to J. B. Smith, 14 April 1865.

[4] *The Times*, 1 Dec. 1865, p. 7, col. f.

[5] Bright Papers, Add. MSS. 43,388. Milner Gibson to Bright, 7 Dec. 1865, f. 110.

[6] Hansard, vol. 181, 320–3.

[7] Ibid., 323.

America had been mooted by Lord Durham. In 1858 A. T. Galt had presented resolutions in the Canadian Assembly favourable to a federal system for Canada and the adjoining eastern and western territories. As the Canadian legislative processes became deadlocked in the early 1860s, both major political parties agreed to work for a federal solution. In the eastern colonies, maritime union was being considered, but its attraction was never widespread, and when Canadian delegates expressed a desire to discuss a wider union, the Charlottetown conference was arranged. At this conference the Canadians made a favourable impression on the Maritimers, the force of their arguments being subsequently fortified by the victories of the North in the American Civil War. Both British political parties gave their support to the proposed union although, as a result of the rather unexpected popular opposition which had developed in New Brunswick and Nova Scotia, it was not until 1867 that Lord Carnarvon piloted the British North America Bill through Parliament.

Before the debate in the House, Bright had had the opportunity of meeting two supporters of the scheme, George Brown of Upper Canada and Dr Charles Tupper[1] from Nova Scotia. He had had one call from Joseph Howe[2] of Nova Scotia, who was the leading opponent of the bill.[3] Bright did not oppose the second reading, but he had strong objections to the proposed federation. One was his opinion that Nova Scotia had been placed within the proposed federation against the wishes of the people of that colony. He requested that the British North America Bill be delayed until Nova Scotia could have an election the following year.[4] He suspected that the uncommon

[1] TUPPER, SIR CHARLES (1821–1915). Edinburgh M.D. 1843; sat in legislative assembly of Nova Scotia 1855–67; prime minister, 1864–7; M.P. in Canadian parliament, 1867–84; in the Canadian cabinet, 1870–3 and 1879–84; appointed High Commissioner for Canada in London, 1883; returned to Canada in 1896 to become leader of Conservatives and prime minister; defeated at polls in 1896.

[2] HOWE, JOSEPH (1804–73). Editor and proprietor of Halifax *Nova Scotian*, 1828–41; elected to legislative assembly, 1836; sat in assembly 1836–63; foremost advocate of responsible government in colony; prime minister in 1860; retired to become fishery commissioner under reciprocity treaty, 1863; in 1866 led anti-confederation forces in Nova Scotia; in 1869 accepted office with Dominion government.

[3] Walling, pp. 294–5.

[4] Hansard, vol. 185, 1181–2.

speed with which the bill was being passed through Parliament was in large part due to the opposition of Nova Scotia to the plan. He had a point here; the bill was read in the House of Commons for the first time on 26 February, for the second on 28 February, and the third on 7 March. Another objection which Bright raised was the provision in the bill for a nominated senate. He saw that such a contrivance was the transplantation of an aristocratic element to a country whose destiny was democratic. He thought that eventually the nominated senate would have to be changed by the Imperial Parliament.[1]

Bright's final reservations concerned the spending of imperial money in the colonies. He stated that if British North America were to come constantly to the imperial exchequer for railway guarantees and help in defence, then it would be better for both Britain and the new federation that the latter should become independent. He thought it was time to make it clear '...that the taxes of England are no longer to go across the ocean to defray expenses of any kind within the Confederation which is about to be formed'.[2]

By 1868 the Nova Scotians who opposed federation, of whom Howe was the leader, were still not satisfied with their lot. C. B. Adderley, the Colonial Secretary in the Disraeli cabinet, admitted in Parliament that there was a great deal of unrest in the colony.[3] Howe once again, in 1868, called on Bright to gain his services for the province. But Howe was having some difficulties. He wrote to Bright, 'I begin to have nearly as bad an opinion of the two Houses of Parliament as you have. Admiral Erskine called this morning to say that Mr. Hadfield, who had put his notice of motion on the paper had, overpersuaded by Cardwell and Adderley, shrunk from moving it last night.' He also felt despondent because it was so difficult to get the prayer of a petition read in the House of Commons.[4] Bright attempted to aid Howe by presenting the petition against confederation on 15 May.[5] In all, Howe paid Bright three visits.[6] Bright relied upon the delegation with

[1] Ibid., 1180–3. [2] Ibid., 1184. [3] Ibid., vol. 192, 1678.

[4] Canadian National Archives, Ottawa. Howe Papers, MSS. MG 24, B29, vol. 10. J. Howe to Bright, 8 March (1868), (draft copy). Admiral Erskine was M.P. for Stirlingshire and G. Hadfield was M.P. for Sheffield.

[5] Walling, p. 325. [6] Ibid., pp. 316, 320, 325.

Howe for support. Two nights before his speech, he wrote, 'This even[g] I am to see some of my Nova Scotians about my speech.'[1] Representations for the other side were made to Bright by Dr Charles Tupper.[2]

On 16 June 1868, Bright moved that a commission be sent to Nova Scotia to ascertain the situation. In the main, his speech had two purposes. One was to show that Canadian federation was based on false premises. He suggested that it had been based on a desire to prevent union with the United States.[3] He made a good point of the fact that confederation had been devised to relieve political deadlock in Canada. However, his chief concern was to show that Nova Scotia had been unfairly treated. The petition that he had presented on 15 May had included the names of seventeen out of nineteen federal representatives, and thirty-six out of thirty-eight provincial members in Nova Scotia.[4] He charged that there had been pressure exerted by the Colonial Office, the Governor and Canadian officials on the electors of Nova Scotia in the recent election.[5] He dealt with the whole history of Canadian federation, attempting to show that Nova Scotia had always shown an antipathy to a wider union of the Canadian colonies, and had displayed interest only in some union of the maritime colonies.[6] He termed Nova Scotia 'the noblest colony',[7] and expressed his fear that unless Britain were to act as he recommended there would be an irresistible attraction to join the United States, a development which he would not like to see if it were based on a 'growing estrangement from England'.[8] These arguments had some effect on the House, because, despite the opposition of both front benches, whose supporters mustered a majority of 183, no less than eighty-seven voted on his side.[9]

The acknowledged strong opinions of Bright on the Nova

[1] Bright Papers, U.C. Bright to his wife, 14 June 1868.

[2] Walling, p. 320. There is an account of the interview given in *Life and Letters of the Rt. Hon. Sir Charles Tupper*, ed. E. M. Saunders, i, 176–7.

[3] Hansard, vol. 192, 1671.

[4] Ibid., 1659–62.

[5] Ibid., 1667. For examples, see P. B. Waite, *The Life and Times of Confederation.*

[6] Hansard, vol. 192, 1659–67.

[7] Ibid., 1666. [8] Ibid., 1673. [9] Ibid., 1697.

Scotia situation led to an exchange of correspondence with the Secretary of State for the Colonies, Lord Granville, after Bright had entered the cabinet. Lord Granville had been requested by the Governor-General of Canada to state the intentions of the British government not to interfere with the British North America Act. Granville thought that the great majority of the cabinet, including Gladstone, opposed interference, but he wished to inform Bright before a decision was taken. Granville thought such an announcement would force more repealers to join Joseph Howe, who had now changed sides in favour of confederation.[1]

Bright replied that he would allow Granville to take whatever decision he wished, and that he would not propose a discussion in the cabinet, but he warned Granville of the danger in the situation. He did not think Howe's desertion would affect the discontent which 'he did not create'. Bright proceeded to argue: 'I condemned the original Act as a gross violation of all the principles on which our Colonies have been governed for 25 years back, & as a great wrong to the Colony of Nova Scotia.... I greatly fear that if we compel Nova Scotia to submit, we shall create a feeling of hostility, not to Canada only, but to England, which may have bad results....*It should not be forgotten that the Colonies of Nova Scotia & New Brunswick are very near to the New England states.*'[2]

Bright followed a consistent policy throughout the mid-nineteenth century in regard to Canada's association with Britain. It was best stated by him in 1867 when he said, 'For my share, I want the population of these Provinces to do that which they believe to be the best for their own interests—remain with this country if they like, in the most friendly manner, or become independent States if they like. If they should prefer to unite themselves with the United States, I should not complain even of that.'[3] He doubted the wisdom of Canada's remaining within the Empire, but he went no further in acting on this doubt than voicing a warning of the possible difficulties with the United

[1] Bright Papers, Add. MSS. 43,387. Granville to Bright, 14 Jan. 1869, ff. 7–9.

[2] Granville Papers, P.R.O. 30/29/52. Bright to Granville, 17 Jan. 1869. (Bright's emphasis.)

[3] Hansard, vol. 185, 1185.

States[1] and continuing his own opposition to imperial guarantees of loans to Canada.

The charges that Bright advocated separation[2] have emanated largely from the debates in 1865 on the defence of British North America. But, as has been seen, many British politicians, including Disraeli, realized that British power was faced with an impossible task in defending Canada. In this circumstance they were anxious to inform Canadian statesmen that independence would not be thwarted if such a step was consonant with their wishes. Undoubtedly in such statements there was a degree of wishful thinking that the Canadians would indeed take the hint. The dilemma was basically between the possible insult to colonial opinion by a clear appraisal of the situation or the false buoying of Canadian hopes by the continued pretences of an impotent protector. As for Bright, he never appreciated the force of Canadian sentiment in favour of the imperial connexion, and thus unwittingly erred on the side of offending colonial loyalties. He made, however, no overt recommendations for joining with the United States. When E. W. Watkin (M.P. for Stockport) insinuated that Bright wanted the British North American colonies to be a part of the United States,[3] the *Star* came to Bright's defence, calling the charge 'a gratuitous and unfounded misrepresentation'. It emphasized the fact that Bright had set before Canada the choice of her own path.[4]

Bright did not want to see Britain the cause of any ill-feeling within a colony. That explains his strong advocacy of the cause of Nova Scotia in 1867–8. If union with the United States were to come, it should be freely contracted, free of any strain or bad relations with the mother country. It could be argued that resentment might be felt in the colonies if Bright's views on the economic relations of mother country and colony were implemented. He seemed to narrow the grounds of discontent that Britain should avoid to political and constitutional ones.

Though Bright said he was not opposed to Canadian con-

[1] Bright said that the danger in North America might arise from a desire on the part of the United States to avenge hostile British measures. It could also result from Canadian impolicy, such as the St Albans affair, concerning which he was very critical. (Hansard, vol. 177, 1615, 1621–9.)

[2] See C. A. Bodelsen, *Studies in Mid-Victorian Imperialism*, p. 34.

[3] Hansard, vol. 185, 1888–9. [4] *Morning Star*, 1 March 1867 p., 4, col. d.

federation in principle,[1] it must be admitted that he was not in the least impressed with the potential of Canada as a nation. From 1865 to the end of his career he thought he saw signs of confederation breaking down. In 1886 he used this argument for declining to support Chamberlain's idea of federation for Ireland based in part on the Canadian principle.[2] He opposed not only money grants to the proposed Canadian Pacific Railway, but the very need for such a line,[3] although construction of this railway did more than just bind the new nation together in a physical sense. It is perplexing to think that Bright believed that a great nation would survive the fratricidal conflicts undergone by the United States, but failed to see how British North America could overcome difficulties, such as sectionalism, of lesser magnitude.

Bright's optimism concerning an eventual union between Canada and the United States indicated a lack of understanding of the direction that nascent Canadian nationalism would take. He could not have understood the sentiments which caused the British Empire Loyalists to leave their homes in the United States after the Revolution. By looking upon the question as one of economics, he overlooked the large part that sympathies and loyalties had to play.

Bright's efforts were directed towards making the concept of empire more flexible, and less concerned with sovereignty. Where the colonies of European settlement were concerned, empire could just as easily be a bond of mutual interests, origins, language and customs, without political claims or economic obligations. Illustrative of this contention is his attitude towards the United States. It was just as much a 'colony' of Britain as the Canadian provinces or the Australian colonies. The United States employed representative government and to some extent shared a common racial background with Britain. He thought that though the forms of government might vary, all 'English' countries had a common destiny of democratic government. He was convinced that the 'English nations are brought together and they must march on together'.[4]

[1] Hansard, vol. 192, 1665.
[2] Chamberlain Papers, J.C. 5/7/30. Bright to Chamberlain, 9 June 1886.
[3] Granville Papers, P.R.O. 30/29/52. Bright to Granville, 17 Jan. 1869.
[4] *The Times*, 9 Oct. 1866, p. 7, col. e.

CHAPTER IV

The Colonies 1870–1889

WRITERS of imperial history have discerned a change in Britain's policy towards the Empire beginning some time after 1870. One writer has called the stage initiated after 1870 'flamboyant imperialism'.[1] Another has written: '1870–71 was a year full of incident, that ushered in an age of incident, of hasty telegrams, frontier clashes, and naval scares.'[2] Professor R. Robinson and Dr J. Gallagher give a later date. They consider that 1882, as far as Britain's relations with Africa were concerned, was the turning point.[3]

The reasons advanced for this change vary. Robinson and Gallagher think that the quest for securing Britain's routes to the East was fundamental to her expansion in Africa.[4] Others postulate that the unity of new European states such as Germany meant greater competition for territorial control, especially in Africa. Furthermore, books such as Dilke's *Greater Britain* (1868) and Seeley's *Expansion of England* (1883) helped to cultivate appreciation of the worth of Empire.[5] In the colonies there was a corresponding development of appreciation of the connexion with Britain, which led to proposals for various forms of imperial federation.

Bright's attitude towards the Empire changed as Britain took increasingly more aggressive steps to consolidate and, in some cases, widen her areas of control. To his earlier opposition to colonies as economic liabilities was now added appreciation of the fact that they could also provide battle grounds for territory-hungry European powers. He noticed that the attrac-

[1] R. Muir, *A Short History of the British Commonwealth*, ii, 602.
[2] Thornton, *The Imperial Idea and Its Enemies*, p. 17.
[3] R. Robinson and J. Gallagher, *Africa and the Victorians*, p. 17.
[4] Ibid., p. 470.
[5] J. E. Tyler, *The Struggle for Imperial Unity (1868–1895)*, pp. 47–8.

tion of imperialism had captured even the Liberal party. In 1882 he wrote, 'Painful to observe how much of the "jingo" or war spirit can be shown by certain members of a Liberal Cabinet.'[1] The years between 1870 and 1889 are the true time of Bright's anti-imperialism.

The new aspect of imperialism which presented itself after 1870 called forth from Bright in 1879 and 1880 criticism of the severest kind. It was his opinion that no such events could have taken place under Gladstone.[2] Until July 1882, Bright tended to regard the question of imperialism as a party matter. In 1881 he wrote, 'We, I speak of the Liberal Party, are endeavouring to promote Peace in India & in South Africa.'[3] After 1882 Bright fought for the traditions of the Manchester School against any extension of empire. In 1885 he said, 'If the Manchester policy be dead, then I say let us humiliate ourselves, for morality and Christianity are dead also.'[4]

There were five main reasons for Bright's antagonism to the imperialism that resulted in such affairs as the Zulu war and the second Afghan war. Underlying all of them was an inherent distrust of empire. Bright believed strongly in the lessons that history could teach. 'No completer ruin has history shown, perhaps, than the great ruin of the conquering and sanguinary Roman Empire.' The punishments of ancient empires, he said, 'will visit modern realms, with their rulers and their people, if they persist in the pursuit of empire and glory, sacrificing uncounted and countless multitudes of human lives. It seems to me that that which has taken place in past times must in this respect take place in times to come. The retribution, sometimes of individuals and sometimes of nations, comes slowly, but it is sure to come'.[5] The activities of Britain in all parts of the world would be thrown on the scales for good or evil, and the final reckoning known.

The strongest reason for opposing extension of empire was his abhorrence of the bloodshed which often accompanied manifestations of imperialism. He wrote, 'It is a matter of grief to

[1] Walling, p. 485.

[2] *The Times*, 27 Oct. 1879, p. 10, col. d.

[3] National Library of Ireland, MS. Autograph A.L.S. Bright to H. Y. Thompson, 16 May 1881.

[4] *The Times*, 30 Jan. 1885, p. 6, col. b.

[5] Ibid., 23 Jan. 1880, p. 11, col. c.

me to observe than [sic] in the discussion of a question of this kind [bombardment of Alexandria], the fact that much blood will be shed, & that multitudes will be slaughtered, never seems in the least to affect the deliberations & conclusions of our statesmen.'[1] Speaking at Birmingham in 1880 Bright asked, '—What is it that makes this endless and terrible slaughter different in its nature from those transactions which we call murder?'[2]

The second reason for Bright's antipathy to empire was the cost which he charged fell with marked weight on the shoulders of the millions in Britain. He said in 1879 at Manchester that the burdens of the Empire fell not upon the Empire, but upon the people of Britain. 'This policy may lend a seeming glory to the Crown, and may give scope for patronage and promotion...to...a favoured class, but to you, the people, it brings expenditure of blood and treasure, increased debt and taxes.'[3]

Thirdly, Bright did not favour the inherent mistrust of other nations that either accompanied the expansion of an empire or could be a fundamental factor in initiating aggressive acts. He upheld the traditional assertion of Cobden that Britain had nothing to fear from Russia. This belief had special application to India. As he said in 1878, 'The interests of this country with regard to Russia in connexion with India is in unbroken amity, and I am sure that unbroken amity would be secured if we could get rid of the miserable jealousy that afflicts us.'[4] In 1879 he prophesied that affairs in Egypt would lead to trouble between Britain and France.[5]

Bright saw that the desire for overseas territory could become a highly dangerous type of competition. Considerations that European control could effect a change for the better in living standards for the people in Africa, it seems, were less important to him than good relations with continental powers. Speaking of Egypt in 1877, he commented on the newspaper articles calling for annexation, by which, he thought, it was under-

[1] Ripon Papers, Add. MS. 43,632. Bright to Ripon, 2 Oct. 1882, f. 94.

[2] *The Times*, 23 Jan. 1880, p. 11, col. c.

[3] Ibid., 27 Oct. 1879, p. 10, col. e.

[4] Ibid., 14 Jan. 1878, p. 10, col. b.

[5] Ibid., 17 April 1879, p. 11, col. c.

stood '...that we are to obtain possession of Egypt as the highway of India and govern it upon the plan which we govern India. I do not say that it might not be found an advantage to these poor wretched subjects of the Khedive, but there is one consideration that these wild and crazy people never for a moment look at. What, do they think, would be thought in Europe if anything of this kind were done? Why this, first of all; that having seized upon something which we thought was useful for us, we left the whole of the rest of the Turkish Empire to be seized by anybody else who was strong enough to seize it'.[1]

The lesson of the cost of India to Britain in terms of money and troops was a further reason for Bright's aversion to imperial obligations. In 1883 he expressed his opinion that ten Cape wars, three China wars, the Persian war, the Abyssinian war, the Crimean war and Egypt had been 'the price we pay for that great, historical, marvellous dependency of the British Indian Empire'.[2]

However, as has been noted, Bright did not recommend the giving up of India. The difference in his attitude to India from that felt towards such countries as Egypt can be judged from the study that Bright devoted to them. He continued to explore the problems of India by extensive reading and personal contacts.[3] But he admitted that he knew little about Africa.[4] Wilfrid Blunt[5] found his knowledge of Egypt disappointing.[6]

Finally, Bright's conception of how the world might be—his utopia, so to speak—did not involve empire building. His belief in free trade ran counter to imperial plans. He wrote, 'For the disbanding of great armies and the promotion of peace I rely on the abolition of tariffs, and on the brotherhood of the

[1] Ibid., 26 July 1877, p. 8, col. b. One of the reasons why Bright doubted the wisdom of granting a charter to the North Borneo Company was that the Company through its operations might 'involve us in difficulties with some of the Continental countries'. (Granville Papers, P.R.O. 30/29/143. Cabinet minute (undated).)

[2] *The Times*, 23 March 1883, p. 4, col. c.

[3] 'I want to read the article on Indian irrigation by Col. Chesney.' Potter Papers, MS. f923.2. Br 13. (68). Bright to T. B. Potter, 4 Dec. 1877.

[4] Granville Papers, P.R.O. 30/29/52. Bright to Granville, 26 Sept. 1873.

[5] BLUNT, WILFRID SCAWEN (1840–1922). Entered diplomatic service, 1858; retired, 1869; a visit to India in 1878 convinced him that Britain was wrong to pursue a course of empire building; took up cause of Arabi Pasha in Egypt; strong supporter of Irish Home Rule.

[6] W. S. Blunt, *Secret History of the English Occupation of Egypt*, p. 359.

nations resulting from free trade in the products of industry.'[1]

If free trade had prevailed in 1876, perhaps Bright's suggestion of that year that the Suez Canal should be placed under the control of the leading powers of Europe might have had a greater chance of success. He thought his scheme for the control of the Suez Canal might be the cause 'of a more strict and generous and peaceable political union among the nations of Europe'.[2]

Bright's attitude, then, could be fairly characterized as 'Britain first'. He resented the amount of time spent in cabinet meetings on foreign and colonial affairs. It was his opinion in 1880 that only a few minutes of every hour was given to the discussion of home affairs.[3] He did not see how the colonies contributed either in men or in money 'to the strength of the people' of the United Kingdom.[4]

II

Bright's introduction to the personal turmoils that he would undergo in this new age of imperialism began after he had returned to Gladstone's cabinet in September 1873. Immediately he was plunged into the difficulties of the Ashanti war. The Ashanti were a warlike tribe who inhabited inland territory on the Gold Coast. They took exception to an Anglo-Dutch agreement in 1871 that handed over certain Dutch forts to British control. Claiming one of these, they invaded British territory early in 1873. The British government decided to take decisive action and sent out Sir Garnet Wolseley to defeat the Ashanti. This campaign was so distasteful to Bright that he contemplated resignation after less than two months in office.[5] Despite his forebodings, Bright, ever anxious for peace, sent to Granville a letter from W. H. Clarke, a man considered by Bright to have an excellent knowledge of West Africa. In his own letter he urged Granville to seek a non-military solution in West Africa. He asked that his letter be sent on to Lord

[1] Leech, p. 39.
[2] *The Times*, 5 Dec. 1876, p. 4, col. c.
[3] Ibid., 30 March 1880, p. 4, col. f.
[4] Ibid., 19 Dec. 1879, p. 4, col. b.
[5] Walling, p. 358.

Kimberley.[1] His fears in the situation were summed up in a letter to Gladstone: 'I confess I dont like the system of a war being undertaken by the War office & the Colonial office, without special directions & restrictions from the Cabinet. *I distrust the soldiers*—promotion is so often their object, & revenge & example the pretext for operations & cruelties which are needless & dishonourable.'[2] Possibly the only mitigating factors for him were that the cabinet's early instructions were for peace[3] and that by his presence in the cabinet after the war had started he could attempt to limit it.[4] He hoped in a cautious way that Sir Garnet Wolseley might be equal to the task of adjusting the differences with the Ashanti,[5] and rejoiced when he succeeded early in 1874.[6]

What was Bright's solution to the difficulties that arose in West Africa? He presented his ideas in this regard to his constituents in October 1873. 'The time will come, I trust, and before long, when Parliament, acting upon the opinion of one of its own committees, will consider that it would be wise to withdraw absolutely from the African coast.'[7] He thought that trade would flourish to a greater extent when there were no forts. Furthermore, it was not a country where English life could expect to be maintained, nor was there a slave trade to suppress. He believed '...the interests and the honour of the country at some not distant time would be best consulted by an entire withdrawal from that coast'.[8]

[1] Granville Papers, P.R.O. 30/29/52. Bright to Granville, 31 Aug. 1873. Lord Kimberley in his reply stated that he did not think the British public would agree to abandoning their Fanti allies to the 'horrible barbarities' of Ashanti rule. (Bright Papers, Add. MSS. 43,387. Kimberley to Granville, 2 Sept. 1873, ff. 83–4.)

[2] Gladstone Papers, Add. MSS. 44,113. Bright to Gladstone, 17 Sept. 1873, ff. 72–3. (Bright's emphasis.)

[3] Potter Papers, MS. f923.2. Br 13 (50). Bright to T. B. Potter, 27 Sept. 1873.

[4] Walling, p. 358.

[5] Bodleian MS. Eng. letter c. 185 (typewritten copy). Bright to Congreve, 31 Oct. 1873, ff. 183–4.

[6] Gladstone Papers, Add. MSS. 44,113. Bright to Gladstone, 6 Feb. 1874, f. 92.

[7] *The Times*, 23 Oct. 1873, p. 5, col. e. Adderley's committee in 1865 had recommended withdrawal from all territory except Sierra Leone. (Parl. Papers, No. 412 (V). *Reports from the Select Committee appointed to consider the state of the establishments on the West Coast of Africa, 1865*. p. 111.)

[8] Ibid., 23 Oct. 1873, p. 5, col. e.

During Bright's third term as a cabinet minister, Transvaal troubles presented themselves to the Gladstone cabinet. Since the 1860s the policy of the British government had been 'to cajole' the republics of the Transvaal and the Orange Free State 'into a federation with the Cape and Natal colonies'.[1] The importance of keeping the Cape route open coupled with a desire to prevent possible difficulties between Transvaal and the Zulus, prompted the British government to annex the Republic of the Transvaal in 1877. This act provoked Boer nationalism against British designs. When Gladstone did not renounce the annexation as had been expected, the Boers became impatient, revolted, and won a surprising victory at Majuba Hill early in 1881.[2]

Although Bright did nothing to avert the march of events that led to this defeat, he was immediately involved in the cabinet crisis which it caused. Joseph Chamberlain and Sir Charles Dilke, who favoured more liberal measures for Ireland, were anxious to gain the upper hand against the Whigs by blocking their aim of suppressing the Transvaal rebels. Chamberlain was influential in persuading Bright to request an interview with Gladstone.[3] One day later, on 3 March, after an hour's discussion with the Prime Minister, he was reassured that a peaceful solution was possible. On 5 March he was able to write in his diary that no member of the government was urging war, though the situation caused him considerable worry until he learned on 22 March of the successful negotiations with the Boers.[4]

Robinson and Gallagher have placed Bright among Gladstone and others who sympathized with the Transvaal struggle for self-determination.[5] It is certain that this was of less consideration with Bright than his desire to maintain peace. He wrote, 'It may be impossible for me to remain with the Govt if a resolute attempt for peace is not made.'[6] To a correspondent

[1] Robinson and Gallagher, op. cit., p. 56.

[2] Ibid., pp. 60–5.

[3] S. Gwynn and G. Tuckwell, *Life of the Rt. Hon. Sir Charles W. Dilke*, i, 368; Gladstone Papers, Add. MS. 44,113. Bright to Gladstone, 2 March 1881, f. 147.

[4] Walling, pp. 458–60.

[5] Robinson and Gallagher, op. cit., p. 67.

[6] Walling, p. 459.

he expressed his wish that a settlement would be made 'satisfactory to the Transvaal people',[1] but there is little doubt that his chief exertion was to avoid bloodshed.

Meanwhile, events in Egypt were moving quickly to a crisis. There the British and French had been in control since 1879 when the financial difficulties of the Egyptian government had prompted them to intervene. Opposition to this Dual Control had the effect of unifying the diverse nationalist movements. Resentment was caused partly by the presence of highly paid European officials. The nominal ruler of Egypt, the Khedive, was not popular, and Arabi Pasha, the nationalist leader, gained control of Egyptian government. Gambetta, the head of the French government, pressed for action to uphold the Khedive.[2] However, when the British government saw in 1882 the need for intervention, Gambetta had lost his place in France, leaving the British to take unilateral military action in the form of the bombardment of Alexandria.

It was not sympathy for Arabi Pasha that led to Bright's resignation.[3] Blunt wrote of Bright speaking 'less sympathetically than Gladstone' of Egyptian nationalism.[4] The overwhelming reason for his resignation is given in a letter to Lord Ripon: 'Had I consented to the Egyptian war my whole political life would have been stained beyond recovery—& I could not have remained on the Treasury Bench to listen to statements in its defence which I felt entirely unable to support. That the war began in self defence is absurd.'[5] Though he claimed to have had the support of two cabinet ministers in his contention that the Suez Canal was not in any danger,[6] this allegiance did not run to the extent of resignation. Unlike the situation a year earlier, during the Transvaal affair, Dilke and Chamberlain had ranged themselves on the other side. The only reason for surprise to his contemporaries was that his

[1] Blind Papers, Add. MSS. 40,125. Bright to K. Blind, 14 March 1881, f. 183.

[2] J. Marlowe, *Anglo-Egyptian Relations 1800–1953*, pp. 112–18.

[3] Bright's resignation was made final on 15 July 1882. (Gladstone Papers, Add. MSS. 44,113, 15 July 1882, ff. 181–2.)

[4] W. S. Blunt, *Secret History of the English Occupation of Egypt*, pp. 235, 359.

[5] Ripon Papers, Add. MSS. 43,632. Bright to Ripon, 2 Oct. 1882, f. 93.

[6] *Goldwin Smith's Correspondence*, ed. A. Haultain, p. 141.

resignation had not taken place at any time within the preceding ten days.[1] The reason for this Bright explained to Chamberlain in 1883. At the time when the ships were sent to Alexandria 'you will remember that the only reason given in & to the Cabinet was that there was danger to English subjects, not that the Forts were to be bombarded'.[2]

Joseph Chamberlain in his *Political Memoir* stated that had Bright led an agitation against the government, he could have destroyed it.[3] In answer to the question why this did not occur, it would now appear that Chamberlain himself might have been partially responsible. Bright wrote a scathing letter of criticism of the government to the Birmingham Liberal Caucus which its officials succeeded in burying.[4] After this outburst, calmer reasoning returned. He explained to Chamberlain in 1883 that he preferred 'to treat the Egyptian incident rather as a deplorable blunder than as a crime'.[5] Were the Tories an alternative? 'Our friend Sir W. Lawson makes his protest—he worries the Govt. & pleases the opposition which is much less to be trusted than is the Govt. itself.'[6]

Bright had the grim satisfaction of seeing his opinions largely vindicated. Chamberlain wrote, '...I am afraid you were right & we were wrong.'[7] Bright had told the cabinet that 'they had lost their heads',[8] and it is significant that modern writers speak of Gladstone 'catching the jitters' of the rest of the cabinet.[9] Mr A. J. P. Taylor traces the beginning of British imperialism from the occupation of Egypt.[10]

III

In the 1860s, when Bright had been aiding the cause of Joseph

[1] See *Birmingham Daily Post*, 17 July 1882, p. 5, col. e.

[2] Chamberlain Papers, J.C. 5/7/20. Bright to Chamberlain, 4 Jan. 1883.

[3] J. Chamberlain, *A Political Memoir 1880–92*, ed. C. H. D. Howard, p. 81.

[4] Peter Fraser, *Joseph Chamberlain*, p. 43.

[5] Chamberlain Papers, J.C. 5/7/20. Bright to Chamberlain, 4 Jan. 1883.

[6] Bodleian MS. Eng. letter c. 185 (typewritten copy). Bright to R. Congreve, 5 March 1884, f. 188.

[7] Bright Papers, Add. MSS. 43,387. Chamberlain to Bright, 14 Jan. 1884, f. 192.

[8] Chamberlain Papers, J.C. 5/7/21. Bright to Chamberlain, 18 Jan. 1884.

[9] Robinson and Gallagher, op. cit., p. 111.

[10] A. J. P. Taylor, *The Trouble Makers*, p. 68.

Howe, the latter had, while in Britain, written a pamphlet stressing the need for colonial representation within the Imperial Parliament. At that time, however, Howe was advocating a course that had little appeal.[1] But, as British fears increased at the threat posed by growing military and commercial rivalry during the late Victorian period, support for imperial consolidation became more widespread. In essence, imperial federation was an attempt to reconcile colonial self-government with imperial unity. One such plan, advocated by the third Earl Grey, concerned the instituting of a committee on which would sit colonial agents who could advise the British government on intended legislation. The idea of imperial federation was first popularized in 1871 by two articles in the *Contemporary Review*. In 1884 was formed the Imperial Federation League, which was the first organization pledged to secure 'the permanent unity of the Empire' by federation.

Bright's attention was drawn to imperial federation through a speech made by Alexander Galt in Edinburgh in 1883. Bright commented that he could not see how it would be possible for Canada to be given any share in the formation of decisions of the British government. Schemes for giving the colonies representation in the Imperial Parliament were, in his opinion, 'absolutely impracticable'.[2]

Early in 1885 at Birmingham Bright condemned imperial federation as 'ludicrous'. To his mind it appeared that the very men who were unable to rule Ireland were the ones who wished to bind the colonies in closer union with the mother country. He claimed that any kind of colonial council, such as Lord Grey had proposed, would not work because it too closely resembled the council of India, which was 'a great evil'. He summed up his opinions on colonial policy and imperial federation by saying, 'The true policy of this country is not to seek to enlarge our Empire. Nor is it to seek to bind the Empire together more closely in the way proposed by the Federation League. The way to deal with our colonies is to deal with them [the way] we do now, to encourage them, to

[1] J. M. Beck, 'Joseph Howe: Opportunist or Empire-builder?', *Can. Hist. Rev.*, xli, no. 5 (Sept. 1960), 200–2.

[2] *The Times*, 23 March 1883, p. 4, col. b.

give them freedom as now, to deal justly and fairly with them on all occasions, to cultivate sympathy and good will towards them; but if we bind or attempt to bind them in a closer tie by meddling with them, by allowing them to give counsel, which perhaps we should not follow, we shall find that instead of their being more our friends they will be less our friends, and that the bond of union will, in all probability, be weakened. I am for friendship.'[1]

Bright had the opportunity in 1885 to discuss imperial federation with one of its supporters, Lord Rosebery. He wrote, 'Much interesting conversation on Colonies and Federation. Mr. Gladstone agreed with me that the wisest plan is to leave Colonies much as they are.'[2]

In succeeding years Bright was not hard put to find terms of abuse for imperial federation. On one occasion he branded it as the offspring of 'the jingo spirit'.[3] But he had also by 1888 adopted three coherent reasons for his distrust. One was Britain's 'blind' foreign policy, which would lead to colonial participation in imperial wars in which the colonies would have no interest.[4] Another reason was the tariff policy of colonies such as Canada and Victoria, which not only divided them from Britain, but caused disunity among themselves.[5] Finally, he did not think the self-governing colonies would allow any interference in their laws or policies by the British government. These colonies would prefer separation to infringement on their sovereignty.[6]

Bright's own hope for further imperial development involved setting up a free trade area embracing Britain, the colonies and the United States. This would, he thought, have tremendous effects not only in the creation of wealth, but also in providing an influence for peace in the world.[7] The imposition of higher tariffs by Canada in 1879 pained him because it ran counter to this vision of what the Empire could accomplish. He showed his concern in Parliament in 1879 when he questioned Sir Michael Hicks-Beach (Secretary of State for the Colonies)

[1] *The Times*, 30 Jan. 1885, p. 6, col. c.
[2] Walling, p. 524.
[3] *The Times*, 14 Jan. 1887, p. 7, col. e.
[4] Ibid.
[5] Ibid., 29 March 1888, p. 10, col. c.
[6] Ibid., 14 Jan. 1887, p. 7, col. e.
[7] Ibid., 19 Dec. 1879, p. 4, col. d.

as to whether the government '...intended to represent to the Canadian Government the impolicy of a war of Tariffs between different portions of the Empire'.[1] The imposition of tariffs by Canada tended to strengthen his feelings that eventually Canada would join the United States. As he said, 'Economic facts are much stronger than Imperial federation leagues.'[2]

Bright was generally less comfortable in regard to imperial affairs between the years 1870 and 1889. He found no cause similar to colonial self-government for which he could struggle in a positive way. Instead he was involved in a series of defensive actions, combating the use of military action and the idea of imperial federation. Nor could Bright adequately explain the causes of the new imperialism. He was apt to ascribe it either to lapses in morality or to vainglorious ambition. His views on non-intervention became increasingly anachronistic, as the young Radicals like Chamberlain and Dilke favoured more aggressive policies. Whereas they had chosen to stand with him in 1881, their changed stance in 1882 meant that his withdrawal from the cabinet was a solitary protest.

Bright spent less time considering colonial problems within the self-governing colonies than he gave to India and the dependent territories between 1870 and 1889. His contacts with leaders in the self-governing colonies had never been extensive. Contacts usually came about as a result of a specific issue such as Nova Scotia's dissatisfaction with confederation. Perhaps his closest friend holding a dominant position in a colony was Sir Henry Parkes,[3] who consulted Bright on problems such as emigration.[4] He also informed Bright of the fortunes of free trade in New South Wales.[5] Other colonial leaders whom he had met included Sir John Macdonald, the Canadian Prime Minister,[6] and Edward Blake, the Canadian

[1] Hansard, vol. 244, 1311.

[2] *The Times*, 30 Jan. 1885, p. 6, col. c.

[3] PARKES, SIR HENRY (1815–96). Powerful working-class agitator; leader of anti-transportation movement in New South Wales; elected member for legislative council; campaigned for responsible government; prime minister, 1872; adherent of free trade.

[4] Sir Henry Parkes, *Fifty Years of Australian History*, i, 158.

[5] Bright Papers, Add. MSS. 43,389. Parkes to Bright, 15 Aug. 1878, ff. 285–6.

[6] Walling, p. 447.

Liberal leader.[1] He tended to withdraw from most colonial issues, and though he was consulted by both sides on the constitutional struggle in Victoria in 1878,[2] it is not evident that he took any action. Some of his vagueness on colonial affairs can be detected in this reference to Edward Blake in one of his speeches: 'Mr. Blake, I believe, is the leader—at least, so it was stated the other day—of the Liberal party, and this Liberal party, I presume, is not the protection party.'[3]

Although the problems resulting from the possession of empire became an increasing source of discomfort to Bright, it is true that occasionally he found arguments in support of causes he favoured by drawing upon the experience of the colonies. This was particularly the case in connexion with his ideas about reform of the British system of representation. In his view, colonial experiments proved the value and safety of the use of the secret ballot and manhood suffrage. In 1858 he signed his name to a memorial to W. Nicholson, the founder of vote by ballot in Victoria, because the success of the innovation 'would promote the improvement of our institutions at home'.[4] In 1865 he praised the system of franchise in British colonies: 'England is the mother of Parliaments.... An Englishman if he goes to the Cape can vote, if he goes to Australia he can vote, if he goes to the Canadian Confederation or to our grandest colonies he can vote.' He commented further that it was the intention of the British government to give representation by population in the proposed Canadian Confederation, and yet there was the belief current that such principles would be 'wholly destructive if applied to this country'.[5]

In addition, the Empire strengthened Bright's demands for non-intervention in Europe. In 1878 he suggested to the House that the difficulties in South Africa and northern India were enough for Britain to solve without attempting to uphold the Ottoman Empire against Russia.[6]

When Bright turned his attention to Ireland, he conveyed the impression that the Empire was one reason why Ireland

[1] Walling, p. 384. [2] Ibid., p. 420.

[3] *The Times*, 30 Jan. 1885, p. 6, col. c.

[4] *Morning Star*, 15 April 1858, p. 2 col. b.

[5] *The Times*, 19 Jan. 1865, p. 9, col. d.

[6] Hansard, vol. 237, 801–2.

should remain in union with Britain. In 1868 at Limerick he offered a share of the Empire to his audience in this way: 'Ireland, like every other country in Europe, had a right to desire national independence, but the time had not come yet for the discussion of that subject, but he offered to Ireland the reciprocity of sentiment of his own countrymen—the members of a great and noble empire, and a share in the glory and prosperity.'[1] From the context of this speech and one other delivered in 1868,[2] it seems possible that Bright was not referring, by these words, to anything more than the United Kingdom. If this is so, it is still of interest, however, as an example of his attempt to induce the Irish to look outward rather than inward. To this question of the relationship between Irish and imperial matters, it is now appropriate to turn.

[1] *The Times*, 15 July 1868, p. 6, col. d.
[2] Ibid., 5 Feb. 1868, p. 12, cols. d–e.

CHAPTER V

Ireland 1843–1857

RUINED cottages in great numbers during the day in Skibbereen, and in almost all the journey. Women sitting or standing about their cabins with countenances of deepest dejection.... Women and girls look much better than men and boys in health; very many widows and orphans among them.

Way to Bantry: Land uncultivated, and undrained, cottages in ruins. Aspect of country most cheerless, the people living in desolation.[1]

Such were the impressions recorded by John Bright while on his second trip to Ireland in 1849.[2] During subsequent visits in 1852, 1866 and 1868, he was to find considerable amelioration, but Ireland remained in his opinion 'a blot' upon 'the reign of the Queen'.[3] What would Bright propose to alleviate the situation? What methods would best effect any solution? Was there any justification for saying that Irishmen might be well advised to press for restoration of their own parliament? These are some of the questions the following pages will attempt to answer.

Bright's assessment of the Irish situation will also be investigated in order to discern any influence exerted upon it by the experience derived from the imperial example. Considering Ireland in conjunction with the Empire would seem appropriate too in that Ireland had occupied until 1800 '...a status which for all practical purposes was colonial'. Though Ireland had its own Parliament, it was 'constitutionally almost impotent'.[4] English control of the Irish Parliament was facilitated

[1] Walling, p. 102.

[2] For the observations of foreign travellers in Ireland see N. Mansergh, *The Irish Question*, pp. 21–41.

[3] Hansard, vol. 181, 694.

[4] Sir D. L. Keir, *The Constitutional History of Modern Britain 1485–1951*, pp. 434–5.

because Catholics were excluded from the franchise, and there was no limit to the number of placemen. Not until 1783, the age of 'Grattan's Parliament', was legislative and judicial autonomy gained, but even then Irish government suffered from the fact that the legislature had no control over the executive.

In 1801 the separate Irish legislature was terminated by the Act of Union which was adjudged to be necessary in the light of the menace posed by revolutionary France and the continuing deficits of the government. Rather than being primarily the product of bribery and intimidation, as it is so often painted,[1] the historian of the Act claims that it did reflect the rather limited public opinion of that day.[2] It abolished the Irish Parliament and allocated twenty-eight lay peers and four bishops to the House of Lords, and 100 Members to the House of Commons. Irish judicial independence ended with the designation of the House of Lords as the supreme court.

Irish government after union was decentralized to a considerable extent. There were over twenty departments which handled mainly fiscal and military matters. However, the British government could exert any amount of policy direction it wanted through the Lord Lieutenant or Viceroy, and the Chief Secretary. The former, as representative of the monarch, was ultimately responsible for Irish conditions. The latter was in charge of matters relating to law and order, and the varied problems connected with the civil and military administration. Because successive Prime Ministers in the nineteenth century took differing attitudes towards these officials, their importance tended to rise and fall depending on whether they were invited to join the cabinet.[3] As a result the partnership between them was frequently 'uneasy'.[4]

After 1801 the political situation was still unsettled. The failure of Pitt to pass a Catholic emancipation bill created an impression in Ireland that the Union had been unfair. Even after Daniel O'Connell succeeded in getting an emancipation

[1] See for example E. Curtis, *A History of Ireland*, p. 348.

[2] G. C. Bolton, *The Passing of the Irish Act of Union*, pp. 216–22.

[3] R. B. McDowell, *The Irish Administration 1801–1914*, pp. 1–28.

[4] R. B. McDowell, 'The Irish Executive in the Nineteenth Century', *Irish Historical Studies*, ix, no. 35 (March 1955), p. 264.

act passed in 1829, Protestants still monopolized important offices in Ireland. The Catholic population was also angered by the ruling that forced them until 1838 to pay tithes and church rates to the established church. The abolition of the forty shilling freehold in 1829 reduced drastically the number of county voters; many of Ireland's county and borough seats were controlled directly by patrons; the influence of landlord and priest was felt in nearly all elections;[1] and finally, the men who were elected had to journey to London, where they often lost touch with the affairs of their constituencies and faced financial difficulties.

To make matters worse, the evils of the Irish land system were becoming all too apparent. Initially separated, except in the north, by a religious barrier, tenants were alienated from landlords by insecure tenure and high rents. The report of the Royal Commission appointed in 1843 stated that poor relations between landlord and tenant constituted the chief cause of Ireland's difficulties.[2] Only in Ulster was there any form of tenant-right, and even there it was customary rather than legal.[3] Absentee landlords felt little sympathy for their tenants, and in many cases were little interested in their estates.

Most people in Ireland lived near the subsistence level, and depended on one crop, the potato, for their survival. Between 1791 and 1841 there was a great increase in the population of Ireland[4] without any corresponding improvement in cultivation. There was therefore an increasing struggle for the land, which carried higher rents in its wake. The soil was poorly cultivated, since good farming methods were not practised. In the great famine of 1845–7, 'the whole crazy system collapsed'.[5] The frequent lawlessness of the Irish peasant was his only weapon against a land system which he regarded as akin to robbery. This challenged the government 'at its most sensitive point, and at its first duty, the maintenance of order'.[6] To make matters worse, English public opinion feared that any

[1] H. J. Hanham, *Elections and Party Management*, pp. 181–2, 408–12.
[2] C. Woodham-Smith, *The Great Hunger*, pp. 20–4.
[3] R. D. Collison Black, *Economic Thought and the Irish Question*, pp. 6–7.
[4] See K. H. Connell, *The Population of Ireland 1750–1845*, p. 25.
[5] Keir, op. cit., p. 441.
[6] Woodward, *The Age of Reform 1815–1870*, pp. 444–4.

amelioration of the Irish peasant's situation would interfere with the rights of property.

Thus the Irish situation that faced Bright and the British House of Commons in 1843 was critical. Sir L. Woodward concludes that 'Irish opinion was justified in holding that after 1824 Ireland gained little positive advantage of an economic kind from the union'.[1] Sir D. L. Keir sums up: 'English administration in Ireland was hopelessly found wanting.'[2]

II

From the time Bright entered Parliament in 1843, he regarded Ireland as suffering a severe form of breakdown and demoralization. As he said, 'The Prisons are crowded, the chapels deserted, society is ruined, and disorganized; labour is useless.'[3] He thought that the only certain remedy was the development of industry 'on which can be reared the enduring edifice of union and of peace'. But industrious activity of any kind had not taken hold in Ireland because the land was not free of feudal fetters, which prevented its free exchange.[4] Thus improvement of the land system assumed a double significance not only as the most immediate necessity for an orderly society, but also as the ultimate foundation of further economic and social progress.

Bright believed that there were natural economic laws of accumulation and dispersion,[5] but that the existing system of land laws had tended to impede the free working of these natural laws, especially those of dispersion.[6] He wished to see free trade in land.[7] He capsulized his thinking on the land problem in a letter to Cobden: 'Our "territorial" system is one which works a wide & silent cruelty.... I should like to join a League sworn or pledged to its entire overthrow—there are facts enough afloat that would suffice to make a revolution in

[1] Ibid., pp. 337–8.

[2] Keir, op. cit., p. 441.

[3] Hansard, vol. 104, 168.

[4] Ibid., 180.

[5] Leech, p. 187.

[6] '...the possession of the soil in vast properties is not the most favourable for the full development of its powers.' (National Library of Ireland, MS. 2149. Bright to J. Kay, 14 Sept. 1850, f. 78.)

[7] 'Now, I want Parliament to remove every obstacle in the way of the free sale of land.' (Hansard, vol. 104, 173.)

opinion with regard to it, & it follows logically on the free trade movement.'[1] Though Cobden expressed his readiness to follow wherever the laws of political economy led,[2] no such organization sprang up, unless the aims of the Land League in Parnell's time could be considered to be synonymous.

Several measures would have to be taken to institute free trade in land. Firstly, land had to be regarded as essentially the same as other property, and not as something sacred.[3] Then legislators would perforce correct a practice like entail which tended to keep land in large parcels[4] for periods of time extending beyond one lifetime. Since the custom of primogeniture also had this effect, Bright thought that if the landower died without a will, then his property should be equally divided among his offspring.[5] He also thought that a man should have the choice of leaving his land to whomever he wished.[6]

Another problem was the exceedingly slow system of transferring land.[7] In 1847 Bright urged Lord John Russell to present an incumbered estates bill to help overcome the dilatory nature and expense of land exchange.[8] In 1848 he predicted that a large amount of capital would be expended on Irish estates if a proper measure were passed.[9] When Russell's ministry presented their bill in 1849 he spoke in favour of it, saying that it protected the safety of the landed class.[10] In 1850 he defended the Act from an attempt by the House of Lords to reduce its effectiveness.[11] Although welcoming the Incumbered Estates Act as a much needed piece of legislation, he thought that more was required 'in the same direction'.[12] He had other suggestions to make. He recommended the registration of land

[1] Bright Papers, Add. MSS. 43,383. Bright to Cobden, 25 Sept. 1851, f. 209.

[2] Cobden Papers, Add. MSS. 43,649. Cobden to Bright, 1 Oct. 1851, f. 207.

[3] Hansard, vol. 104, 174.

[4] Ibid., vol. 101, 537.

[5] Ibid., vol. 104, 175.

[6] *Northern Whig*, 5 Oct. 1852, p. 2, col. a.

[7] There are some excellent references to the ineffective working of Chancery in Charles Dickens, *Bleak House*.

[8] Hansard, vol. 95, 987.

[9] Ibid., vol. 104, 172.

[10] Bright said he did not wish legislation to maintain the property of one class as against another. (Hansard, vol. 104, 916.)

[11] Ibid. vol. 113, 922–5.

[12] Bright Papers, Add. MSS. 43,383. Bright to Cobden, 17 Sept. 1849, f. 191.

as was done in many European countries. He would reduce to a nominal level the charge for stamps that had to be affixed to all documents. To open up new farm land, he could see no objection to the government's encouraging purchasers for waste lands.[1]

The ideas of Bright and Cobden on the free sale of land were upheld in Ireland by two prosperous Quakers, Jonathan Pim and Joseph Bewley.[2] In addition, the Central Relief Committee of the Society of Friends, which had done such valuable work during the famine, had concluded that the free sale of land was necessary to improve conditions in Ireland. Another supporter was Neilson Hancock, Professor of Political Economy at Dublin University.[3] When Charles Gavan Duffy[4] set up a Freehold Land Society to enable tenants to pool their resources to buy land, Bright encouraged the project.[5]

The suffering Bright encountered in Ireland in 1849 impressed him deeply.[6] What he perceived to be most immediately required was a plan of tenant security. To this end, while in Dublin, he formed a committee of Professor Hancock, Sir Robert Kane,[7] James Perry, a Quaker, and others, which was to draw up a bill for this purpose.[8] Bright thought such a bill necessary because of 'the war between the tenants & the lords of the soil'.[9] He wrote further, 'The people *must* & *will* live, & all the rights or privileges of property will break down under the great necessity.'[10] Upon his return to England, he continued to press for such a measure, bolstering his argument by pointing out that tenant compensation had already been recommended

[1] Hansard, vol. 104, 175–6.

[2] Black, op. cit., p. 33.

[3] Ibid., pp. 33–4.

[4] DUFFY, CHARLES GAVAN (1816–1903). Journalist; founded *Nation* in 1842; founder of Young Ireland party; arrested, 1848; paper suppressed; M.P. for New Ross, 1852; emigrated to Victoria, 1855; rose to be prime minister and speaker; K.C.M.G. in 1873; returned to Europe, 1880.

[5] Sir Charles Gavan Duffy, *My Life in Two Hemispheres*, ii, 17.

[6] For a full account, see Walling, pp. 101–07.

[7] KANE, SIR ROBERT (1809–90). Professor of chemistry, Apothecaries Hall, 1831; wrote *Industrial Resources of Ireland*, 1844; president, Queen's College, Cork, 1845; knighted in 1846.

[8] Bright Papers, Add. MSS. 43,383. Bright to Cobden, 17 Sept. 1849, f. 191.

[9] Friends Historical Collection, Dublin. (Portfolio 5a, 29.) Bright to J. Pim, 17 Sept. 1849.

[10] Ibid. Bright to J. Pim, 27 Sept. 1849. (Bright's emphasis.)

by the Devon Commission. In addition, he urged the wisdom of granting leases as a means of creating a new spirit in Ireland.[1]

It is useful to point out distinctions in the meaning of the term tenant-right. R. D. Collison Black shows that tenant-right encompassed both the idea of 'tenant-right of occupancy' and the 'tenant-right of compensation for improvements'.[2] It was the latter idea that Bright embraced, while to the former, known as 'fixity of tenure', he showed a marked hostility until 1880–1. Bright's idea of tenant-right was that compensation should include the tenant's investment in buildings, drainage and fences. In parts of Ireland where tenant-right in some form existed (in Ulster), he thought that compensation should be retrospective for twenty years. Where tenant-right did not exist, he thought that compensation should date from the passing of a bill.[3]

Meanwhile, in Ireland there was another group of men coming to conclusions on the question of tenant-right. In the summer of 1850 Fred Lucas,[4] Dr John Gray,[5] and Gavan Duffy formed a Tenant League. They adopted a radical programme, including fair rent, free sale and security of tenure.[6] Bright's opinion was quite unfavourable. He wrote: 'The "Tenant League" in Ireland is complicating a question already difficult enough—how disgusting it is to see men of powerful intellect like my cousin *Lucas* lending themselves to such impostures!'[7]

Bright's remedy for the land problem was embodied in his own land bill which he had completed by June of 1850.[8]

[1] *The Times*, 5 Jan. 1850, p. 3, col. c.

[2] Black, op. cit., p. 26.

[3] *Northern Whig*, 5 Oct. 1852, p. 2, col. b.

[4] LUCAS, FREDERICK (1812–55). Son of Quaker merchant; devoted much attention to Irish politics at University of London; called to the bar in 1853; converted to Catholicism in 1839; started weekly London newspaper, the *Tablet*, in 1840; supported ultramontane views; M.P. for Meath, 1852–5; a skilful debater; was related to Bright by marriage.

[5] GRAY, SIR JOHN (1816–75). Journalist; Glasgow M.D., 1839; editor and part proprietor of *Freeman's Journal*, 1841; sole proprietor, 1850; tried and sentenced with O'Connell in state trials, 1844; returned three times unopposed for Kilkenny; knighted, 1863.

[6] J. H. Whyte, *The Independent Irish Party 1850–59*, pp. 9–12.

[7] Bright Papers, Add. MSS. 43,383. Bright to Cobden, 12 Oct. 1850, f. 202.

[8] Friends Historical Collection, Dublin. (Portfolio 5a, 30.) Bright to Pim, 1 June 1850.

He was prompted to act by his assessment of the situation in Ireland: 'You see the murders in the north of Ireland—by & bye [sic] it will be worth while trying my Bill or some other Bill to settle the relations of Landlord & Tenant.'[1] He experienced, however, some difficulty in getting his committee in Ireland to produce a draft plan.[2] It was Professor Hancock who eventually drew up the bill sent to Bright. Pim's view of its intention was that it would give 'full power to landlords & tenants, whether under settlements or not, to deal with the land, as if they were perfectly free'. As for Pim himself, though he professed to want to institute the *laissez-faire* principle in land, this did not imply a quiescent policy on the part of the government. Rather, his aim was to put landlord and tenant on terms of legal equality, chiefly by altering the law of eviction.[3]

Bright's bill may have been oriented more in the direction of the tenants, as he confessed not to find Pim 'liberal' enough.[4] Early in 1852 he distributed his bill to Irish Members, some of whom approved of it, but since 'it did not meet the views of a large class in Ireland who were moving in relation to this matter', he said he preferred not to go ahead without their approval.[5] This refers to the members of the Tenant League, who found his proposals too moderate. Lord John Russell revealed in the House that Bright had sent his proposals to him, he in turn had sent them to Ireland for study by the Privy Council, the Irish executive and the law officers of the Crown, whose opinions were adverse.[6] His bill had proved too moderate for the extremists and too advanced for the government.

One man who was advocating the cause of tenant-right in Parliament in a manner which Bright could approve was W. S. Crawford,[7] whose measure for tenant-right was less radical than that of the Tenant League. In February 1852, Bright

[1] Bright Papers, Add. MSS. 43,383. Bright to Cobden, 3 Jan. 1852, f. 232.

[2] Friends Historical Collection, Dublin. Pim MSS. i 32. Bright to Pim, 24 Jan. 1850.

[3] Ibid., portfolio 5a, 78. Pim to Bright, 12 March 1850 (draft).

[4] Bright Papers, Add. MSS. 43,383. Bright to Cobden, 24 Oct. 1851, f. 213.

[5] Hansard, vol. 119, 366.

[6] Ibid., 359–60.

[7] CRAWFORD, WILLIAM SHARMAN (1781–1861). Large landowner in Co. Down; about 1830 resolved to make Ulster custom into a legal enactment for all Ireland; M.P. for Dundalk, 1835–41; M.P. for Rochdale, 1841–52; an advanced Radical who accepted Chartist principles.

gave his support for leave to bring in Crawford's tenant-right bill,[1] and his speech was praised as 'fair' and 'generous' by the *Irish Tenant League*,[2] the organ of the Tenant League, which also endorsed Crawford's bill. At the end of the debate on the bill, Bright extended an invitation to Irish Members '...that he was ready to co-operate with any of the Irish Members in bringing forward some other measure based upon the considerations he had been urging upon their attention'.[3] These possibilities of co-operation improved when in August 1852, to accommodate Crawford's views, the Tenant League gave up their demands for security of tenure, in return for his support.[4]

There were still areas of difference. In late 1852 Bright was invited by several leading Liberals of Belfast[5] to attend a banquet in that city. He had made no contacts there[6] before, but Crawford approved of the idea;[7] and thus on 5 October he addressed about 240 of the 'influential liberals of Belfast'.[8] During his speech he outlined his views on tenant-right,[9] while stating that 'It is not necessary that every man who helps a great project should have precisely the same views upon it that every other man has.'[10] Crawford acknowledged that 'His friend, perhaps, was not disposed to go to the full length of what he [Crawford] would be disposed to go.'[11]

The first disagreement was not crippling to plans of co-operation. Bright was unconvinced that 'all improvements of the soil and works of every description' should be the wording of a tenant compensation bill. He and William Shee[12] thought

[1] Hansard, vol. 119, 365–8. [2] *Irish Tenant League*, Feb. 1852, p. 115, col. c.

[3] Hansard, vol. 119, 368. [4] Whyte, op. cit., p. 32.

[5] W. S. Andrews and W. Girdwood. Bright Papers, Add. MSS. 43,383. Bright to Cobden, 7 Sept., 1852, f.249. W. Girdwood was a Presbyterian minister. (Sir C. Gavan Duffy, *The League of North and South*, p. 323, n. 2.)

[6] Smith Papers, MS. 923.2, S.344 (7). Bright to J. B. Smith, 7 Sept. 1852.

[7] Bright Papers, U.C. Bright to his wife, 11 Sept. 1852.

[8] Bright Papers, Add. MSS. 43,383. Bright to Cobden, 15 Oct. 1852, f. 251.

[9] See p. 124.

[10] *Northern Whig*, 5 Oct. 1852, p. 2, col. a. [11] Ibid.

[12] SHEE, SIR WILLIAM (1804–68). Called to the bar in 1828; became queen's serjeant in 1857; M.P. for Kilkenny 1852–7; took charge of tenant-right bill when Crawford left parliament in 1852; received knighthood in 1863; in 1863 became first Roman Catholic to be appointed to the Court of Queen's Bench since the Revolution.

that compensation should be given for 'the more usual, more expensive, and most easily appreciable improvements'. The general reason for this was that it would not offend 'the landed proprietors of the United Kingdom'.[1] The other disagreement, so far as the *Freeman's Journal* was concerned, was more serious. It conceded that Bright was 'in advance of most English statesmen', but it could not sanction his plan as long as he was not willing to extend retrospective compensation throughout the rest of Ireland.[2] The *Northern Whig* took the view that the differences in opinion over the retrospective features of a tenant-right bill could be overcome.[3]

Between 1853 and 1857 nothing practical was done to soothe the relations of landlord and tenant. Bright did co-operate in 1853 with William Shee in the preparation of clauses for a tenant compensation bill,[4] but his main concern in that year was the renewal of the East India Company charter. In 1854 the Crimean war began, and early in 1856 he was struck down with his first 'nervous breakdown'. Difficulty was also created for him by the fact that some of his associates thought he was going too far to meet Irish demands. Even though he could not meet the views of either the moderate Crawford or extremist Lucas, he was accused by one of his political friends, C. P. Villiers, of having sacrificed his principles on the matter of tenant-right.[5] Lord Palmerston's dictum that 'tenant-right is landlords' wrong' was a general opinion held by British statesmen. Bright believed that tenant-right was being held back because a large number of Irish proprietors within Lord John Russell's cabinet were 'difficult to manage'.[6] Then there were difficulties among the Irish M.P.s. The defection of W. Sadleir (M.P. for Athlone) and J. Keogh (M.P. for Co. Carlow) from the Tenant League demoralized Irish representatives.[7] The defeat of Crawford in July 1852, was a serious blow. The

[1] W. Shee, *Papers, Letters, and Speeches in the House of Commons on the Irish Land Question*, p. 56.

[2] *Freeman's Journal*, 6 Oct., 1852, p. 2, col. b.

[3] *Northern Whig*, 7 Oct. 1852, p. 2, col. c.

[4] Walling, p. 143.

[5] Bright Papers, Add. MSS. 43,386. C. P. Villiers to Bright, 25 Sept. 1852, f. 96.

[6] Friends Historical Collection, Dublin. Pim MSS. i 23. Bright to Pim, 31 Jan. 1848.

[7] Sir C. Gavan Duffy, *The League of North and South*, pp. 237–8.

decision of the Tenant League to work independently of all English parties[1] made it more difficult for men like Bright to sympathize with their aims.

Though efforts to pass a tenant-right bill were unavailing, Bright had raised some hope that Irish grievances could be rectified within the Imperial Parliament. Crawford, for example, was convinced that Bright would be of aid to the tenant-right cause.[2] William Shee, more moderate than Crawford, was in complete agreement with Bright.[3] The *Northern Whig* valued his efforts because it might engender a competition among parties for the favour of Ireland.[4] Bright was anxious to assure those interested in the question that there was growing English concern for the plight of tenants. He wrote to one Irish correspondent, 'When your deputation is in London, I shall be glad to have an opportunity of meeting the gentlemen of whom it will be composed. I am very anxious to see a generous & just Bill & give security & compensation to the Irish Tenantry.'[5]

Bright also tried to point out to Irishmen that the correction of their depressed economy did not lie in the directions that they often assumed. In 1849 he expressed the opinion that Ireland could not be saved by any adjustment of the poor-rates.[6] He warned that emigration was a false panacea, and the money involved in effecting it might be better spent at home.[7] Capital alone, without a change in land tenure, was worthless. According to Bright, £14,000,000 had been borrowed by Irish landlords between 1837 and 1847, but had had a negligible effect so far as he could see.[8]

Though it probably had little influence on the willingness of the landlords to accede to Bright's arguments, he always stressed that his recommendations were in their best interests. He wrote, 'The landlords don't perceive that they are large sharers in everything which begets improvements and investments on the soil.... All advance in the classes below them tends

[1] Whyte, op. cit., p. 88.
[2] *Northern Whig*, 5 Oct. 1852, p. 2, col. d.
[3] Shee, op. cit., pp. 56–7.
[4] *Northern Whig*, 12 Oct. 1852, p. 2, cols. d–e.
[5] Belfast Public Record Office, T. 1765/3. Bright to J. Greenfield, 23 March 1850.
[6] Hansard, vol. 102, 286.
[7] Ibid., vol. 104, 176–7.
[8] *The Times*, 5 Jan. 1850, p. 3, col. b.

to their good without exertion on their part.'[1] If land could be freely exchanged, then young people would be filled with the hope of owning it. Owning a plot of land would transform a man, Bright thought, from a rebel to a conservative.[2]

III

In his earlier years in Parliament Bright tended to regard the political aspects of Irish affairs as the most demanding of attention. He wrote, 'I would not appear to under rate the importance of the political branch of the Irish malady. I am sure it is important & but for its glaring evil, I have no doubt the economical & social wrongs of the country would long ago have been remedied.'[3]

What was preventing the political stability of Ireland? He concluded from his visit in 1849 that, 'Here we have in perfection the fruits of aristocratic & territorial occupation & privilege—& unless these restrictions are removed, industry will be, as hitherto, impossible.'[4] In his maiden speech to Parliament on 7 August 1843, Bright charged that 'Land-owners have been our law-makers, and yet everywhere there is suffering, and the land-owners are everywhere charged with the mischief.'[5]

In addition to the landlords' holding back needed legislation on the land, he claimed they had forced upon the people of Ireland the 'blot' to the name of Christianity in Ireland, the Protestant established church.[6] It was in every way a political church with 'political power and political privileges'.[7] In 1845 he declared his opinion that the Protestant church was the root of the difficulties in Ireland. Everything was Protestant in Ireland, including the Viceroy, landlords and soldiers.[8] While in Ireland he observed the bitterness resulting from attempts of the established church to gain converts from among the Catholic population.[9] It angered him greatly that English

[1] Walling, p. 100.
[2] *The Times*, 5 Jan. 1850, p. 3, col. c.
[3] Friends Historical Collection, Dublin. Portfolio 5a, 29. Bright to Pim, 27 Sept. 1849.
[4] Bright Papers, U.C. Bright to his wife, 2 Sept. 1849.
[5] Hansard, vol. 71, 341.
[6] *The Times*, 18 Jan. 1847, p. 6, col. f.
[7] Ibid., 5 Jan. 1850, p. 3, col. c.
[8] Hansard, vol. 79, 820.
[9] Bright Papers, U.C. Bright to his wife, 28 Sept. 1852.

politicians were afraid to touch the Irish church because it might set in motion a chain reaction that would endanger its English counterpart.[1]

Bright's philosophy, instilled by his Quaker background, was that a state alliance with religious groups was not only inimical to religious liberty, but was also destructive of vitality in a religious body.[2] This led him to oppose the grant to Maynooth College passed by Sir Robert Peel in 1845. Maynooth College was an educational institution for Irish priests, and Bright regarded the bill as a 'sop given to the priests'.[3] In his words, 'Ireland was suffering, not from the want of another Church, but rather because she already has one Church too many.'[4] The same attitude led him to disapprove of the Regium Donum, a grant of money to the Irish Presbyterians, and in 1850 he moved that there be a gradual reduction of this grant.[5] The £1,000,000 given to the established church was even more galling to his regard for religious equality. In his opinion the fact that the majority of people in Ireland were not adherents of the church was an unanswerable argument against the grant.[6] Furthermore, the established church had been instituted by a 'foreign and conquering power'. From this unpromising beginning it had come to be associated 'with a course of political action which has not been considered favourable, or liberal, or just, to the greater portion of the population of Ireland'.[7] All this had the effect of making Catholicism not only a faith but also a patriotism.[8]

Another political drawback, in Bright's opinion, was the poor quality of Irish representatives. Commenting on one particular parliamentary debate, Bright wrote, '... the Irishmen take up nearly all the time,—saying worse than nothing'.[9] He revealed his attitude more fully in a letter to Pim: 'The fact is that too many of your members do not represent Ireland, & my honest belief is that their indifference as to measures of a general, & imperial, & therefore of necessity, *Irish character* &

[1] Hansard, vol. 127, 947–8.
[2] Ibid., vol. 79, 823.
[3] Ibid., 820.
[4] Ibid., 821.
[5] The attempt failed. (Hansard, vol. 113, 265–8.)
[6] *The Times*, 5 Jan. 1850, p. 3, col. c.
[7] Ibid., 7 Oct. 1852, p. 7, col. b.
[8] Ibid. p. 7, col. c.
[9] Bright Papers, U.C. Bright to his wife, 10 Dec. 1847.

import is much more observable than is that of English members to measures strictly Irish.' He claimed that the only agreement ever reached among Irishmen occurred when something was to be demanded from the Chancellor of the Exchequer.[1] His trip to Ireland in 1849 strengthened his opinion; he found the Irish representatives were held in open scorn by most people.[2]

From this evidence Bright was not willing to conclude that Ireland would never be able to produce capable representatives. He blamed Ireland's sham representative system, under which 40,000 electors from among a population of eight million chose the M.P.s. It was a 'fraud' upon the people of Ireland to hold out the idea of a representative system without investing them with its benefits.[3] The violence of election time in Ireland was, to Bright, disgraceful in every way.[4]

Bright was not hesitant in offering remedies for these political defects. One of the fruits of his 1852 visit to Ireland was a plan for the disestablishment of the Irish church, written in the form of a letter to Dr Gray, to be addressed to a group of Irishmen meeting in Dublin to discuss the church question. He rejected Lord John Russell's 1843 proposals for concurrent endowment and Lord Grey's 1845 proposals for allowing Catholic bishops in the House of Lords. His ideas of religious equality admitted neither financial nor political privilege. If complete equality were accepted, the chief problem would be to disendow the funds of the State church. To do this he recommended a 'Church Property Commission' to hold in trust church titles and properties and to dispense gifts of £1,000,000 each to the Presbyterians, Catholics and the Episcopalians. This would leave £7,000,000 which he recommended should be used for strictly Irish purposes, such as improving education. All grants similar to that given to Maynooth College would

[1] Friends Historical Collection, Dublin. Portfolio 5a, 29. Bright to Pim, 27 Sept. 1849. (Bright's emphasis.)

[2] Bright Papers, Add. MSS. 43,383. Bright to Cobden, 17 Sept. 1849, f. 189.

[3] Hansard, vol. 100, 516–18. Professor Gash remarks of the 1832 Reform Act, 'But justice to Ireland was measured by different standards on the other side of St. George's Channel.' (Gash, *Politics in the Age of Peel*, p. 63.)

[4] Bright once recalled a talk with an Irish Member who told of one of the most orderly elections Ireland had had—only three killed and twenty-eight wounded. (Hansard, vol. 190, 1651.)

cease.[1] More than a plan was required. He advised Irish Liberal members to make religious equality 'the cardinal question in their political movements.'[2] In 1853 he supported a motion by G. H. Moore (M.P. for Mayo) for the appointment of a select committee to inquire into ecclesiastical revenues.[3]

In Bright's view, the surest way to deal with the established church and lesser political problems was a complete reform of the Irish representative system. He wanted to extend the franchise to anyone who was rated to support the poor.[4] Needed too was a redistribution of seats more in accord with property and population. He thought Ireland had a just claim to more than 105 representatives in the House of Commons.[5] He advocated the secret ballot as a means of ending violence in Ireland and giving liberty of conscience to voters. In 1850 he gave his support to the Parliamentary Voters (Ireland) Bill,[6] which resulted in quite a large increase in the county voters in Ireland, but, because of amendments passed by the Lords, ended by reducing the borough voters.[7]

Finally, Bright believed that the state of Irish politics could be vastly improved by a union of English and Irish Liberals.[8] One of the reasons for his going to Ireland in 1852 had been his reluctance to 'throw away an opportunity of doing anything that... [might] serve to unite Irish & English Liberal politics & action'.[9] A closer union with Irish Liberals was a development desired by both Bright and Cobden.[10] From his 1849 trip Bright had surmised that the English Liberals would in future receive a steadier support from the Irish Members. At that time he

[1] Leech, pp. 99–111. Bright's plan was in part based upon suggestions advanced by Cobden in the 1830s. (Read, *Cobden and Bright*, p. 193.)

[2] Hansard, vol. 127, 951.

[3] Ibid., 946–51.

[4] Bright objected to the payment of rates as a criterion because a trade slump could throw many off the electoral rolls. (Hansard, vol. 108, 1303–4.)

[5] *The Times*, 5 Jan. 1850, p. 3, col. c.

[6] Hansard, vol. 108, 1302–6, 1359–61; vol. 109, 250, 257, 1077–8; vol. 113, 551–9.

[7] R. B. O'Brien, *Fifty Years of Concessions to Ireland*, ii, 169.

[8] 'Liberals' was not the only term used to describe the followers of Bright and Cobden—also used were 'free trade party', 'Reformers', 'Manchester School'.

[9] Bright Papers, Add. MSS. 43,383. Bright to Cobden, 7 Sept. 1852, f. 250.

[10] Cobden had inquired of the possibilities of such a union after Bright's 1849 trip. (Cobden Papers, Add. MSS. 43,649. Cobden to Bright, 14 Sept. 1849, ff. 137–8.)

thought that the Repeal movement had lost its force, but that it would take time for Repealers and those Liberals who had upheld the Union to begin work together.[1]

In 1850 at Manchester Bright urged Irishmen to meet together and discuss the problems of their country. They could count on the support of the 'great free trade party', who were anxious to atone in the future for the calamities of the past.[2] In Belfast in 1852 he denounced those people who claimed that no union could take place. Surely, he argued, co-operation in recent years on such great issues as the Reform Bill, slave emancipation and free trade was rejoinder enough to such a contention.[3]

It is extremely difficult to estimate the success of Bright's efforts. Political parties and allegiances at this time were very fluid. However, it was the opinion of C. P. Villiers in 1852, and it may be a minimum estimate, that Bright could count on the personal support of only three Irish M.P.s 'from gratitude or regard or because you were right'.[4] On the other hand, the sizeable contingent of Irishmen in the India Reform Society was, in part, indicative of Bright's standing with them. And his visit to Belfast in 1852 called forth enthusiastic praise in that city for the Manchester School.[5] The *Northern Whig* stated that a union of Irish and English reformers was desirable because the Whigs and Tories were in trouble.[6] There is little doubt that Bright improved his co-operation with W. S. Crawford, W. Shee and their supporters. It is an indication of the degree of their understanding that Bright exposed in Parliament in 1853 the measures used against Crawford in the 1852 election.[7]

[1] Bright Papers, Add. MSS. 43,383. Bright to Cobden, 17 Sept. 1849, f. 190.

[2] *The Times*, 5 Jan. 1850, p. 3, col. d. [3] Ibid., 7 Oct. 1852, p. 7, col. c.

[4] Bright Papers, Add. MSS. 43,386. C. P. Villiers to Bright, 25 Sept. 1852, f. 96. Villiers does not name the supporters of Bright.

[5] *Northern Whig*, 5 Oct. 1852, p. 1, col. f. [6] Ibid., 7 Oct. 1852, p. 2, col. c.

[7] Hansard, vol. 128, 217–19. In the 1852 election M. J. O'Connell (M.P. for Kerry Co.) established contact with Manchester which resulted in a League lecturer being sent to Ireland. In addition, £50 was donated to his campaign fund. That not more was done in a general way to uphold supporters of free trade was due to Bright who was quite reluctant to loosen the League purse strings, and it was really Cobden who seemed most enthusiastic for the project. Bright feared the combination of ceaseless demand in Ireland and strict accountability in Manchester. (Wilson Papers, Manchester Central Reference Library. M. O'Connell to G. Wilson, 8 March, 9 March, 26 July 1852; Bright to G. Wilson, 22 March, 1 April 1852; Cobden to G. Wilson, 9 March, 12 March 1852.)

The effectiveness of this co-operation was slightly reduced by the political impotence of the northern tenant farmer.[1]

Political rapport with the Tenant League was made extremely difficult by the League's pledge to remain independent of English parties. The *Irish Tenant League* repudiated the idea of a union with the Manchester School for the stated reason that they had never shown much capacity in the House.[2] Bright had had some contact with Fred Lucas and Charles Gavan Duffy in 1851 on the tenant-right question,[3] but he never hoped to do much with this extreme group even during his visits to Ireland.[4] There was another difficulty. The Manchester School was never properly a political party. As Cobden was reported to have said to Gavan Duffy, 'there is no attempt to create a party because we have none of the necessary agencies. We have no office or honours to promise, no court holy water to distribute; we can only state our opinions and leave them to take their chance outside the House as well as inside'.[5] The defection of Keogh and Sadleir from the Tenant League was another example of the maxim that a political party needs more than a cause to attract adherents.[6]

Bright set up an ideal of political treatment of the Irish people. As he said, it was the duty of the government to bring 'six-sevenths of the population of Ireland in opinion, more in harmony and accordance, with the people and Government of this country.'[7] He thought in 1850 the true policy for Ireland was one of liberality and 'generosity'.[8] Though he voted for coercion in the pre-Christmas session of 1847, he did not do so before assuring himself that the corrective medicine was of a mild solution.[9] In 1851 at the time of Lord John Russell's

[1] Hanham, op. cit., p. 182.

[2] *Irish Tenant League*, April 1852, p. 136, cols. a–b.

[3] Bright Papers, U.C. Bright to his wife, 22 Feb., 15 March 1851.

[4] Ibid., Add. MSS. 43,383. Bright to Cobden, 15 Oct. 1852, f. 251.

[5] Gavan Duffy, *My Life in Two Hemispheres*, ii, 54. Bright mentions a talk with Gavan Duffy and Cobden in 1851. (Bright Papers, U.C. Bright to his wife, 17 March 1851.)

[6] Cobden attributed the repeal of the Corn Laws not to a party, but to ten 'earnest & united' men. (Cobden Papers, Add. MSS. 43,649. Cobden to Bright, 16 Oct. 1852. f. 283.)

[7] Hansard, vol. 99, 6.

[8] Ibid., vol. 113, 558.

[9] Bright Papers, U.C. Bright to his wife, 1 Dec. 1847.

abortive attempt to control the appointment of Roman Catholic bishops by means of the Ecclesiastical Titles Assumption Bill, Bright took to writing to oppose the measure. In the *Manchester Examiner and Times* he wrote an editorial entitled 'Who Wrecked the Ship'.[1] In it he warned that Ireland could not be ruled on the basis of 'No Popery'. Anything that further weakened the connexion between Ireland and Britain was too great a price to pay for the gratitude of Protestant fanatics.[2]

A desire that Ireland should be treated fairly led Bright to consider various schemes by which Irish opinion could be given freer expression in the House and Irish legislation considered more fully. In 1850 he presented a plan whereby the House would be divided into sections to consider the details of bills and to leave the whole House to consider principles.[3] He also urged English Members 'to take into consideration most seriously' the wishes of Irish M.P.s when a majority of English Members threatened to upset their legislation.[4]

Bright had little to say regarding Repeal. He considered the movement to be extinguished.[5] The basis of his appeal to Ireland was to teach the Irish people that they could expect justice from England;[6] so underlying his work for Ireland was a belief in the Union. As for the differences between Ulster and the rest of Ireland, he criticized the reluctance of the northern Irish to pay a rate-in-aid in 1849 to help their stricken brethren in the south and west. He declared that 'if this Bill [Rate-in-aid] can succeed in making Ulster a part of Ireland in interests and sympathies, I think it will be attended with a very happy result'.[7]

IV

What caused Bright to take an interest in Ireland? According to Bright himself, his attention was aroused by his reading the

[1] Walling, p. 119.

[2] *Manchester Examiner and Times*, 1 March 1851, p. 4, cols. c–e.

[3] Hansard, vol. 113, 1040.

[4] Ibid., vol. 127, 949. Bright said in 1867 that he had suggested in the House more than fourteen years before a plan for an all Irish session. (*The Times*, 2 Feb. 1867, p. 5, col. c.) I can find no reference to such a plan in his speeches 1851–4.

[5] Bright Papers, Add. MSS. 43,383. Bright to Cobden, 17 Sept. 1849, f. 190. The wording would suggest that Bright did not discount its possible resurrection.

[6] *The Times*, 5 Jan. 1850, p. 3, cols. c–d.

[7] Hansard, vol. 104, 165.

account of an agrarian outrage.[1] This is consistent with his abhorrence of bloodshed. His interest also arose from his residence in Lancashire, where large numbers of Irish immigrants were a pressing problem, especially in times of depression. In a speech in the Commons in December 1847, he said, 'I protest most solemnly against a system which drives the Irish population to seek work and wages in this country and in other countries, when both might be afforded them at home.'[2] He saw too that the emigration of discontented Irishmen to other parts of the world had dangerous implications. If trouble should develop between the United States and Britain, it was certain that Irishmen in America would throw their weight against Britain.[3] Concern for financial economy[4] also aroused his interest in Ireland. He regarded the presence of 26,000 soldiers and 12,000 police in Ireland as unnecessary if proper action were taken to remove grievances.[5] Then, too, there were problems that affected Britain that also beset Ireland, quite often in a more severe form. The extension of the franchise, the ballot, and redistribution of seats were common needs of both countries. The land problem was more critical in Ireland because of the lack of industry to absorb the overflow of rural people. Bright summed up his reasons for interest in Ireland in 1852 when he wrote, 'I have endeavoured to study it [the problem of the established church], and to regard it as becomes an Englishman loving justice and freedom, anxious for the tranquillity of Ireland, the welfare of the empire, and the honour of the imperial government.'[6]

To gain his information, Bright studied Irish problems with great care. It was his boast in 1884 that he had studied the report of the Devon Commission of 1845 more thoroughly than anyone else.[7] His service on various parliamentary committees

[1] Joseph Kay, *The Social Condition and Education of the Poor in England and Europe*, i, 315–18.

[2] Hansard, vol. 95, 988.

[3] Ibid., vol. 101, 534.

[4] Bright said that representatives were sent to Parliament with the express purpose of seeing that public funds were not voted without proper reason. (Hansard, vol. 107, 283.)

[5] Hansard, vol. 97, 1183–6.

[6] Leech, p. 110.

[7] *The Times*, 31 Jan. 1884, p. 10, col. a.

enabled him to gain information on Ireland.[1] His two visits to Ireland in 1849 and 1852 put him in touch with practical men who were familiar with the problems of Irish land tenure and industry. Sir Robert Kane had written a book on the industrial resources of Ireland.[2] During a part of Bright's stay he was accompanied by W. T. Mulvany, a Commissioner of the Board of Works.[3] In local areas he quite often had the aid of a priest familiar with neighbourhood conditions.[4]

In 1852 Bright renewed his acquaintance with Kane and Professor Hancock.[5] He stayed with W. Kirk (M.P. for Newry)[6] and while in Belfast dined with Robert Grimshaw (D.L.), who had chaired his meeting, and W. S. Crawford.[7] He met Dr Gray, editor of the *Freeman's Journal*, in 1849[8] and John Lamb, occasional writer for the *Northern Whig*, in 1852.[9] Those from whom he sought information he described as men who had 'great practical knowledge, & great legal knowledge'.[10]

Equipped with the knowledge that these men could impart, and with a deep belief in the absolutes of generosity and justice, Bright tried to find a common ground for co-operation with Irishmen to solve the problems of church and land. In this he was hindered somewhat by his own devotion to the laws of political economy and by the slow build-up of Irish distrust of English statesmanship. However, he did make admirable use of the floor of the House and the public platform to dwell on the theme that Ireland demanded the attention of Parliament. William Shee wrote of him as 'our only hearty English friend'.[11] He did a great deal to create an opinion that Irish Members could look to the support of English Members for parliamentary correction of their grievances.

[1] He served on the Irish Poor Law Committee in 1849. (Hansard, vol. 104, 161.) In 1853 he took part in the Irish tenant-right committee. (Bright Papers, U.C. Bright to his wife, 2 March 1853.) In 1854 he served on the Irish Corruption Committee. (Bright Papers, U.C. Bright to his wife, 10 March 1854.)

[2] See R. Kane, *The Industrial Resources of Ireland.*

[3] Bright Papers, Add. MSS. 43,383. Bright to Cobden, 17 Sept. 1849, f. 189.

[4] Walling, p. 104.

[5] Bright Papers, U.C. Bright to his wife, 11 Sept. 1852.

[6] Ibid., 12 Sept. 1852.

[7] Ibid., 5 Oct. 1852.

[8] Ibid., 14 Aug. 1849.

[9] Ibid., 5 Oct. 1852.

[10] Ibid., Add. MSS. 43,383. Bright to Cobden, 17 Sept. 1849, f. 191.

[11] Shee, op. cit., p. 167.

CHAPTER VI

Ireland 1857–1870

FROM 1857 to 1870 Bright continued to press for Irish reforms. He evolved a new plan to deal with the land question that received legislative sanction from Parliament in 1870. The disestablishment of the Irish church in 1869 was the culmination of a long campaign by Bright against the evils of the established church. He continued to stress the need for closer union between Irish and British Liberals, but progress in this direction was exceedingly difficult. Bright, however, expected that Irish discontent would diminish with the consequent benefit of a more secure Union.

II

Bright returned to politics in July 1857, when he accepted the nomination to stand at Birmingham. Though his treatment of the Irish land question was to be relatively insignificant until 1864, he had made up his mind in approximately 1857 that the land question was the key to the Irish difficulty.[1]

From 1857 to 1865 Bright had two solutions to offer on the land question. One was a tenant's compensation bill which he continually advocated. He proposed that compensation should not be left to free contract between landlord and tenant, but should be secured by Parliament.[2] By the dictates of political economy Bright could not see his way to support either fixity of tenure or fair rent. He wrote to Gladstone, '...I know nothing more dangerous than the Irish land question. I have read an article...by Professor Cairnes—it has alarmed me a good deal.

[1] See Rathbone Papers, University of Liverpool, R.P. xviii 2, 3. (1). Bright to W. Rathbone, 1 Dec. 1879.

[2] *The Times*, 31 Oct. 1866, p. 12, col. c.

...He defends a "fair rent" to be settled by some authority above Landlord & Tenant.'[1] Drawing Lord Granville's attention to the same article, he expressed his amazement that such a belief was held not to be 'at variance with the true teaching of political economy'.[2] His other solution continued to be what he called 'Free Land'. This could be achieved by breaking down the laws of primogeniture and entail so that a beginning could be made of enabling 'the Irish people' to become 'the possessors of the soil of Ireland'.[3]

In 1866 Bright unfolded a new scheme which he hoped would create a 'middle' proprietary between the large landowners and the many tenants. He recommended a parliamentary commission, stocked with £5,000,000 of government money, to negotiate with absentee landlords for the sale of their land, which was to be resold to the tenants. To induce such sales, the landlord should receive 10 per cent above London prices. The tenant would pay a certain rent each year, and anything paid above that amount would go towards the purchase price of the farm.[4] While defending the plan in 1868, Bright argued that it could work along the same lines as the rent banks in Prussia. He cited, too, the example of Prince Edward Island, where the government had bought such lands to the advantage of the people.[5] The Tory land bill of 1866, according to him, had provided for loans for improvements. Was it not potentially a much more worthwhile step to lend money to help tenants to become owners? He thought also that there was much saved money in Ireland that would issue forth under favourable circumstances. A more energetic cultivation of the soil would also produce greater savings.[6]

Bright's scheme did not emanate from any preference for state action. It was dictated by the exigencies of the situation. He would not countenance the plan proposed by J. S. Mill (M.P. for Westminster) to make the state the landlord of all

[1] Gladstone Papers, Add. MSS. 44,112. Bright to Gladstone, 1 Jan. 1870, f. 118.

[2] Granville Papers, P.R.O. 30/29/52. Bright to Granville, 2 Jan. 1870.

[3] Leech, p. 112.

[4] *The Times*, 3 Nov. 1866, p. 5, col. e.

[5] Ibid., 5 Feb. 1868, p. 12, cols. c–d.

[6] Hansard, vol. 190, 1645–8.

Irish tenants.[1] His general reluctance to allow state interference in business can be seen in the controversy over Irish railways within the Gladstone cabinet, of which he had become a member in December 1868. In May 1869, he sent Gladstone a memorandum strongly dissenting from Lord Clanricarde's view that the state should take over control of the railways.[2] Gladstone, who at the same time was being pressed by Bright to adopt his land purchase plan, was led to query why 'Bright should strain at a gnat about Railways and yet should swallow without difficulty such a camel as the notion of making the State a great Land Jobber'.[3] In the latter part of 1869, when Gladstone was busy trying to draft legislation both on the land and railways, he encountered further opposition from Bright. The latter thought that railways were too expensive for a poor agricultural people. Gladstone, perhaps remembering Bright's exhortations in this regard in another country, wrote the one word 'India' in the margin.[4]

A month later Bright consulted the expert, James Murland of Dublin, who thought that government loans to enable large and small lines to amalgamate would be the best remedy.[5] Gladstone without committing himself to the idea of loans, thought that such a merger would be the best idea.[6] When he submitted to Bright a tentative plan for the railways Bright was willing to support it, but only if Gladstone was certain that some scheme was inevitable.[7] Gladstone eventually gave up his plans when a commission headed by the Duke of Devonshire did not recommend any considerable change.[8] It can be seen from this account that Bright could not easily be brought to the idea of state purchase.

[1] Hansard, vol. 190, 1650. Mill claimed that this was a misrepresentation of his intentions. See J. S. Mill, *Autobiography of John Stuart Mill*, p. 205.

[2] Gladstone Papers, Add. MSS. 44,420. Memorandum. Bright to Gladstone, 3 May 1869, f. 166.

[3] *The Political Correspondence of Mr. Gladstone and Lord Granville 1868–76*, ed. A. Ramm, Gladstone to Granville, 24 May 1869, i, 22.

[4] Gladstone Papers, Add. MSS. 44,112. Bright to Gladstone, 15 Oct. 1869, f. 98.

[5] Ibid., 24 Nov. 1869, f. 101.

[6] Bright Papers, Add. MSS. 43,385. Gladstone to Bright, 25 Nov. 1869, f. 52.

[7] Gladstone Papers, Add. MSS. 44,112. Bright to Gladstone, 29 Nov. 1869, ff. 103—4.

[8] J. Morley, *Life of W. E. Gladstone*, i, 877 n.1.

What, then, prompted Bright to advocate land purchase? From his correspondence it is clear that it was an attempt to forestall even wilder schemes that could develop if no remedy were applied. As he observed in a letter to Gladstone, the condition of Ireland could become worse, '& measures far beyond anything I now contemplate will be necessary'.[1] A tenant who contracted to purchase his farm would have 'fixity of tenure',[2] and thus meet the objections of those who were so strongly in favour of it.

Bright was careful to point out that he did not wish to interfere with property rights.[3] Only landlords and tenants who were willing to bargin would be affected.[4] Only in the case of lands held corporately by the London Companies—the Fishmongers, Drapers and others[5]—would he insist on compulsory sale.[6] He set up the ideal that any man of moderate means 'should, if he could, became the possessor of land or of his farm'.[7]

Bright proclaimed the fundamentals of this idea in Dublin in 1866 upon the request of twenty-three Irish Liberal M.P.s to attend a banquet in his honour.[8] Upon returning to Britain he revealed in a speech to his constituents the details of his scheme.[9] On the floor of the House he defended land purchase as tending not only to the well-being of tenants, but also to the landlord's prosperity and honour.[10]

What support did Bright receive for his plan? The editor of the *Freeman's Journal* offered the opinion that Bright's scheme was too advanced to gain immediate acceptance. He thought that a sound plan of tenant-right would be more acceptable

[1] Gladstone Papers, Add. MSS. 44,112. Bright to Gladstone, 21 May 1869, f. 87.

[2] Hansard, vol. 190, 1648. Sir John Gray (M.P. for Kilkenny) was the leader of those in Ireland who supported fixity of tenure.

[3] Ibid., 1645–6.

[4] This marks a departure from his stand in 1866 when only the tenants of absentees were to be given aid.

[5] O. Robinson, 'The London Companies as Progressive Landlords in Nineteenth Century Ireland', *Econ. Hist. Rev.*, 2nd series, xv, no. 1 (1962), 118.

[6] Hansard, vol. 190, 1648–9.

[7] Ibid., 1646.

[8] *The Times*, 6 Sept. 1866, p. 9, col. a.

[9] Ibid., 5 Feb. 1868, p. 12, cols. c–d.

[10] Hansard, vol. 190, 1649–52.

to both landlords and tenants.[1] The O'Donoghue,[2] who had taken the chair at the two speeches made by Bright in Dublin, continued to uphold the same view.[3] The *Freeman's Journal* was more willing, however, to accept Bright's proposal in regard to the tenants on church land, whose position would come into question with the disestablishment of the Irish church.[4] Eventually Bright's scheme in this regard was accepted by the Gladstone government, and the Church Temporalities Commission succeeded in making sales to 6057 of 8432 tenants.[5]

The greatest support in Ireland for Bright's plan came from the section termed by the *Freeman's Journal* as the 'intellectual and commercial representatives of the citizens of Dublin',[6] who met in the Mansion House in November 1869. Sir Dominic Corrigan and Judge Little both supported land purchase as recommended by Bright. Most of the speakers denied that they were afraid of fixity of tenure, but regarded Bright's plan as best, for varying reasons, including one who said it conformed to human nature.[7]

Bright's land purchase scheme was criticized from both extremes. Some thought it might work so well that it would lead to a multiplicity of small plots,[8] while others contended that it would not be universal enough in its application.[9] *The Times* represented more of a centre position. In 1869 it was non-committal.[10] By 1870 its only worry was the financial aspect. It considered that at least 25 per cent of the purchase money should be advanced by the tenant.[11]

[1] *Freeman's Journal*, 2 Nov. 1866, p. 2, col. f.

[2] O'DONOGHUE, DANIEL (1833–89). 'The O'Donoghue'; M.P. for Tralee, 1857–62, 1865–85; bankrupt 1870; advocated Catholic university and tenant-right.

[3] *Freeman's Journal*, 4 Feb. 1867, p. 2, col. e.

[4] Ibid., 28 Jan. 1869, p. 2, col. f.

[5] J. E. Pomfret, *The Struggle for Land in Ireland*, p. 89.

[6] *Freeman's Journal*, 25 Nov. 1869, p. 2, col. e.

[7] Ibid., p. 3, cols. d–i.

[8] See speeches of W. H. Gregory (M.P. for Galway Co.) and H. Bruen (M.P. for Carlow Co.), Hansard, vol. 190, 1706–18, 1731. Gladstone, on the other hand, feared that the land would inevitably return to a few owners. (Bright Papers, Add. MSS. 43,385. Gladstone to Bright 22 May 1869, f. 32.)

[9] See comment of J. E. Thorold Rogers in *Freeman's Journal*, 6 Oct. 1869, p. 3, col. b. Also, speech of Marquess of Clanricarde, Hansard (Lords), vol. 185, 793–6. See comments of Sir J. Gray and H. D. Hutton below.

[10] See *The Times*, 27 Oct. 1869, p. 6, col. e.

[11] Ibid., 16 Feb. 1870, p. 9, col. c.

However, it was the opinion of the *Freeman's Journal* and its proprietor, Sir John Gray, that would be most vital to the acceptance or rejection of any land measure in Ireland. The weight and importance of Gray's views are indicated by the fact that the Prime Minister had been warned that success or failure of the Land Bill depended on Gray's newspaper.[1] Gray, himself, when speaking in Manchester in October 1869, emphasized that he had no objection to Bright's scheme as far as it went, but he added that 'this proposal would not cover the whole ground'. It would apply, he thought, only to absentee landlords, whose estates were not the worst managed. At best only 40,000 tenants would be affected by the measure, leaving over 500,000 unprotected.[2] On 19 January 1870, his publication sharply criticized Bright's views. It refuted the idea that the land question was very complex,[3] a point made by Bright in an address to his constituents in January 1870.[4] The *Freeman's Journal* thought that primogeniture and entail only 'have great interest for the student or for the votary of political economy'.[5] It conceded that such questions as the creation of a small proprietorship might be complex, but what absorbed Irish hearts was the much more simple problem of landlord and tenant.[6]

Criticism of a similar kind came from Dublin barrister H. D. Hutton (who himself devised a plan for occupying ownership).[7] Hutton doubted whether anyone but 'the better class' of tenant would have saved enough money to secure the state's advances, and pointed out that therefore Bright's plan would be too slow in its operation.[8]

As Professor Black points out, there was little support for Bright's remedy from either the tenants or the economists. But the influence of his name was enough to attract considerable attention to land purchase.[9] Sir James Caird thought that Bright's scheme or an expanded version of it would be prac-

[1] J. Morley, *Life of W. E. Gladstone*, i, 926.
[2] *Freeman's Journal*, 22 Oct. 1869, p. 4, col. a.
[3] Ibid., 19 Jan. 1870, p. 2, col. g. [4] *The Times*, 12 Jan. 1870, p. 7, col. d.
[5] *Freeman's Journal*, 19 Jan. 1870, p. 2, col. g. [6] Ibid.
[7] Black, *Economic Thought and the Irish Question*, p. 57.
[8] B.M. 8145 bbb 5(8). H. D. Hutton, *The Irish Question*, pp. 17–20.
[9] Black, op. cit., p. 58.

ticable.[1] Bright took care that Caird's views were made known to Gladstone.[2] What was surprising was the amount of support given to the idea of land purchase by the landed interest in both Ireland and England. Lord Salisbury declared in favour of Bright's proposals, saying that the widening of the basis of property was politically desirable.[3] In *The Times*, an Irish landlord, John Ussher, advocated it strongly.[4] Marcus Goodbody, a landowner in King's County, believed that the Irish people would not become attached to the Crown until an occupying proprietorship were established.[5] J. L. O'Beirne (M.P. for Cashel) in 1867 sought to obtain an advance of £1,000,000 to carry out land purchase.[6]

Though no exact estimate of Bright's support can be made, much of it came from the commercial interests in Ireland; from those landlords who did not set their face against any concession, and particularly those who opposed fixity of tenure; from a wide variety of M.P.s including Irish (if an effective tenant-right bill were passed); and finally from partial concurrence of writers such as Hutton and Sir J. Caird. There was, in addition, the support received from the National Association within which the clerical element, in particular, was in favour of land purchase.[7]

What kind of difficulties faced Bright within the cabinet? In 1867 he wrote that the Irish question might not be fairly grappled with because of the Whig peers who had not the 'courage to attempt anything great'.[8] He suspected in 1868 that Gladstone had not studied the land question,[9] though Gladstone proved in 1869 to be in favour of the principle of a peasant proprietorship.[10] He had to contend with the strong opposition of Lowe and Cardwell within the cabinet. The

[1] B.M. 8145 bbb 3(8). James Caird, *The Irish Land Question*, p. 30.

[2] Gladstone Papers, Add. MSS. 44,112. Bright to Gladstone, 15 Oct. 1869, f. 97.

[3] Hansard (Lords), vol. 202, 75–6.

[4] *The Times*, 15 Sept. 1869, p. 10, col. f.

[5] Gladstone Papers, Add. MSS. 44,112. M. Goodbody to Bright, 7 Jan. 1870, f. 127.

[6] Black, op. cit., p. 60.

[7] E. R. Norman, *The Catholic Church and Ireland in the Age of Rebellion*, pp. 390–5. For a definitive account of the National Association see esp. pp. 135–90, 282, 409.

[8] Northy Papers, Add. MSS. 44,877. Bright to Northy, 26 Dec. 1867, f. 16.

[9] Leech, p. 114.

[10] Bright Papers, Add. MSS. 43,385. Gladstone to Bright, 22 May 1869, f. 31.

former was a firm believer in freedom of contract. He thus had no ally in the cabinet for his plan, while his opponents (Lowe, Cardwell, Argyll) could count on mutual support.

While still involved in the Irish church issue, Bright urged upon Gladstone his plan for land purchase as he had outlined it in Dublin in 1866.[1] He was also anxious to have a competent observer sent to Prussia to report on land reform being carried out there.[2] Gladstone did not take up this suggestion,[3] nor was he any more enthusiastic about adopting Bright's land plan. He thought it would involve the state in the position of a land jobber who paid high prices. The fact that it could be adopted for only a limited number of tenants would not solve the problems of the others.[4] Granville concurred with Gladstone, but he was also worried that the question could break up the cabinet because Bright, who was so enamoured of his scheme, would be extremely annoyed at having his plan 'snuffed out'.[5] There seemed little prospect for the realization of land purchase. Gladstone concluded from a talk with Bright that he would be no great obstacle in the way of a land bill.[6] As Gladstone commented, if Lord Russell were to speak to him about Bright's plan he could honestly say that '...we have thrown him over quite as much as Lord R. would have done'.[7] In October Bright was not confident that his scheme had a chance of acceptance in the cabinet.[8]

Despite Gladstone's initial comments, Bright determined to prepare a memorandum incorporating not only his land purchase scheme but also a proposal to remove the impediments to free land exchange, such as entail and settlement laws.[9]

[1] See p. 139.

[2] Gladstone Papers, Add. MSS. 44,112. Bright to Gladstone, 21 May 1869, f. 88.

[3] Black, op. cit., p. 63.

[4] Bright Papers, Add. MSS. 43,385. Gladstone to Bright, 22 May 1869, ff. 31–2.

[5] *The Political Correspondence of Mr. Gladstone and Lord Granville 1868–76*, ed. A. Ramm, Granville to Gladstone, 26 May, 1869, i, 23.

[6] Ibid., Gladstone to Granville, 27 May 1869, p. 24.

[7] Ibid., 21 May 1869, p. 22.

[8] Clarendon Papers, Bodleian MS. Clar. dep. c. 499, folder 6. Bright to Clarendon, 14 Oct. 1869.

[9] Gladstone Papers, Add. MSS. 44,112. Bright to Gladstone, 29 Nov. 1869, ff. 104–5. I have not found the actual memorandum, but Gladstone's letter of 4 Dec. 1869, to Bright comments on it. (Bright's Papers, Add. MSS. 43,385. Gladstone to Bright, ff. 56–9.)

Gladstone thought these latter proposals should be dealt with in conjunction with England and Scotland, and could not be accommodated in an Irish land bill.[1] As for land purchase, Gladstone expressed no little exasperation with Bright's wish to place the proposals on tenant-right of the Irish Secretary, C. Fortescue, in the second order of discussion for the cabinet. Gladstone's former objections to land purchase remained steadfast.[2]

How, then, did the 'Bright clauses'[3] appear in the Irish Land Act of 1870? No doubt Bright's determination and influence were greater factors to contend with than Lord Granville had expected. Bright was a figure almost as important as Gladstone in the Liberal party, possibly more prominent in Ireland, and one that Gladstone could little afford to alienate. There was no doubting his determination. In 1883 he put it on record that the rejection of the scheme would have entailed his withdrawal from the government.[4] Moreover, a spirit of compromise did exist in the cabinet. Bright gave way on the matter of state purchase of waste lands[5] in favour of Gladstone's device that any purchaser, including landlords, could buy them.[6] Finally, though the purchase clauses were inserted in the Act, they were so circumscribed in their application that little of practical value resulted except, perhaps, in providing a precedent. By the purchase clauses the Board of Works was entitled to advance two-thirds of the price to tenants on an annuity rate of 5 per cent for the sale of any land in the hands of the Landed Estates Court.[7] To encourage large scale transfers, the same provisions were extended to the tenants of any purchaseable estate where four-fifths of them wished to become owners. Lastly, to induce the sale of individual farms by landlords, an attempt was made to overcome inconveniences to purchase by allowing the state to guarantee a title to the purchaser. But

[1] Bright Papers, Add. MSS. 43,385. Gladstone to Bright, 30 Nov. 1869, f. 54.

[2] Ibid., 4 Dec. 1869, ff. 56–8.

[3] R. R. Cherry, *The Irish Land Law and Land Purchase Acts 1860 to 1901*, pp. 191–202.

[4] *The Times*, 15 June 1883, p. 10, col. d.

[5] Gladstone Papers, Add. MSS. 44,122. Gladstone to Fortescue, 10 Dec. 1869 (draft), f. 99.

[6] J. Morley, *Life of W. E. Gladstone*, i, 925.

[7] Cherry, op. cit., pp. 195–8.

even here the difficulties for the most part proved too great. Only 877 tenants took advantage of the Bright clauses. Their ineffectiveness resulted mainly from the lack of sufficient capital. Tenants who often paid immoderately high rent were unable to accumulate enough money to purchase their farms. Furthermore, because the tenant security portion of the Land Act failed, there was little reason for the landlord to sell. It was not until the dual ownership principle was accepted in the 1881 Act that landlords felt sufficiently pressured to want to sell. Large-scale transfers did not take place, however, until the Act of 1885 provided for the advance of the full price to the tenant.[1]

However, despite cabinet opposition and 'luke-warm' support in Ireland, Bright had almost single-handedly secured the insertion of the purchase clauses in the 1870 Act, thus providing a precedent for future land bills which recognized the necessity for widening the basis of land ownership in Ireland. His motives had not changed since his early years in Parliament. A middle proprietary would 'awaken industry' and create loyalty and tranquillity.[2]

III

Bright continued to regard the landed interests as the chief obstacle to Ireland's improvement. He held that 'the peace of Ireland & the unity of the Empire has already for generations been sacrificed' for the sake of the Irish landlords.[3] What did he regard as the solution? Cobden and Bright agreed that nothing could be done 'on this question of the land with the House as at present [1864] constituted'.[4] In addition to an adequate reform bill, there was a necessity for the secret ballot in Ireland.[5] As for redistribution, he thought that Ireland should have a

[1] Pomfret, op. cit., pp. 89–90; Mansergh, *The Irish Question*, p. 41; J. C. Beckett, *The Making of Modern Ireland 1603–1923*, pp. 373, 391, 394.

[2] Hansard, vol. 190, 1651–2.

[3] Gladstone Papers, Add. MSS. 44,420. Memorandum. Bright to Gladstone, 3 May 1869, f. 166.

[4] Cobden Papers, Add. MSS. 43,652. Cobden to Bright, 30 March 1864, f. 166.

[5] National Library of Ireland, MS. 894. Bright to G. H. Moore, 1 Dec. 1858, pp. 640–1.

slight addition in Members,[1] as well as an increased number of seats for such places as Dublin, Belfast, Kilkenny, Limerick and Cork.[2]

He considered that the best method of achieving these ends was by a workable union of English Radicals with the Irish 'popular' or Liberal party. In his view the major aims of both groups were inter-related. Irish Liberals could help swing the balance in favour of such measures as parliamentary reform. In 1858 he wrote to one Irish Liberal, 'I hope we shall have a hearty cooperation from all the Liberal Party in Ireland in our attempt to improve our system of representation.'[3] While in Dublin in 1866 he pointed out that Irishmen had a great interest in British reform schemes because even if their 105 Members were completely independent, it would still be a bad Parliament if the English Members were under the thumb of the landlord.[4] In return the English Radicals could aid Irishmen in reform matters as well as the all-important affair of disestablishing the Irish Church.

In 1858 Bright was in sufficiently close contact with several Irish Liberals to consult them about his plans for a reform bill that he was drawing up. He maintained a liaison with W. S. Crawford, who, though not then in Parliament, was of considerable importance in Ulster. To gain advice on his bill he also conferred with J. F. Maguire (M.P. for Dungarven).[5] Another Irish Member whom he consulted was G. H. Moore.[6]

The failure of reform plans in 1858–9 and Bright's overwhelming pre-occupation with American affairs at this time tended to set the Irish question in abeyance and weaken his lines of contact with Irish M.P.s. But early in 1865 at Birmingham he served notice that it was time to attend to Ireland's

[1] Bright Papers, Add. MSS. 43,384. Bright to Cobden, 14 Nov. 1858, ff. 144–5.

[2] *The Times*, 18 Jan. 1859, p. 7, col. d.

[3] National Library of Ireland, MS. 894. Bright to G. H. Moore, 1 Dec. 1858, p. 641.

[4] *The Times*, 3 Nov. 1866, p. 5, col. c.

[5] Belfast Public Record Office, D856/D/139. Bright to W. S. Crawford, 9 Jan. 1859.

MAGUIRE, JOHN FRANCIS (1815–72). Called to Irish bar 1843; founded *Cork Examiner* in 1841; M.P. for Dungarven, 1852–65; M.P. for Cork, 1865–72; vigorous upholder of disestablishment, tenant-right, and public education.

[6] National Library of Ireland, MS. 894. Bright to G. H. Moore, 1 Dec. 1858, p. 641.

needs, chief of which was the disestablishment of the church.[1] In Parliament he called for an equality of laws between Ireland and England. In particular reference to the poor laws, he thought that more outdoor relief, as in England, should be given. In general he thought that no greater humiliation attached itself to any country for the treatment of another than that of Britain for the condition of Ireland.[2]

Such advocacy on behalf of Ireland did not go unnoticed there. In late 1864 Bright was invited by Irish Liberal M.P.s—J. F. Maguire, Major O'Reilly (M.P. for Longford Co.), The O'Connor Don (M.P. for Co. Roscommon)—and Roman Catholic church officials to attend a meeting in Dublin. He could not go, but suggested a slogan of 'Free Land' and 'Free Church' for the Liberal party. He thought such aims could be gained if they united 'with the popular party in England and Scotland for the advance of liberal measures'. He hoped the meeting would provide 'a more distinct policy and a better organization' for the future.[3]

As a result of the meeting, the National Association was formed on 29 December 1864, with the aims of disestablishment of the Irish church, a tenants' compensation bill and freedom of education in all its branches.[4] One of the speakers (Professor Sullivan) paid tribute to Bright's influence. 'You all heard the admirable letter of Mr. Bright dictated by his love of justice.... We now call upon them [the English Liberals] to aid us to return to an effort to render victorious our three causes, described in the words of Mr. Bright's "free land, free church" and free education also.'[5] The *Freeman's Journal* thought the most hopeful aspect of the meeting was the desire of the Irish to unite with 'the advancing Liberal party'.[6]

Bright continued to sympathize with Ireland's difficulties in Parliament and in the provinces. In Birmingham in 1865 he warned that Ireland would not be peaceful as long as the established church existed.[7] When Parliament met for a special session on 17 February 1866, to suspend Habeas Corpus in

[1] *The Times*, 30 Jan. 1864, p. 5, col. e.
[2] Hansard, vol. 173, 1879–84.
[3] *The Times*, 31 Dec. 1864, p. 9, col. e.
[4] *Freeman's Journal*, 30 Dec. 1864, p. 4; Norman, op. cit., pp. 141–51.
[5] *Freeman's Journal*, 30 Dec. 1864, p. 4, col. g.
[6] Ibid., p. 2, col. e.
[7] *The Times*, 14 Dec. 1865, p. 9, col. e.

Ireland, he castigated the record of imperial control since the Act of Union. Saying that he had never before risen under such a strong feeling of shame, he called upon Gladstone and Disraeli to forget party spirit, so inimical to Ireland's interests, and to legislate wisely so that Ireland could become a credit to the Empire.

Although Bright said that he would not vote against coercion, he felt it would be perilous to let another session pass without introducing remedial legislation. To him the 'statesmanship' of the past had rubbed the veneer of respectability from the word. Statesmanship consisted of more than merely guarding the Crown. It meant doing 'justice' to the people.[1] J. B. Dillon (M.P. for Tipperary Co.) praised his speech as one of 'the most generous, most true, and most noble' that he had ever heard.[2]

In consequence of the continued appreciation in Ireland of Bright's stand, Dillon extended an invitation to him to attend a public banquet in Dublin.[3] It was signed by 140 names,[4] including twenty-three M.P.s—among them: J. F. Maguire, The O'Donoghue (M.P. for Tralee) and John Gray.[5] Bright replied that 'as so many among you are of opinion that something may be done to make a more perfect union between the Liberals of Ireland and the Liberal party here, with a view to wiser legislation for your country and for ours, I have not felt myself at liberty to refuse the invitation'.[6]

The proposed meeting at the Rotunda in Dublin came to be known as the 'Bright Banquet'. It was a momentous occasion. The *Freeman's Journal* had to refer to the days of O'Connell to find a comparison.[7] Unfortunately, Dillon had died, but The O'Donoghue's eloquent speech as chairman welcomed Bright as 'the tried and trusty friend of Ireland'.[8] Bright's purpose was revealed in his opening remarks: 'How is it that we or Parliament can act so as to bring about in Ireland contentment and

[1] Hansard, vol. 181, 685–95. [2] Ibid., 702.

[3] *The Times*, 6 Sept. 1866, p. 9, col. a.

[4] Ibid., 31 Oct. 1866, p. 12, col. a.

[5] Ibid., 6 Sept. 1866, p. 9, col. a. For complete list see Appendix II.

[6] Ibid., 6 Sept. 1866, p. 9, col. a.

[7] *Freeman's Journal*, 31 Oct. 1866, p. 5, col. b.

[8] *The Times*, 31 Oct. 1866, p. 12, col. a.

tranquillity and a solid union between Ireland and the rest of Great Britain? And that means further, how can we improve the condition and change the minds of the people of Ireland?'[1]

Bright began by citing the ills of Ireland. The disgraceful panorama of famine, secret societies, and discontent resulted from the control of the Tory party, whose principles, he felt, had always had fullest expression in Ireland. It was little wonder that Irishmen should look to the west for their deliverance.[2] For remedies he disclosed his land purchase scheme, in addition to giving as his opinion that disestablishment would create a new political and social atmosphere. Legislation on the Irish church and land would be expedited if Irishmen realized that the reform movement in Britain was as much their concern as it was of the English and Scottish.[3]

Bright's visit to Ireland was of great value to those Irishmen who felt that they could look to the Imperial Parliament for the amelioration of their country's ills. He became a symbol of hope, so much so that the mere mention of his name could be guaranteed to elicit long and appreciative cheering on the part of Irish audiences.[4] His reputation in 1866 attracted contingents of enthusiastic Irishmen from all over the country to listen to his speech in Dublin.

Bright's visit was instrumental in the creation of a Reform League in Dublin under the presidency of The O'Donoghue.[5] It hoped to work in conjunction with reformers in England and Scotland to widen the franchise in Ireland. In February 1867, Bright, his brother Jacob (M.P. for Manchester) and T. B. Potter (M.P. for Rochdale) were made vice-presidents of the organization.[6] In that same month The O'Donoghue, in his capacity as President, spoke in Manchester on the same platform as Bright, Potter and others.[7] In a letter to his supporters early in 1867, The O'Donoghue informed them that he

[1] Ibid., cols. a–b.

[2] Ibid., cols. b, c.

[3] Ibid., col. d.

[4] See *Freeman's Journal*, 3 Jan. 1867, p. 4, col. c.

[5] Ibid., 22 Nov. 1866, p. 4, cols. b–d. One representative of the Irish Reform League directly acknowledged that he had been converted by Bright. (*Freeman's Journal*, 4 Feb. 1867, p. 3, col. a.)

[6] Ibid., 27 Feb. 1867, p. 4, col. e.

[7] Ibid., 4 Feb. 1867, p. 2, cols. a–f.

was receiving more and more support from English reformers.[1] The *Freeman's Journal* was high in its praise of the efforts of The O'Donoghue. It commented, 'The Irish people are too quick-witted not to perceive that a dozen JOHN BRIGHTS in the House of Commons would vastly accelerate the redress of their grievances. Hence their powerful sympathy with the Reformers of England.'[2] One important reason why the Irish looked to Bright so earnestly was well brought out by a speaker in Cork. He said that 'Mr. Bright's advocacy was important, for he represented not a constituency but millions of the people.'[3]

Bright's influence was felt too in the lobby. A survey of the parliamentary division lists in 1867 and 1868 shows remarkably little divergence between Bright and the twenty-three Irish M.P.s who asked him to speak in Dublin in 1866. Some of them, such as The O'Donoghue and J. A. Lawson (M.P. for Portarlington) and Edward Sullivan (M.P. for Mallow) never opposed Bright in these two years. When it occurred that Bright and Gladstone went into opposing lobbies, three times as many Irish Liberals always voted with Bright, although they were in a minority.[4] Although there was certainly no compact of any kind, this did not prevent Irish Tories such as J. Whiteside (M.P. for Dublin University) from commenting that the Tenant-Right Bill of 1866 was 'the honourable performance of the compact between the Liberal party and Irish Members' contracted by Bright in his letter in 1864.[5]

But most Irish Liberals preferred to retain the right to vote on any issue as they saw fit rather than be tied down to a party commitment. Even N. D. Murphy (M.P. for Cork City), who did not, in fact, vote against Bright in the years 1867–8, had worded his letter of acceptance to the banquet in 1866 by pointing out that '...all may not agree in everything that Mr. Bright has said or written'.[6] Sir John Gray, although he attended several meetings in London on behalf of the Irish

[1] *Freeman's Journal*, 10 Jan. 1867, p. 4, col. f.

[2] Ibid., 6 Feb. 1867, p. 2, col. h.

[3] Ibid., 19 Oct. 1866, p. 4, col. g.

[4] House of Commons, *1867 Divisions*, pp. 119–20 and pp. 151–3, and *1867–68 Divisions*, pp. 161–2.

[5] Hansard, vol. 183, 1111.

[6] *Freeman's Journal*, 19 Oct. 1866, p. 4, col. f.

Reform League,[1] always retained freedom of action to work with any party that promised good measures.[2] When P. J. Smyth (elected M.P. for Westmeath, 1871) was enrolled in the Reform League, he made it clear that his support for reform did not involve an alliance with 'any English faction'.[3]

The Reform League itself did not blossom as its founders had hoped. After one year it had expired. The membership had never come within a fraction of the 100,000 prophesied at its outset.[4] The leadership of The O'Donoghue was at its best aloof, and he never had the support of many other M.P.s. As The O'Donoghue himself said in London in 1867, 'I have been condemned for urging upon the Irish people to join you in this movement by many of my friends.'[5] When Ernest Jones came to lecture at the Reform League in Dublin in 1867, The O'Donoghue was the only M.P. present.[6] The two most immediate reasons for the League's downfall were the espousal of the cause of Garibaldi by the London Reform League[7] and the hanging of the 'Manchester Martyrs'.[8]

There were many reasons why Bright, right up to the split in opinion with those who supported fixity of tenure, retained the confidence and support of the Irish people and most Liberal M.P.s. One was his attitude to Fenianism. The Fenian Brotherhood, though led by Irishmen, was planned and organized in the United States, and had for its object the establishment of an independent Irish republic. When the Civil War was over, experience and discipline were mingled with a daring, almost reckless courage; they sought to overthrow British rule. Several outrages were committed in England that did their cause no good.

On the outbreak of Fenianism in March 1867, Bright took a very lenient view. He considered the revolt as a proof of the results of the misgovernment of Ireland.[9] He expressed this view in the House while presenting a petition on behalf of

[1] Ibid., 7 Dec. 1866, p. 4, col. c.
[2] Ibid., 3 Jan. 1867, p. 4, col. a.
[3] Ibid., 7 Dec. 1866, p. 4, col. c.
[4] Ibid., 22 Nov. 1866, p. 4, col. c.
[5] Ibid., 9 May 1867, p. 2, col. e.
[6] Ibid., 3 Sept. 1867, p. 3, col. f.
[7] Ibid., 5 Nov. 1867, p. 8, col. c.
[8] Ibid., 26 Nov. 1867, p. 4, col. c.
[9] Northy Papers, Add. MSS. 44,877. Bright to E. Jones, 4 Oct. 1867, f. 153.

Richard Congreve and others of his Positivist leanings.[1] It stated that there was legitimate ground for unrest in Ireland, of which Fenianism, though in error, was the expression. The petition sought to secure the revision of past sentences on Fenians. It asked for lenient punishments because such offences as Fenians committed were in aid of a cause 'free from dishonour'. Bright stated that he agreed with the general spirit of the petition.[2]

On diverse other matters Bright took a position sympathetic to liberal Irish views. In Dublin in 1866 he discussed the difficulties of the Irish representatives in London, where because they were not unanimous they could rarely raise sufficient voice to influence the progress of legislation.[3] In May 1867, he defended the courage of J. F. Maguire who had gone to America and had come back with dire warnings of things to come from the Irish race in America unless Irish grievances received immediate attention.[4] In 1868 he eloquently defended J. F. Maguire's motion for an inquiry into the state of Ireland.[5] He protested against the practice of English Members absenting themselves from debates such as the Irish Reform Act. This tended to delay needed legislation and created a bad impression in Ireland.[6] In 1867 at Manchester he proclaimed his belief that if measures were passed on disestablishment and land reform, the prison doors could be opened to political prisoners.[7] He also defended the right of Irishmen to seek the restoration of their parliament if they thought it advantageous to do so.[8]

The Irish Liberals had good cause to appreciate Bright's efforts to disestablish the Irish church. The Irish church had failed, by Bright's reckoning, in the two spheres for which it had been set up. Firstly, it had failed as a religious institution; it had made Ireland more Romanist than any other Catholic

[1] See Harrison, *Before the Socialists* for an account of the Positivists in British politics at this time, esp. p. 279.

[2] Hansard, vol. 186, 1929–31. Before the end of the year, however, he censured the Fenian movement in very strong terms. (*The Times*, 24 Dec. 1867. p. 3, col. d.)

[3] *The Times*, 1 Nov. 1866, p. 8, cols. e–f.

[4] Hansard, vol. 187, 959–60.

[5] Ibid., vol. 190, 1642–63.

[6] Ibid., vol. 188, 777–8.

[7] *The Times*, 2 Feb. 1867, p. 5, col. c.

[8] Ibid., 5 Feb. 1868, p. 12, col. b.

country in Europe. Secondly, as a political institution, it had not secured the Union.[1] He set up the ideal of free churches in Ireland which would leave no man with a grievance against the Imperial government.[2]

Bright took steps to sound out Gladstone on this issue. In 1864 he elicited from him the assurance that a settlement of the Irish church would be one of the great purposes of the Liberal party when it was 'restored to life'.[3] By November 1867, Gladstone told Bright that he was entirely willing to suppress the state church.[4] In December Bright sent Gladstone his letter of fifteen years earlier on the Irish church.[5] He asked for a careful study of it because his standpoint, as a Dissenter, would have to be considered by any statesman who took up the church question.[6] Gladstone thought the basis of Bright's plan was the best he had ever seen.[7]

1868 marked the year that Bright ceased to be a Radical and became a Liberal. He was even persuaded not to speak on occasions when his own inclinations were to do so. He was invited to attend what he called an 'Opposition Cabinet Meeting' on several occasions. Social engagements increased his rapport with leading Liberals. Bright's attack on Disraeli in the House on 7 May was the direct outcome of a talk with Lord Clarendon, who expressed the view that Disraeli was poisoning the mind of the Queen on the Irish church issue.[8] Indeed, Bright's acceptance by fashionable society dates from 1868. Even the Queen's attitude towards him had changed. After his entry into the cabinet, Clarendon wrote, 'Eliza [Queen Victoria] so far from being afraid of Bright has quite a predilection for him.'[9]

During 1868, both in and out of Parliament, Bright insisted continually upon the need for disestablishment. On 22 April he took the chair at Spurgeon's Tabernacle to address a crowd

[1] Hansard, vol. 191, 649–52.
[2] Ibid., vol. 190, 1656.
[3] Walling, p. 276.
[4] Ibid., p. 313.
[5] See pp. 131–2.
[6] Gladstone Papers, Add. MSS. 44,112. Bright to Gladstone, 9 Dec. 1867, ff. 63–4.
[7] Bright Papers, Add. MSS. 43,385. Gladstone to Bright, 10 Dec. 1867, ff. 20–1.
[8] Walling, pp. 315–19.
[9] *My Dear Duchess*, ed. A. L. Kennedy, p. 247.

of 7000 on the subject.[1] On 3 June he went to Liverpool to protest against the 'Protestant and political ascendancy' in Ireland.[2] In the House he gave his support to the three resolutions of Gladstone, the chief of which called for the disestablishment of the Irish church.[3] On 4 May he claimed that as long as Disraeli stayed in office, the opportunity to strengthen the nascent feelings of amity towards Westminster growing in the west and south of Ireland would be wasted.[4]

After quitting London before the end of the session, Bright combined a trip to Ireland with an election campaign that, according to *The Times*,[5] resulted in an outpouring of nearly 34,000 words. In this way he prepared public opinion to accept the Irish question as the prime issue of the election.[6] His visit to Ireland was mainly for pleasure, although he addressed a public breakfast in Limerick on 14 July. From his contacts in Ireland during this interval he concluded, 'I am evidently deemed an authority on Irish matters in this country!'[7]

The reputation earned by Bright on the subject of disestablishment meant that church officials sought him for consultation. His plans for disestablishment were 'favourably criticized' by several Anglicans, including Dr Guthrie and Dr Newman Hall.[8] Bright's impression of a deputation from the Irish Presbyterians, including Montgomery, their Moderator, was much less favourable. He rebuked their 'miserable subservience to the Tory and Church party'.[9]

It was the need for Bright's assistance on the Irish Church Bill that Gladstone emphasized to gain Bright for his cabinet. It was the appeal to his sense of duty that overcame his self-conscious dislike of work and official position[10] and led him on

[1] *The Times*, 23 April 1868, p. 5, col. a.

[2] Ibid., 4 June 1868, p. 5, col. c.

[3] R. B. O'Brien, *Fifty Years of Concessions to Ireland*, ii, 239–40.

[4] Hansard, vol. 191, 1739.

[5] *The Times*, 25 Nov. 1868, p. 5, col. e.

[6] Royden Harrison endorses Marx's contemporary opinion that among the working classes the Irish question overshadowed other issues. (Harrison, *Before the Socialists*, p. 160.)

[7] Bright Papers, U.C. Bright to his wife, 12 July 1868.

[8] Walling, p. 317.

[9] Ibid., pp. 324–5.

[10] Bright Papers, U.C. Bright to his wife, undated letter marked 'Very Private'. Evidence suggests 5 December 1868.

9 December 1868, to accept office in Gladstone's administration. Within the cabinet he joined Gladstone, Granville and others in a committee to draw up a disestablishment bill. In a speech which Kimberley praised as 'superb', he warned that it was intolerable that the Irish people should suffer religious insult any longer.[1] After the rejection of the bill by the Lords he contributed little to the eventual compromise. His letter to the secretary of the Birmingham Liberal Association printed in *The Times*, criticising the action of the Lords,[2] merely embarrassed the Liberal party. His major role had already been completed; he had gathered the players together, and it was Gladstone and Granville who had to work out an acceptable ending.

What contributions had Bright made to improve the political atmosphere of Ireland? He had been one of the first prominent English Members both to support the idea of disestablishment and to produce a plan for carrying it out. He had also advocated the principle of disendowment rather than concurrent endowment, and in this he had the support of the Roman Catholic hierarchy in Ireland.[3] He contributed to the preparation of a public feeling that disestablishment was necessary. As late as January 1868, he considered the English people to be quite ignorant of Irish wrongs.[4] In addition, because of the Reform Act, there were nearly a million additional voters to inform in 1868 who had never before exercised the franchise.[5] He convinced many of them that questions of Protestantism or Popery had nothing to do with the Irish church question.

Bright also kept Gladstone informed of Nonconformist opinion in the House of Commons. After a conversation with H. Richard (M.P. for Merthyr Tydfil) and E. Miall (M.P. for Bradford), Bright wrote to Gladstone complaining of what generally appeared to be the too favourable terms being ex-

[1] John Wodehouse, First Earl of Kimberley, *Journal of Events during the Gladstone Ministry 1868–74*, ed. E. Drus, pp. 2–3.

[2] *The Times*, 15 June 1869, p. 11, col. c.

[3] Norman, op. cit., p. 285.

[4] Leech, p. 114.

[5] Hanham, *Elections and Party Management*, p. ix. But see also Blake, *Disraeli*, pp. 475–6.

tended to the Anglicans as compared with the Presbyterians.[1] Gladstone discounted such charges.[2] On another occasion Bright warned that, considering the temper of the House, especially with the Scottish Members, it would be extremely rash to give any money to the Catholics from the church funds unless the feeling of the House changed.[3]

Undoubtedly Bright over-estimated the beneficial effects of disestablishment. Sir William Gregory, though influenced by O'Connell to regard the church as an intolerable injustice, wrote that the Irish masses cared little about the matter.[4] The Tithe Commutation Act of 1838 had made it less of a grievance among Irish peasants.[5] Bright's over-emphasis was quite often a by-product of rhetoric. He had made clear in April 1869, his belief that disestablishment would not affect agrarian crime.[6] But no more would there be a Catholic grievance.

Despite the willingness of the Liberals to tackle long-standing problems, Bright's hope for a closer union with Irish Liberals was but briefly realized. Criticism of his land scheme has already been noted.[7] Unfortunately the church issue also adversely affected his position with the Irish. This resulted from his increasing disposition to treat too generously the claims of the Anglicans pursuant to any disestablishment of the church. In 1868 he stated that congregations of the Church of Ireland should be allowed to maintain possession of their churches and parsonages.[8] Regarding this as much too generous, many Irish reformers began 'to lose faith in him'.[9] There were other problems. The O'Donoghue, on whom Bright relied, was of rather unstable character. The gap between expectations aroused in Ireland by a Gladstone government and the actual

[1] Gladstone Papers, Add. MSS. 44,112. Bright to Gladstone, 14 Feb. 1869, ff. 83–6.

[2] Bright Papers, Add. MSS. 43,385. Gladstone to Bright, 15 Feb. 1869, ff. 28–9.

[3] Gladstone Papers, Add. MSS. 44,112. Bright to Gladstone, 9 Jan. 1869, ff. 74–5.

[4] Sir William Gregory, *Sir William Gregory K.C.M.G.*, ed. Lady Gregory, p. 255.

[5] R. B. O'Brien, *Fifty Years of Concessions to Ireland*, ii, 175.

[6] Hansard, vol. 195, 2016.

[7] See pp. 142–3.

[8] Hansard, vol. 190, 1658.

[9] Norman, op. cit., p. 343. This refers most specifically to the National Association.

results achieved led to disillusionment. To take one example, the failure of the Land Act to include fixity of tenure embittered an influential number of Irish Liberals.

IV

Bright's trip to Ireland in 1866 resulted in greater speculation on his part regarding problems relative to Britain, Ireland and the Empire. From his visit he learned that there was a considerable 'party' who believed that more responsible government would result if Ireland were severed from England. He then made this unequivocal statement in February 1867: '...I proceed from the basis that the political union of Great Britain and Ireland is a thing decided and fixed for a long time, and therefore upon that basis we should consider what can be done for Ireland.'[1] Never before had he felt called upon to make such a forthright declaration. That it occurred in 1867 is indication enough of the transitory and tenuous nature of the Anglo-Irish *rapprochement*.

In a speech at Birmingham in 1868 Bright remarked on the identity of language and interests between Ireland and Britain, the closeness of family ties, and then said, '...I shall never consent myself to any measure that would disturb legislative union till it is proved that in England statesmanship is absolutely dead, and till it is proved in Ireland that right and justice have failed to influence mankind.'[2] That is why he was so determined to see the Irish church disestablished, because if it were not, those who argued for a Dublin parliament would find their arguments 'not only immeasurably strengthened, but I should say conclusive'. The issue was a challenge to the British people to ascertain whether they were capable of ruling the 'Irish nation'.[3] In this instance there was no question in his mind that it was improper for one nation to rule another. The only consideration was whether it could govern justly. History might show that empires were dangerous, but economics raised compelling doubts regarding the wisdom of Balkanization. Whether

[1] *The Times*, 2 Feb. 1867, p. 5, col. c.
[2] Ibid., 5 Feb. 1868, p. 12, col. b.
[3] Ibid., 4 June 1868, p. 5, col. f.

the Irish Sea was a bridge or a barrier was in the eyes of the beholder.

Bright entertained great hopes that the stage had been reached when Ireland would no longer be disaffected or disloyal. One of his constant scources of hope for this lay in the example of Scotland. It seemed reasonable to him that if the Scots could be made happy in their union with England, why could not the Irish?[1] He believed that if the land and church issues were properly handled, the obstacles to closer co-operation with the Irish would disappear. They would then be like the Scottish Members: ready to unite on measures for their own country, but also willing to participate in matters of general interest to the United Kingdom.[2]

If Ireland were loyal then the results of the 'evil of our misgovernment' in the form of Fenian threats to colonies such as Canada would end.[3] Though Bright did not think that the Fenians could overthrow the power of England, 'the discontent is not the less discreditable to us, and it is scarcely less hurtful to the Empire than if it were more powerful and more able to contend with England'.[4] But even here where it might seem that he was viewing the Empire as a unit, it was more properly a concern for the removal of a cancer within the United Kingdom that degraded its moral standing in the world.

In his last speech on Irish affairs before his illness in 1870, Bright praised the conduct of the Irish Members. Recent conversations with them convinced him that there was a growing confidence in Parliament on the part of the Irish. There had never been 'more honourable, more intelligent, or more patriotic [Members], than that which we have now in honour and happiness to meet'.[5]

Despite this, Bright was most cautious in recommending the release of Fenian prisoners. In Ireland G. H. Moore was leading a vigorous campaign to gain their freedom. Bright's position was that it would only be safe to allow release if the political climate were improved by the successful operation of Liberal legislation. When Gladstone asked for his advice in

[1] *The Times*, 14 Dec. 1865, p. 9, col. e.
[2] Ibid., 5 Feb. 1868, p. 12, col. d.
[3] Ibid., 23 April 1868, p. 5, col. b.
[4] Hansard, vol. 187, 960.
[5] Ibid., vol. 198, 89.

late 1869[1] Bright regretted that the recent meetings in Ireland made it impossible to act for the moment, as it would be unwise to give the appearance that action was taken as a result of such agitation. His suggestion was for the executive to go over the list of prisoners and pick out those who might be safely liberated. To this advice Gladstone added the marginal comment, 'I have tried this: it can not be done.'[2] In early January 1870, Bright wrote to Gladstone, '...if the Land Bill should *look* well & *go* well thro' Parlt, it may be wise if not indeed necessary, to reconsider the amnesty demand before the Session is over'.[3] Soon afterwards, he was so seriously attacked by illness that he could take no further part in public affairs, and it was not until July that he again proposed that the prisoners should be released.[4]

From the attitude that Bright took at this time, it is clear that he was certain that a 'final solution' of the Irish problem had been reached. The two great problems of the church and land had been legislated upon. All that was needed now was 'to make an appeal to all thoughtful men in Ireland to make this the last occasion in which political prisoners will have to be dealt with'.[5] The events of the next few years were to reveal the illusion of this hope.

[1] Bright Papers, Add. MSS. 43,385. Gladstone to Bright, 13 Oct. 1869, ff. 46–7.

[2] Gladstone Papers, Add. MSS. 44,112. Bright to Gladstone, 15 Oct. 1869, ff. 96–7.

[3] Ibid., 5 Jan. 1870, f. 120. (Bright's emphasis.)

[4] Ibid., 4 July 1870, ff. 138–9.

[5] Ibid., 29 Sept. 1870, f. 153.

CHAPTER VII

Ireland 1870–1889

IT IS a salient fact that on 8 June 1886, John Bright entered the lobby opposing Gladstone, and by his example carried enough dissident Liberals with him to defeat the Liberal Home Rule Bill. The importance of this defeat to subsequent British history cannot be estimated, for the bill might have been the answer to the interminable Irish question. It is important to know why Bright decided to oppose Gladstone's measure. This chapter will also investigate the post-1886 period to see what position Bright took towards the new political situation.

Bright's contemporaries were apt to explain his decision on the Home Rule Bill on the basis of his recognized antipathy towards the Irish parliamentarians.[1] One quoted Bright as having said that Parnell had 'the eye of a madman'.[2] Modern writers have also laid great stress on Bright's hostility to the Irish Members. J. L. Hammond wrote, 'Bright soon lost all perspective, and his old Irish sympathies...were extinguished by what seemed to him the base ingratitude of the Irish party.'[3] Trevelyan gave this attitude as one reason for Bright's decision. As a second he offered Bright's consistent opposition to the idea of Home Rule.[4] No doubt this was important, but it leaves one to ponder again (as Trevelyan did) this extract from Bright's diary for 22 March 1885: 'Long talk...on Ireland. I suggested a mode of dealing with Irish question. Ireland; 32 Counties, 32 County Boards; 64 representatives to a Central Council in Dublin for internal affairs...leaving to it Education, Local

[1] T. M. Healy, *Letters and Leaders of My Day*, i, 171. Note Blunt's similar opinion: W. S. Blunt, *The Land War in Ireland*, pp. 36–7. Also, Sir George Leveson Gower, *Years of Content 1858–1886*, p. 243.

[2] W. McCullagh Torrens, *Twenty Years in Parliament*, p. 246.

[3] J. L. Hammond, *Gladstone and the Irish Nation*, p. 213.

[4] Trevelyan, *The Life of John Bright*, pp. 444–5.

taxation and Control. The question a great difficulty, but some solution must be found.'[1]

It would seem from this that Bright was aware of the seriousness of the problem which Gladstone felt obliged to take up. It might indicate, too, that any one explanation will not suffice to answer the question posed at the beginning of this chapter. Indeed, there are reasons that would lead one to think that Bright would have aided Gladstone's cause.

Certainly one of these factors was a belief Bright had in the Liberal party that amounted almost to a faith. Many of his speeches in the years 1875 to 1882 were eulogies of the achievements of the Liberal party.[2] Another factor was his devotion to Gladstone, as illustrated in Dilke's diary: 'Says Bright to Dodson: "You were put into the Cabinet to vote with Gladstone. Surely you ought not to oppose him." Says Dodson indignantly, "A man may have an opinion." "But why express it?" said the old Quaker.'[3]

The force of these loyalties was severely reduced by the British bombardment of Alexandria. On 8 June 1885, when noting the defeat of the Gladstone government, Bright displayed little remorse: 'Thus, after 3 years, my foretelling is proved correct—that the bombardment of Alexandria would destroy the Government.'[4] After the Home Rule split, Bright wrote this comment on Britain's foreign policy: 'Tory and Liberal Administrations commit much the same blunders and crimes.'[5]

Economic considerations were the decisive factor in Bright's decision. He had long argued that economics lay at the bottom of the Irish question. In 1879 he wrote, 'The Land question is the great question for Ireland. I have said this for more than 20 years & before long it will be generally admitted to be so.'[6] It was Chamberlain's opinion that the main reason for Bright's entering the cabinet in 1880 was to have a voice in the Irish Land Bill.[7]

[1] Walling, p. 525.
[2] See for example *The Times*, 27 Oct. 1879, p. 10, col. d.
[3] Gwynn and Tuckwell, *The Life of the Rt. Hon. Sir Charles W. Dilke*, i, 368.
[4] Walling, p. 528.
[5] *The Times*, 19 March 1887, p. 6, col. e.
[6] Rathbone Papers, xviii, 2, 3. (1). Bright to W. Rathbone, 1 Dec. 1879.
[7] Chamberlain Papers, J.C. 5/5. Chamberlain to J. Morley, 16 April 1880 (draft).

Bright presented his plan for the Irish Land Bill in December 1880. He wished to make the purchase clauses of the 1870 Act more effective by setting up four Commissioners in Dublin, Belfast, Cork and Limerick who would be empowered to exchange the lands of voluntary owners and buyers. The state should set aside five million pounds yearly, and the amount advanced to each purchaser from this fund could be determined by the Commissioners or the Irish executive. Compulsion to sell could be used in the cases of properties held by corporations or of owners of waste lands who were unwilling to improve them. To help the poorer tenants, especially in Connaught, the government could reclaim waste lands, create farms, and rent them at a low rate. Bright put great faith in his scheme. He thought this plan would give new life to the Irish farmer, would increase his industry, and fill his heart with hope.[1]

When discussions had advanced into March, Bright was urging an even stronger bill,[2] presumably to improve the tenant security clauses.[3] It was to his speech in Birmingham on Irish land[4] that the Duke of Argyll turned to see if his moderate views could be reconciled with Bright's more advanced ideas.[5]

Bright's transition from radicalism to conservatism on the land issue after 1881 was swift. He defended the Liberal Land Bill ably in Parliament,[6] and as soon as it was passed in July 1881, he expressed his hope that the question of Irish land had finally been settled. It was now up to Ireland to make herself prosperous.[7] His previously professed views on land underwent change. In 1883 he expressed concern over the 'advanced' views of Lord Thurlow. 'Dined with Lord Reay.... Among guests, Lord Thurloe, whose opinions on Land question very advanced: thinks many great estates and few landowners a serious peril to the nation.'[8] Such a passage contrasts vividly with

[1] Gladstone Papers, Add. MSS. 44,625. Memorandum, 17 Dec. 1880, ff. 26–9.

[2] Ibid., Add. MSS. 44,642, note, f. 152.

[3] In late February Bright wrote that the Land Bill required 'more strength in some particulars, especially as to tenure'. (Walling, p. 457.)

[4] *The Times*, 17 Nov. 1880, p. 6.

[5] Gladstone Papers, Add. MSS. 44,625. Memorandum, 24 Nov. 1880, ff. 10–12.

[6] Hansard, vol. 261, 94–112.

[7] *The Times*, 5 Sept. 1881, p. 8, col. d.

[8] Walling, p. 498.

Bright's words in 1850: 'I see in your [Irish] territorial aristocracy a class who have not only neglected every duty, but whose very existence in our day is incompatible with the elevation of your labouring & cultivating population.'[1]

Bright came to place more and more importance on the retention of the landlord power in Ireland. In 1879 in Parliament he said that it was only the power of Britain that stood between confiscation and the rights of property.[2] By 1886 he was as much against Gladstone's land purchase scheme of that year as he was opposed to a Dublin parliament. He still thought the 1881 Act had gone as far as necessary. He doubted the wisdom of buying out the landlords. Gladstone's contention that he would be helping the landlords by this act[3] failed to convince Bright, though the argument appealed to the same spirit of landlord self-interest that he had so often used. He was convinced that without the proprietary class the Irish nationalists thought 'they could unite the whole of Ireland in hostility to England.'[4]

In a well-argued speech to his constituents in July 1886, Bright maintained again that the seat of the Irish difficulty was not political but economic. He claimed that the political argument was being pushed to the fore with the hope that its success would enable the land to be rented at a cheaper rate, or that there would be no rent at all if the landowners could be expelled. It was only the political question (Home Rule) that was making the land question (the proposed land bill) necessary. His most telling blow against the two bills was that the Home Rule Bill did not entrust to the Dublin parliament the control over land. This failure to hand over the first duty of government—i.e., the preservation of property—was in his eyes an admission of failure.[5]

Bright's determined opposition to the Land League is not, then, to be wondered at. It angered him that men were going about Ireland telling tenants that their rents were too high.[6]

[1] Friends Historical Collection, Dublin. Pim MSS. i 32. Bright to Pim, 24 Jan. 1850.

[2] Hansard, vol. 245, 1652.

[3] Walling, pp. 536–7.

[4] *The Times*, 14 Nov., 1887, p. 7, col. f.

[5] Ibid., 2 July 1886, p. 10, col. b.

[6] Hansard, vol. 257, 1561–2.

The failure of the 1881 Act he blamed entirely on the agrarian agitation of the Land League.[1]

Bright's knowledge of the readiness of the colonies to set up tariffs against British manufactures was a further economic reason for his rejection of Home Rule. In Gladstone's efforts to secure a workable Home Rule bill, many possibilities were considered, including one plan whereby Irish delegations might occasionally attend the Parliament at Westminster to give their opinions and votes on specified subjects.[2] Hammond has described this as 'a hint of a plan for Imperial co-operation'.[3] Bright refused to countenance any comparison between the government of the colonies and that of Ireland. He did not think any such scheme of Home Rule as practised in the colonies would be advisable in Ireland because 'the colonies manage their own military affairs & make their own laws—impose *revenue & protective Tariffs as they like*—& are not in fact under the direction of our Parlt'.[4] On 20 March 1886, Bright questioned Gladstone about the possibility of Irish protective duties being instituted against British goods. Gladstone replied that although he did not think it would happen, he would not object if it did.[5] After the split in the Liberal party, Bright opposed Chamberlain's plan for a federation of Britain and Ireland based on the Canadian model as he refused to go to the colonies for an example.[6] He thought such a scheme in Ireland would inevitably tend towards separation.[7]

To measure Bright's attitude to the Irish representatives in the House, it is significant that the very year with which this chapter begins (1870) was marked by the founding in Dublin of the 'Home Government Association of Ireland'.[8] Isaac Butt's leadership in the House for Home Rule had drawn away many of those Liberals who had co-operated with Bright in the 1860s.

[1] *The Times*, 14 Nov. 1887, p. 7, col. f.

[2] Hammond, op. cit. p. 510.

[3] Ibid., p. 512.

[4] Rathbone Papers, xviii, 2, 3. (1). Bright to W. Rathbone, 1 Dec. 1879. (Bright's emphasis.)

[5] Walling, p. 536.

[6] Chamberlain Papers, J.C. 5/7/30. Bright to Chamberlain, 9 June 1886.

[7] Rathbone Papers, xviii, 2, 3. (1). Bright to W. Rathbone, 1 Dec. 1879.

[8] Woodward, *The Age of Reform 1850–1870*, p. 364.

(Many others had either left Parliament or died.) A case in point was the example of The O'Donoghue. He had been an ally of the Liberal government, and because of his own financial troubles had, at the suggestion of Bright, applied for the Chiltern Hundreds in 1873.[1] He wrote to Gladstone, 'I must say for myself that I am the only Irishman that has come boldly to the front and taken up, in opposition to the Home Rule movement, the only tenable position, viz. that Ireland can obtain full and complete justice in the Imperial Parliament.'[2] By 1880 he was forced to side with Parnell for the reason, as he said, that he would be very sorry to lose his seat.[3] Subsequently he himself drew a comparison between the Anti-Corn Law League and the Land League in Parliament[4] to which Bright took great exception.[5] The falseness of the position of The O'Donoghue was revealed in 1886, for after leaving Parliament he came out strongly against Home Rule.[6] Such was the pervasive influence of Parnellism once it gained momentum.

If Home Rule was a cause of division between Bright and the Irish M.P.s in the 1870s, the principles of fixity of tenure and fair rent were another dividing line. Though Bright accepted the 'three F's' (fixity of tenure, free sale and fair rent) in 1880, he had not been able to give fixity of tenure or fair rent his support before that time. It was The O'Donoghue who had presented bills incorporating such principles each year to Parliament, but Bright had thought he was wrong for doing so, as they would not gain the support of the English Members.[7] Butt, with whom Bright might have found it easier to work, because of his greater moderation and respect for Parliament, supported The O'Donoghue on land questions, while Parnell and Biggar (M.P. for Co. Cavan), with whom Bright could not work, gave their support to land purchase.[8]

[1] Gladstone Papers, Add. MSS. 44,440. The O'Donoghue to Gladstone, 12 Oct. 1873, f. 187.

[2] Ibid., Add. MSS. 44,439. The O'Donoghue to Gladstone, 31 July 1873, f. 233.

[3] C. C. O'Brien, *Parnell and His Party 1880–90*, p. 25 n. 1.

[4] Hansard, vol. 257, 1540.

[5] Ibid., 1559–60.

[6] L. G. Rylands, *Correspondence and Speeches of Mr. Peter Rylands*, i, 361–3.

[7] Potter Papers, MS. f. 923.2 Br 13 (55). Bright to T. B. Potter, 3 April 1874.

[8] Hansard, vol. 234, 177–8.

Although this alignment restricted opportunities for Bright's co-operation with Irish Members, he was able in the 1870s to find men with whom to work. In 1873, in company with J. Pim (M.P. for Dublin) and D. C. Heron (M.P. for Tipperary Co.), he brought in a bill to increase the facilities for purchase established in the 1870 Act.[1] In 1879 he was in consultation with W. Shaw (M.P. for Co. Cork), The O'Connor Don (M.P. for Co. Sligo) and P. J. Smyth (M.P. for Tipperary) in an effort to gain support for his plan to make Galway College a strictly Catholic university.[2] The O'Connor Don[3] was a large landowner and moderate in his views; P. J. Smyth was a Whig in sentiment;[4] while Shaw[5] was eventually to lead the moderate Home Rulers.

In 1880 it was Chamberlain's opinion, and there is little reason to doubt it, that Bright still represented to the Irish 'the extreme of English sympathy and concession'.[6] Bright had gone out of his way several times to defend the actions of Irish Members involved in a tussle with the government. Defending O'Connor Power's (M.P. for Mayo) motion to adjourn the House in 1879, he advised everyone to have a little more patience with the Irish Members.[7] He had more than once supported extension of the borough franchise in Ireland.[8] He had supported a motion for the release of political prisoners in 1876.[9] According to one biographer, even Parnell was willing in 1881 to take into consideration Bright's past efforts on behalf of Ireland to excuse what his party regarded as Bright's wrong course on the Coercion Bill.[10]

[1] Hansard, vol. 216, 151. The bill was never brought up for a second reading.

[2] Chamberlain Papers, J.C. 5/20/31. Chamberlain to A. Dale, 15 July 1879 (draft).

[3] T. M. Healy labels The O'Connor Don as virtually the last Liberal to fight a seat in Southern Ireland against a nationalist (1883). (*Letters and Leaders of My Day*, i, 192.)

[4] C. C. O'Brien, op. cit., p. 29.

[5] Bright was also in consultation with Shaw in 1881 when the latter suggested a plan to relieve, by government payments, the difficulty of tenants who owed arrears of rent. (Gladstone Papers, Add. MSS. 44,113. Bright to Gladstone, 27 May 1881, ff. 151–2.)

[6] Chamberlain Papers, J.C. 5/1/. Chamberlain to Harcourt, 25 Jan. 1880 (draft).

[7] Hansard, vol. 247, 711.

[8] Ibid., vol. 250, 865–70; vol. 237, 1965–71.

[9] Ibid., vol. 231, 302–6.

[10] R. B. O'Brien, *Life of Charles Stewart Parnell*, p. 212.

When the 1881 session began in January, the first Irish measure brought up was the Protection of Person and Property (Ireland) Bill. Bright had maintained right into December 1880, that if an effective land bill were introduced, coercion might not be necessary. He thought the cabinet wrong for introducing coercion before the Land Bill.[1]

However in 1881 Bright made up his mind very quickly that the obstructionist techniques of Parnell's party were not the actions of loyalists, and as early as 10 March 1881, even before the introduction of the Land Bill, had written in his diary of the 'Irish rebel party'.[2] By May he was using the term in his private correspondence.[3] They were rebels to him because he was convinced that their main object was the break-up of the United Kingdom.[4]

When Bright stood by the government and defended the Coercion Bill in the House,[5] delivered a stiff rebuke to Irish Members in May,[6] and defended the Prevention of Crime Bill in June 1882,[7] he became a target for Irish scorn, the bitterness of which was increased because of his previous sympathy for Ireland. None, perhaps, was crueller than Sexton's (M.P. for Sligo) gibe in 1882 when, taking up Disraeli's description for the 1868–74 cabinet, he said, 'The right hon. Gentleman...was the most complete extinct volcano at present existing in the world.'[8]

Bright first publicly branded the Parnellists as rebels in Birmingham on 14 June 1883. But his main object of attack at that time was not the Irish, but the Tory party for its alliance with them.[9] It would seem that he considered ostracism of Parnell as the only method of dealing with him. Could anyone be really surprised that he refused to co-operate with the Parnellists in 1886?

Bright's certainty that Britain was dealing with rebels prevented him accepting Home Rule. He wrote, 'If the *rebel*

[1] This is inferred from Walling, p. 454.
[2] Walling, p. 459.
[3] Northy Papers, Add. MSS. 44,877. Bright to Northy, 16 May 1881, f. 84.
[4] Gladstone Papers, Add. MSS. 44,113. Bright to Gladstone, 4 Oct. 1881 f. 160.
[5] Hansard, vol. 257, 1555–65.
[6] Ibid., vol. 260, 1987–93.
[7] Ibid., vol. 271, 275–80.
[8] Ibid., vol. 268, 365.
[9] *The Times*, 15 June, 1883, p. 10 col. d.

party were not *rebels* an arrangement would not be difficult—but with *rebels* how can you negotiate with or trust them?'[1] The truth was that he never really understood Parnellism. He did not appreciate, as did Gladstone, that Parnell stood for a restraining influence in Ireland.[2] It is likely that he credited Parnell with more influence than he actually had, especially with Davitt. Despite his comments concerning the 'lying' statements of the Parnellists, he stated in 1887 that he believed their speeches implicitly.[3] The speeches of T. P. O'Connor and T. Healey at an Irish convention in Chicago in 1881 disturbed him deeply, and he raised the matter once at Birmingham and twice in the House.[4] He did not take into account that in most cases the tone of Irish speeches depended on the audience and the place.[5]

Bright's fixed opinion that Parnell and his party were rebels makes it difficult to understand why he was usually greatly opposed to the suspension of Habeas Corpus. Granted, he fell foul of Labouchere and Radicals who followed him for supporting the Prevention of Crime Bill in 1882,[6] but he had a generally liberal record in the cabinet for opposing coercion. The reason for this seeming paradox was undoubtedly contained in this excerpt from a speech in Birmingham in 1882: 'I believe that all over Ireland there are great numbers of honest and honourable and sensible men who are as anxious for tranquillity in that country as we are.'[7] His chief hope in advising Gladstone to denounce Parnell in 1881 had been to stimulate the 'good' men in Ireland to favour order.[8] Probably, he could never quite believe that the Irish Members were the true representatives of the Irish people. Gladstone's conviction

[1] Chamberlain Papers, J.C. 5/7/26. Bright to Chamberlain, 4 Feb. 1886. (Bright's emphasis.)

[2] Morley, *Life of W. E. Gladstone*, ii, 310.

[3] *The Times*, 21 March 1887, p. 10, col. e.

[4] Hansard, vol. 271, 278–9, 295–8; vol. 268, 325–7. *The Times*, 4 Jan. 1882, p. 6, col. c. T. M. Healy recounts the story of the Convention in *Letters and Leaders of My Day*, i, 140–7.

[5] C. C. O'Brien, op. cit., p. 350.

[6] See *Truth*, 20 July 1882, p. 111. I am indebted to Mr R. Hind for this reference.

[7] *The Times*, 4 Jan. 1882, p. 6, col. b.

[8] Gladstone Papers, Add. MSS. 44,113. Bright to Gladstone, 4 Oct. 1881, f. 162.

that the voice of Ireland had spoken did not impress Bright, who remained certain that at least two million people remained loyal to the Imperial Parliament.[1]

The moral considerations stand clear as a primary element in Bright's distrust of Parnell and his followers. He advised Gladstone to denounce Parnell for his 'lying statements &...the immoral sentiments he is spreading among the Irish people'.[2] He had already branded the results of the Land League in the House as 'illegal and evil'.[3] He felt that their tactics of requiring receipts from tenants for payment of rent destroyed their 'honest feeling and sense of honour'.[4] In 1885 he said that he would be quite prepared to assist any Irish association if it were not concerned in 'criminal actions' and respected the 'moral laws'.[5]

Religious reasons for Bright's vote against Home Rule were closely allied with the question of Ulster. When discussing the case in 1879 for a committee to look into the opinion of Irishmen on Home Rule, he wrote, '...the sentiment of the North would probably be opposed to much of the sentiment of the South—& who should decide?'[6] This predisposition to deal with Ulster separately revealed itself in 1886. He wrote to Gladstone, 'I cannot consent to a measure which is so offensive to the whole Protestant population of Ireland & to the whole sentiment of the province of Ulster so far as its loyal & Protestant people are concerned.'[7] In a letter printed in *The Times* in 1887, Bright said he thought that Ulster might be a 'nationality' differing as much from the rest of Ireland as Wales did from England. His further charge that Gladstone spoke as if there were no province of Ulster[8] led to a public exchange of correspondence between the two. Bright thought that Gladstone's

[1] Northy Papers, Add. MSS. 44,877. Bright to Northy, 27 July 1886, f. 106.
[2] Gladstone Papers, Add. MSS. 44,113. Bright to Gladstone, 4 Oct. 1881, f. 160.
[3] Hansard, vol. 257, 1559.
[4] Ibid., 1562.
[5] Ibid., vol. 300, 265.
[6] Rathbone Papers, xviii, 2, 3. (1). Bright to W. Rathbone, 1 Dec. 1879.
[7] Gladstone Papers, Add. MSS. 44,113. Bright to Gladstone, 13 May 1886, ff. 224–5.
[8] *The Times*, 9 June 1887, p. 6, col. e.

willingness to deal with a 'well considered desire' on the part of the 'Protestant population' had not been acted upon. He thought that Ulster had a definite claim on Gladstone for some expression of opinion as to its future government.[1]

To assess the religious reasons for his opposition to Home Rule, it should be noted that Bright felt a latent hostility towards the papacy. He thought the priests in Rome were 'pulling the wires' in European politics. He wrote, '...I think ...that the madmen of the ultra Popish Party will drive Christian States to some combination by which the Papal power will be limited or suppressed'.[2] One occasion when his anti-Catholic views were exposed in the House occurred in 1881 when he made reference to the time lost in industry because of an excessive number of holy days.[3] This was deeply resented by the Irish Members, who criticized his anti-Catholic tone.[4] He may have been influenced too by the general Quaker antagonism to Home Rule for Ireland. In January 1886, he was visited by two Irish Friends, Jonathan Hogg and T. Pim, who were seeking interviews with influential English M.P.s to advise against surrendering to the Parnellists.[5]

Whatever there was of nationalism in the Home Rule movement, Bright failed to understand. One clear reference to the subject occurred in a speech at Birmingham in 1868. Referring to the contention that there was 'a positive hunger' for a separate Irish nation, Bright said, 'I shall not deny this, although I do not admit it'. He went on to say that, if 'justice' were done to Ireland, healthy nationalism could survive, as in Scotland, without 'the irritation and passion' which so often seemed the necessary concomitant of national feeling.[6] The implication was that nationalism could be overcome by good government. He still maintained that any grievance could be adequately redressed without recourse to a Dublin parliament. The failure of the legislation of the 1880s to achieve a contented

[1] Leech, pp. 145–8.
[2] Potter Papers, MS. f. 923.2 Br 13 (56). Bright to T. B. Potter, 28 Dec. 1874.
[3] Hansard, vol. 260, 1991.
[4] Ibid., 1995, 1998–2000.
[5] Walling, pp. 533–4.
[6] *The Times*, 5 Feb. 1868, p. 12, cols. d–e.

people did not for a moment cause him to appreciate the nationalistic basis of Home Rule.[1]

If Gladstone's handling of Chamberlain was less than perfect in 1885 and 1886, his treatment of Bright as an ex-cabinet minister and close associate was not much better. The last time the subject of greater legislative autonomy for Ireland had been raised in their correspondence was in 1873, and even at that time the first signs of the eventual gulf could be seen. Bright had objected to any representative body in Dublin,[2] and Gladstone wrote, '...I am not certain that I would not go a *step* further than you do.'[3]

No criticism of Gladstone could be made if he had acted throughout as though Bright did not matter. But he made every effort at a late date to acquire Bright's services. As late as 12 May 1886, he called Bright from Rochdale to discuss the Irish question.[4] During Bright's visit to Hawarden in October 1885, Gladstone had given him no hint of the specific measures he had in mind to relieve 'the weight of impending questions'.[5] It is doubtful, though, whether even the wisest handling of Bright could have made him agreeable to Gladstone's scheme.

In addition, Bright strongly resented the treatment of the Liberal party by Gladstone. He felt that when Gladstone urged the country for a majority large enough to be independent of the Irish Members, the voters understood this to mean a request for power to resist Parnell, not to surrender.[6] He also resented the dissolution of Parliament on 10 June 1886, which he regarded as a greater calamity for the Liberal party than the presentation of the Home Rule Bill.[7] He could not help but

[1] Hammond, op. cit., on p. 730, deals with Irish nationalism. Gladstone, he writes, believed that Irish nationalism was an 'inextinguishable passion' which had to be satisfied. His opponents believed it could be 'appeased by material concessions'. Bright fits most closely to the latter category, though as far as concessions were concerned, he was at the end of his tether.

[2] Gladstone Papers, Add. MSS. 44,113. Bright to Gladstone, 7 Oct. 1873, f. 76.

[3] Bright Papers, Add. MSS. 43,385. Gladstone to Bright, 10 Oct. 1873, f. 238. (Gladstone's emphasis.)

[4] Ibid., 12 May 1886, ff. 346–7.

[5] Walling, p. 531.

[6] Leech, p. 131.

[7] Chamberlain Papers, J.C. 5/7/28. Bright to Chamberlain, 1 June 1886.

contrast, also, the way in which great questions such as franchise reform and free trade were put to the country and discussed, while the Home Rule Bill seemed to have been sprung without warning.[1] It is difficult to know whether a 'cooling off' period would have induced him to support Gladstone.

Less important as a factor in Bright's objection to Home Rule was his certainty that such a step would lead inevitably to the separation of Ireland from Britain.[2] This did not arise from his distrust of Parnell and his men, but rather from a conviction that a parliament in Dublin would lead to independence and separation. He had expressed this belief in a letter to The O'Donoghue in 1872.[3] In 1879 he wrote, 'I can understand an Irish independent nation—but...an Irish Cabinet—& still Union with Great Britain & under the English Crown—seems to me of all schemes the most "unworkable" than [sic] can be imagined.'[4] The advent of Parnellism reinforced his earlier fears in this regard.

To a man who took a certain pride in his own consistency, his long opposition to Home Rule would have made it extremely difficult for Bright to give it his support. He commented, 'Honesty and capacity in a member are with some of small value in comparison with the suppleness which permits and enables him [Gladstone] to "turn his back upon himself".'[5] A man whose great causes, such as free trade, parliamentary reform and support of the North during the American Civil War, had all seemed afterwards, even to his opponents, as the right courses, would find it difficult to consider that he might be wrong.

[1] *The Times*, 6 Aug. 1887, p. 10, cols. a–b.

[2] The importance that one attaches to this point depends on the interpretation given to the word 'arrangement' on p. 170. This writer believes that Bright would have acceded to an Irish demand for Home Rule if it were based entirely on an agitation free from any suspicion of violence, disloyalty or confiscation of land. It might be argued that no movement with such a restricted armoury could be effective. Nevertheless, if such an entity can be imagined, Bright's pragmatism might have enabled him to leap over the bounds of consistency.

[3] Leech, p. 123. In his letter to his Birmingham constituents in 1886, Bright quoted the salient points of this letter. (*The Times*, 25 June 1886, p. 11, col. f.)

[4] Rathbone Papers, xviii, 2, 3. (1). Bright to W. Rathbone, 1 Dec. 1879.

[5] *The Times*, 26 June 1886, p. 9, col. f.

II

What was Bright's conception of himself and his role in relation to Irish affairs after June 1886? He saw himself and the Liberal Unionists as defenders of the political Union between Ireland and Britain in the same manner as Lincoln and his party defended the Union in the United States. In 1882 he referred to T. Healy and T. P. O'Connor, representatives to an Irish American conference in Chicago, as 'the Mason and Slidell of this new secession'.[1] He regretted the aid America was giving to the cause of the Parnellists, but felt that '...American opinion will have no influence here in the settlement of the Irish question. The Americans settled their secession difficulty, tho' the prevalent opinion here was against them & we shall settle our Irish difficulty without submission to the opinion of... American Irish upon it.'[2]

Bright's last years in public life were a tragedy. Conservative in all but name, he preferred not to attack Gladstone, entertaining as he did such high opinions of his career.[3] This situation made him a particularly strong supporter of Liberal Unionism. To maintain this party he advised Lord Hartington not to join the Salisbury government in December 1886, after the resignation of Lord Randolph Churchill. He did not feel that he or many of Hartington's supporters could follow him to the other side of the House.[4]

Developments in the Home Rule question soured Bright so much that he is found defending many aspects of politics for which his previous approval would have been unthinkable. For example in 1887 he said, 'Therefore, when you find the House of Lords, with its enormous influence, against this policy [Home Rule], I think it behoves men to consider how far they are right.'[5] Though this excerpt demonstrates his firm opposi-

[1] Hansard, vol. 268, 326.

[2] Friends Historical Collection, Dublin. Portfolio 5a 29a. Bright to George Grubb, 10 Dec. 1887.

[3] Bright gave this reason for refusing Hartington's suggestion to speak during an important debate in April 1887. (Hartington Papers, 340.2119. Bright to Hartington, 12 April 1887.)

[4] Hartington Papers, 340.2075. Bright to Hartington, 28 Dec. 1886.

[5] *The Times*, 6 Aug. 1887, p. 10, col. b.

tion to Home Rule, it was, nevertheless, the first time that he had ever invoked the House of Lords to his defence.

Bright's attitude to *The Times* is another indication of his change. In his early career he had often condemned the principles of this paper, and once spoke of its managers as 'the most unprincipled set of ruffians in the world'.[1] But when *The Times* published its articles on 'Parnellism and Crime', he did not for a moment consider that they might be false. He wrote of *The Times* that it had 'done much to expose, and I hope break down, the criminal gang in Parlt. and in Ireland'.[2]

Bright defended his conservatism by saying, 'I am against anything like a revolution or anything like convulsion in the nation. I do not propose anything and do not like anything that is particularly startling or that is described as particularly heroic.'[3] This is indeed unfamiliar coming from a man who has led so many 'revolutions', albeit peaceful ones, in his lifetime.

What solution did Bright see for the Irish difficulty? It is significant that his only recommendation after 1886 was an elaboration of the one that he had first unfolded to an Irish Member in 1876.[4] His idea was that a committee of Irish Members should be set up which would appoint its own chairman to conduct an investigation of each bill that related to Irish affairs. By majority vote they would amend each bill and then return it to the House, where it would go immediately into the report stage, thus bypassing the second reading.[5] He thought that if the Irish Members were loyal, the House would be willing to defer to their opinion in most cases. He made this strong point when discussing his plan: 'Now, if my plan were to fail because of that persistent disloyalty of the Irish, then this plan of the Government must fail from the same continued cause.'[6] By late 1887 he conceded that his plan would not work as long as the 'rebel leaders' were assured of the support of Gladstone's 'hobby'.[7]

With the exception of this one suggestion, Bright's general feeling after 1886 was that it was better to show where Glad-

[1] *The Amberley Papers*, eds. Bertrand and Patricia Russell, i, 471.

[2] Walling, p. 557.

[3] *The Times*, 2 July 1886, p. 10, col. e.

[4] See Walling, p. 384.

[5] *The Times*, 2 July 1886, p. 10, col. d.

[6] Ibid., col. e.

[7] Ibid., 23 Nov. 1887, p. 9, col. f.

stone's plan was bad than to attempt to suggest anything better.[1] His sentiments are best revealed in a letter to Lord Hartington: 'As to the Irish question I should advise the Govt. [Lord Salisbury's] to do nothing in the way of giving substitutes for Mr. Gladstone's policy. There are improvements & reforms probably much needed in Dublin & in Irish administration but I would not yield to the clamor or the threats of the rebel party, which I hope & suspect will become weaker, as the Govt. resolution & strength are more distinctly manifested.'[2]

One is little surprised, then, to find Bright in 1887 supporting the coercive measures adopted by the Conservative Government.[3] In 1887 he wrote, 'I now support the Government in their endeavour to suppress the rebel movement of the National League, which is the Land League under another name.'[4] Hammond has written of the Plan of Campaign of the National League as 'in many respects an excellent scheme'.[5] Bright regarded it as one more attempt to plunder the landlord and to teach a hatred of England.[6]

Bright's idea was to stand firm; Gladstone's was to concede to Parnell's wishes, hoping that Ireland '...would set out on her new career in a spirit of good will'.[7] Both men had become possessed of an *idée fixe*—Gladstone that Ireland's leaders must be trusted; Bright that they could not be trusted. With some reason, historians have tended to approve the course followed by Gladstone. Bright had enunciated the phrase 'Force is not a remedy',[8] but what else did he have to offer after 1886? When one remembers that Bright's advocacy of colonial self-government was in part based on the supposition that loyalty within a colony would be alienated by closer imperial control, it seems a contradiction in principles for him to have upheld closer control in Ireland. But in his mind, Irish and imperial affairs were clearly dichotomized. Thus he did not see, arch anti-imperialist though he was, the irony of his position. But

[1] Chamberlain Papers, J.C. 5/7/30. Bright to Chamberlain, 9 June 1886.

[2] Hartington Papers, 340.2075. (A & B.) Bright to Hartington, 28 Dec. 1886.

[3] For his comment on the Conservative bill, see *The Times*, 26 Aug. 1887, p. 8, col. a.

[4] *The Times*, 5 Oct. 1887, p. 8, col. c.

[5] Hammond, op. cit., p. 564.

[6] *The Times*, 5 Oct. 1887, p. 8, col. c.

[7] Hammond, op. cit., p. 736.

[8] *The Times*, 17 Nov. 1880, p. 6, col. d.

to be fair to him, it is surely true that nationalism now wears a less romantic glow than it did in the nineteenth century. Not only that, but the geographical contiguity of Ireland makes the case somewhat different than if he had wanted to subjugate North Africa, for example. The crux of the matter is that Gladstone chose better means for the ends Bright had in mind.

Conclusion

JOHN BRIGHT takes a deserved place in the line of liberal Indian reformers. In many respects it would not be wrong to regard him as a throwback to the reformers of the Bentinck, Macaulay and Metcalfe type; he regarded Bentinck as the prototype of British Governors-General in India.[1] In a similar manner he favoured the westernization of India, for only in this way could its wealth and progress be ensured. However, he lacked their general optimism concerning the possible success of such an undertaking, as he regarded British rule as unnatural and in many ways dangerous. The British presence in India could only be justified by virtue of the fact that it was in expiation of the original sin of conquest. Thus India had a special claim upon British statesmanship. An event such as the Indian mutiny made him doubt, however, whether British statesmen could ever attain the level of unselfishness and wisdom requisite to gain the honour of duty properly discharged. Nevertheless, Britain could not withdraw from India until this obligation had been in some way fulfilled, even though it was unbecoming for one people to be in subjection to another. It was apparent to him that with increasing education the Indian people would not tolerate British dominion; this would make it imperative that Britain recognize the necessity for eventual withdrawal. In upholding this principle he performed a valuable service by reinvigorating the idea that British rule in India was in the form of a trust. Thus Bright links hands with the reformers of an earlier generation who saw the eventual necessity for the emancipation of India and that more exclusive group in a later period who kept alive the idea of trust. Indeed, when one paints in the

[1] Hansard, vol. 158, 1146–7.

background to his views, his importance is even more apparent. Dr Mehrotra writes: 'And so, concerned primarily with the maintenance of British rule in India, unable or unwilling to visualize that it could develop into something else, with their highest ideal a benevolent despotism in India, blind to the inevitable tendency of their own work in that country, British statesmen in the last quarter of the nineteenth century—with a few noble exceptions such as Bright, Gladstone, Ripon—almost lost the sense of a mission or purpose.'[1]

Eventual self-government was only a part of a programme of principles which Bright felt should govern Britain's relations with India. It was also necessary to rule by the standard that the good of India must take priority over any possible advantage to Great Britain. This in itself was admirable, but critics might contend that Bright himself transgressed this rule of disinterest. Were railways into agricultural districts in accord with the true interests of India's economy? Was free trade? These examples should not, entirely detract from an otherwise admirable record which included demands for the ending of the salt tax, the opium duties, the high cost of government, and wars of annexation.

Bright also wanted to ensure that Indians were given an increasing opportunity to participate in the governing of their country. But progress was difficult in this sphere when it was possible for responsible men like Lord Curzon to speak of Indians 'in tones normally reserved for pet animals'.[2] As late as 1939, less than half of the posts in the Indian civil service were held by Indians.[3]

Bright also wanted to use the resources of the state to aid in the economic development of India. He saw it as the duty of the government to provide favourable conditions for capital investment by the building of transportation[4] and irrigation facilities. His recommendations for the development of India's transportation system were realized within his lifetime. £95 million were invested by British companies in guaranteed

[1] Mehrotra, *India and the Commonwealth 1885–1929*, p. 29.

[2] S. Gopal, *British Policy in India 1858–1905*, p. 227.

[3] *The Evolution of India and Pakistan 1858 to 1947*, eds. C. H. Philips *et al.*, p. 535.

[4] See D. Thorner, *Investment in Empire*, pp. 158–9, 178–9.

railways in the years 1847 to 1875, providing India with a 'basic network of communications'.[1] His attitudes towards governmental activity in India (and Ireland) gives credence to the 'multi-dimensional character of political attitudes' recently championed by Professor W. O. Aydelotte.[2] Further, there is support for W. L. Burn's conclusion that although the hold of *laissez-faire* thinking on mid-Victorian politics has been greatly exaggerated, it is true that any legislative interference with the natural system had to justify itself by clear proof of necessity.[3]

Finally, consideration must be given to Bright's proposal for the decentralization of India. In retrospect, it seems a very arbitrary and artificial scheme. Though a certain amount of decentralization was introduced into Indian government, no ministry ever adopted his specific plan. It seems to have been of more use to the supporters of centralization as a spectre to frighten the uncommitted. In 1912 Lord Curzon warned the House of Lords that disaster would come to India '...if you are going to contemplate...a policy of separate States in India, a sort of Home Rule all round—Mr. John Bright's idea of an India divided into separate States, with separate Governments'.[4] Such an admonition was not without value, as Bright had misjudged the direction that Indian nationalism would take, as well as the historical basis for unity in India.[5]

In order to carry out his aims Bright surrounded himself with a group of able and expert men. J. B. Smith took special interest in the cotton question and finances. Dickinson was an expert on Indian government and relations with the native states. Sir Arthur Cotton was uniquely familiar with public works. Lalmohun Ghose of Calcutta, another acquaintance of Bright's, was trained in law and conversant with Indian conditions.

The efficacy of the methods used by Bright is best observed

[1] W. J. Macpherson, 'Investment in Indian Railways 1845–1875', *Econ. Hist. Rev.*, 2nd series, viii, no. 2 (1955), 177.

[2] W. O. Aydelotte, 'The Conservative and Radical Interpretations of Early Victorian Social Legislation', *Victorian Studies*, xi, no. 2 (Dec. 1967), 236.

[3] W. L. Burn, *The Age of Equipoise*, p. 134.

[4] Hansard (Lords), 5th series, vol. 11, 165.

[5] See D. P. Singhal, 'Some Consequences of Nationalism in India', *Australian Journal of Politics and Economics*, vii, no. 2 (Nov. 1961), 216–17.

in the 1850s. Through his connexion with the India Reform Society and his association with the Manchester merchants, he was able to apply pressure upon the unsteady Aberdeen coalition to expedite the building of public works in India. He also used the more direct approach of writing to Gladstone when he was concerned over British policy, particularly in the realm of finance.

As Bright became more concerned with emphasizing the goal of self-government, there was a corresponding change in his methods. In the years 1847 to 1858 he concentrated on parliamentary debates, and his public appearances in Manchester were attempts to influence specific decisions of the government. After 1858 his work in Parliament declined, and his opinions on India were given from the public platform. As his aims became increasingly long-range, he found this medium, perhaps, more conducive to changing the views of the electorate, the ultimate arbiters of Indian government.

One can see in the course of Bright's relationship with India a process of growth at work. In the years preceding 1857 he opposed Company rule because India was not producing its potential of cotton. Increasingly within this period he was coming to the view that the condition of India affected the imperial prestige and moral standing of Great Britain. After 1857 his aim was to transform the government of India so that additional cotton would be one minor result of many benefits that would accrue to India and Britain. As a result Bright's stature as an Indian reformer both during and after his lifetime grew to such proportions that he was revered by Indians as a man who understood their wish for self-government.[1]

One can determine much about Bright's view of the Empire by examining his attitude towards the United States. He regarded that country as a 'colony' of Great Britain. A 'colony' was not just a territory that acknowledged the sovereignty of the Queen, but a country that carried on the traditions of democratic government and the use of the English language. He viewed with consternation the threatened breakdown in Anglo-

[1] See Mody, *Sir Pherozeshah Mehta*, i, 275–6; ii. 526; Sir P. Griffiths, *The British Impact on India*, pp. 254–63.

American relations in 1865 because it would shatter his conception of the unity of the Anglo-Saxon nations. His hope was that the Empire, within which he included the United States, would become a free trade area where peace and prosperity would flourish. While discussing British relations with the United States in 1865, he said: 'I believe that these two great commonwealths will march abreast, the parents and guardians of freedom and justice, wheresoever their language shall be spoken and their power shall extend.'[1]

Because Bright favoured such loose ties among fraternal nations one must consider whether he was a separatist. Looked at from the vantage point of the colonial, no doubt he was seen as a threat.[2] All those, colonial and Briton alike, who were concerned with the maintenance of a valued connexion were justifiably ruffled by his willingness to see man's ambition hidden in every imperial endeavour. But Bright displayed no particularized animus when he objected to spending on colonial projects, for he defended the taxpayer against similar depredations for domestic purposes. Nor should a desire to reform a system necessarily imply a demand for its complete dismantling. In a sense both Bright and his critic were right. His strictures on colonial policy, though representing a certain callousness at the time, proved eventually to be the most effective basis for imperial co-operation, which, ironically for Bright, 1914 and 1939 were to show.

The weight of evidence, then, would suggest that Bright did not view separation as inevitable, except in the case of Canada, where economic necessity on the one side and inexorable power on the other would lead naturally to continentalism. Nevertheless, he was most anxious that Britain should not be the agent responsible for breaking the link with any colony. It should be made clear that Bright never went so far as Cobden in his condemnation of the colonial system. Within the Manchester School, Bright was much less radical in colonial affairs than was Cobden. In 1862 it was Cobden who called Bright's

[1] Hansard, vol. 177, 1633.

[2] Tupper was convinced that the 'Cobden and Bright party' favoured separation. (*Debates and Proceedings of the House of Assembly of Nova Scotia, 1866*, 5 April 1866, pp. 202–3.)

attention to a letter written in the *Daily News* by Goldwin Smith calling for colonial emancipation. Cobden thought Bright would find certain passages 'too revolutionary'.[1] Not only did Cobden not regard them as 'too revolutionary', it was he who urged Smith to have them published in book form.[2] The cost of the colonial system did not become the same crotchet with Bright as it did with Cobden. Bright took a more positive interest, as in the case of Nova Scotia, in redressing colonial grievances. Still there was quite a difference in the amount of attention he paid to colonial problems compared with the study he devoted to India. In general, he had infrequent contacts with colonial leaders; they usually came about because of a specific interest aroused in him by an individual such as Joseph Howe. Nor did he cultivate men who were well-informed in colonial problems. He took an interest when he thought a great wrong had been committed or when an important principle was at stake, but otherwise he tended not to involve himself in colonial affairs.

Bright was pre-eminently a mid-Victorian politician, and this was nowhere more true than in imperial matters. Before 1870 he attacked a colonial system that was yielding to his own concept of what the Empire should be, whereas after 1870 he tilted with a system that was growing beyond his own efforts to control. He was a desolate figure after the Egyptian crisis, because the party system could then provide no refuge from folly. While painfully observing the growth of jingoism within the Liberal party, he wrote of himself: 'There seems not a single friend of mine with whom I can consult.'[3] He was unable to accept the reasoning that because Britain was an imperial power she should take up the 'white man's burden'. Britain's record in India was no inducement to think that she could perform the task faithfully. Moreover, how could expansionism lead to anything but estranged relations with the rest of Europe? Then too, there was the threat posed to amicable relations with the self-governing colonies by the growing popularity of imperial federation. Little wonder he could write

[1] Cobden Papers, Add. MSS. 43,652. Cobden to Bright, 31 Aug. 1862, f. 42.
[2] Wallace, *Goldwin Smith*, p. 184.
[3] Walling, p. 486.

in 1880: 'There seems only clouds and dangers about us.'[1]

Though little transpired in Bright's lifetime to efface this gloom, there was in the influence he exerted on the future course of empire some recompense for his tenacity. His conception of the Empire as free of any political subservience or economic obligation presaged the basis of the modern Commonwealth as contained in the Balfour Report of 1926. Bright and his political allies deserve the tribute paid to them by Professor Underhill when he wrote, 'The truth is that the new British Commonwealth of Nations...bears a remarkable resemblance to the ideas of the Manchester men in the 1860s....[They] have turned out to be much better prophets of the future course of imperial development than either Disraeli or Chamberlain.'[2] If this passage relates more to the Commonwealth in its status-obsessed stage, then Bright's example is no less relevant today when questions of race threaten the very existence of the organization. This is in despite of the fact that his recommendations of financial responsibility and Christian morality in dealings with native tribes, would have been as nugatory as any other remedies applied in such trouble-spots as the South-African frontier. The other major influence he exerted sprang from his uncompromising anti-imperialism which he helped to inject into the Radical wing of the Liberal party, the element that never succumbed to the lure of imperialism. From them a small tributary at least joined the many streams of anti-imperialism which went into the make-up of the Labour party. One historian of the movement contends that the 'creed of internationalism of the Bright and Cobden variety' became a basic tenet of the party.[3]

The final impression is that Bright's views were paradoxical. However much he deplored the idea of empire in public or in private, he led no campaign for disruption of the imperial structure. Though greatly stirred by the problems of economic development in India, the opportunities for improving conditions in colonial areas did not impress him. A man whose ideas were thought by some of his contemporaries to mean the end

[1] Ibid., p. 446.

[2] F. H. Underhill, *In Search of Canadian Liberalism*, p. 92.

[3] H. Pelling, *A Short History of the Labour Party*, p. 124.

of Empire appears to have upheld the policies that were to become the mortar of the modern Commonwealth.

Bright's decision in 1886 to vote against Home Rule for Ireland was consistent with his entire political career. Even in the days when he was regarded as the 'friend of Ireland', his prime motive was to render Ireland content with her connexion with Britain. Looking at the situation in a rational way, he could see no reason for a separate Irish parliament when the ties of family, business and geography had bound them together. A wide franchise and a Liberal government would be able to upset the land system and the established church, the chief obstacles to reconciliation with the British. By working more closely with Irish politicians, a sense of common purpose could be instilled into their relationship. Unlike many British politicians, he was willing to study Irish problems by direct personal observation.[1] However, when the remedial legislation of 1869, 1870 and 1881 failed to transform Irish opinion, he concluded that Irish leaders would settle for nothing less than separation. Yet how could Britain sacrifice loyal citizens, particularly in Ulster, to men who seemed so clearly associated with violence and the desire to confiscate the land? In this case resolute government, not surrender, was called for.

Imperial considerations, in so far as Home Rule would either strengthen or weaken the Empire, played little part in Bright's decision. He did not apply to Ireland the principles that he espoused in regard to responsible government in the colonies of European settlement. Though he could see that tightening the bonds of political control over the colonies might cause great irritation, he did not appreciate the argument that maintaining the authority of the British government over Ireland was having the same effect. In fact, the colonial experience swayed Bright in the other direction because the loose bonds of connexion, characteristic of the Empire, could be too easily snapped.

By exerting his influence against Home Rule in 1886, Bright did nothing to prevent the eventual separation of Ireland and

[1] See Mansergh, *The Irish Question*, pp. 48–55. Bright, however, visited Ireland for the last time in 1868.

Britain. Perhaps by the time Gladstone chose to act there was no solution other than what 1921 brought. Nevertheless, Gladstone's course seemed to offer more hope than 'twenty years of absolute government'. But it is one of the ironies of history that Gladstone's attempt at political conciliation bore no results, while Bright's idea of land purchase became the basis for the land system of modern Ireland.[1]

Essential to the understanding of Bright's views on the Empire and Ireland is to realize his complete failure to understand the force of nationalism. This is not to say that he did not recognize the right of all people to aspire to democratic government. He supported colonial wishes in this regard, and later strongly endorsed India's claim for the same rights. The fact that democratic and nationalistic aims overlapped, however, was purely fortuitous. It was not operative in the case of the Irish, whose full representation at Westminster left them with no legitimate grievance. His decentralization scheme for India taken in conjunction with his views on the future of Canada reveal his predilection for regarding boundaries as political and economic conveniences, not demarcations of sentiment. In the case of Irish Home Rule, the democratic wishes of the entire population of Great Britain and Ireland had to be taken into account; to act solely upon the strongly felt claims of one limited part was a spurious misapplication of a principle. The fact that he entertained the view that Irish nationalist demands could be satisfied in 1886 by an amendment of parliamentary procedure to allow Irish committees to amend bills, or that Irish opinion would wilt after 1886 in the face of governmental determination, shows how little he understood the nationalistic basis of Home Rule. For him, the Scottish example sufficed, and he felt no disposition to glance at the Italian model on the continent.

Basically, Bright distrusted the breakdown of larger political units. The world, in his view, ought to have been growing closer together, not breaking apart for the most intangible of reasons. During the American Civil War Bright raised the question of the withdrawal of smaller units from larger political

[1] G. M. Young, *Victorian England*, p. 130 n. 1.

organizations: 'I want to know whether it has been admitted by politicians and statesmen or by any people that great nations can be broken up any time by the will of any particular section of those nations.' He concluded that Europe provided a sorry example of the disorder that resulted from the extreme breakdown into national states.[1]

Bright's belief in Quakerism and cosmopolitan free trade left him ill-equipped to understand the mechanics of a national upsurge. Moreover, his earliest political experience in Great Britain was as a politician intimately allied with the interests of an economic class. He never entirely shed this cocoon. It revealed itself in a tendency to see events determined by economic factors. Nowhere was this more evident than in his opinion on Canada's future relationship with the United States. Irish Home Rule was viewed as a vast subterfuge for confiscating the land.

A noteworthy feature of Bright's career concerns the ease with which the positive and negative aspects of his political causes dovetailed. Recommendation of Indians for employment in the civil service was at the same time a way of breaking down establishment control over India. Supporting Sir Charles Trevelyan was also a method of revenge against the apostasy of James Wilson. Efforts to effect Colonial reform could act as a protest against the ponderous pace of the Lord John Russell government. Nova Scotia's discontents served as a battering ram against Canadian confederation. The fight for tenant-right in Ireland was in line with his battle on a wider front against the landed aristocracy. When all are fitted together, they point to Bright's desire for a liberal, free-trade United Kingdom, and a gentlemen's agreement among Anglo-Saxon nations to work for peace, prosperity and progress.

Bright's greatest triumph was that he came to represent British Liberalism in its most appealing forms. He was idealized by the Indians because of his willingness to battle any odds in their interests. The Irish felt much the same way about him before 1881. Cobden expressed well the reasons for Indian and Irish gratitude when he wrote: 'If there be a task of superhuman difficulty, such as fathoming Irish bogs, or clearing

[1] *The Times*, 6 Dec. 1861, p. 6, cols. a–b.

Indian jungles, you are sure to undertake it.'[1] Bright was remembered in the self-governing colonies for precisely the opposite reason. It was his unwillingness to interfere in their affairs that distinguished him, especially in the minds of minority or oppressed groups. A comment of Henri Bourassa in the Canadian House of Commons during the Boer War reveals what Bright meant to this representative of a nationality which felt outraged by the new imperialism: '... I am a Liberal of the British school. I am a disciple of Burke, Fox, Bright, Gladstone, and of the other little Englanders, who made Great Britain and her possessions what they are.'[2] To another colonial politician, Jan Smuts, who was even more intimately involved in that same war, Bright's memory provided considerable solace: 'Yet suddenly there arose within him the memory and vision of a different England, of a great and magnanimous nation with whom his own small people might have lived in peace. He turned... and said—"If there were only another John Bright." '[3]

[1] Cobden Papers, Add. MSS. 43,649. Cobden to Bright, 9 Sept. 1852, f. 279.

[2] Quoted in F. H. Underhill, *The Image of Confederation*, p. 40.

[3] W. K. Hancock, *Smuts. The Sanguine Years, 1870–1919*, p. 106.

APPENDICES

1. M.P.s who belonged to the India Reform Society 1853

T. Barnes (Bolton-Le-Moors)
J. Bell (Guildford)
W. Biggs (Newport)
J. F. B. Blackett (Newcastle on Tyne)
G. Bowyer (Dundalk)
J. Bright (Manchester)
H. A. Bruce (Merthyr Tydfil)
Lt. Col. J. Caulfield (Armagh)
J. Cheetham (South Lancashire)
J. Crook (Bolton-Le-Moors)
M. J. Fielden (Blackburn)
Sir J. FitzGerald (Clare)
M. Forster (Berwick-on-Tweed)
F. French (Roscommon Co.)
R. Gardner (Leicester)
T. Milner Gibson (Manchester)
Viscount Goderich (Kingston-upon-Hull)
G. Hadfield (Sheffield)
L. Heyworth (Derby)
C. Hindley (Ashton-under-Lyne)
E. J. Hutchins (Lymington)
T. Kennedy (Louth)
F. Lucas (Meath)
J. (W. H.?) Magan (Westmeath)
E. Miall (Rochdale)
G. H. Moore (Mayo)
B. Oliveira (Pontefract)
A. J. Otway (Stafford)
G. M. W. Peacocke (Harwich)
Apsley Pellatt (Southwark)
J. G. Phillimore (Leominster)
T. Phinn (Bath)
J. Pilkington (Blackburn)
W. Scholefield (Birmingham)
Danby Seymour (Poole)
W. D. Seymour (Sunderland)
J. B. Smith (Stockport)
G. Thompson (Aberdeen)
J. A. Wise (Stafford)

2. M.P.s who extended an invitation to Bright to speak in Dublin in 1866

J. F. Maguire (Cork City)
D. J. Reardon (Athlone)
J. B. Dillon (Tipperary Co.)
Sir J. Gray (Kilkenny Bo.)
N. D. Murphy (Cork City)
Sir P. O'Brien (King's County)
M. W. O'Reilly (Longford)
J. Esmonde (Waterford Co.)
G. Bryan (Kilkenny Co.)
J. Bagwell (Clonmel)
The O'Donoghue (Tralee)
E. Sullivan (Mallow)
J. Brady (Leitram)
J. A. Blake (Waterford City)
R. J. Devereux (Wexford Bo.)
B. Whitworth (Drogheda)
Sir C. M. O'Loghlen (Clare)
Sir J. Power (Wexford)
J. A. Lawson (Portarlington)
R. Armstrong (Sligo Bo.)
G. R. Barry (Cork Co.)
C. R. Barry (Dungarvan)
C. Moore (Tipperary)

BIBLIOGRAPHY

PRIMARY SOURCES

A. Manuscript Material

This list attempts to give the chief sources of manuscript material in the book.

British Museum:
Bright Papers, Add. MSS. 43,383–92.
Cobden Papers, Add. MSS. 43,649–52.
Gladstone Papers, Add. MSS. 44,112–13.
Layard Papers, Add. MSS. 38,985.
Northy Papers, Add. MSS. 44,877.
Ripon Papers, Add. MSS. 43,632.
Sturge Papers, Add. MSS. 43,723; 43,845.
Bodleian Library:
Congreve Papers, MS. Eng. Letter C.185.
Birmingham University:
Joseph Chamberlain Papers.
Manchester Central Reference Library:
T. B. Potter Papers, MS. f 923.2 Br 13.
J. B. Smith Papers, MSS. 923.2 S.344–5.
Friends Historical Collection, Dublin:
J. Pim Papers, Letters of John Bright to J. Pim.
The Library, Chatsworth:
Lord Hartington Papers, Letters of John Bright to Lord Hartington.
London Public Record Office:
Second Earl Granville Papers, PRO 30/29/52.
University College London:
Bright Papers, Letters of John Bright to his wife.
National Library of Scotland:
E. Ellice Papers, MS. Acc. 1993.

B. Parliamentary Sources

Hansard's Parliamentary Debates, Third Series, 1843–89.
House of Commons, *Division Lists.*
Parliamentary Papers:
No. 412 (V). *Reports from the Select Committee appointed to consider the state of the establishments on the West Coast of Africa. 1865.*
No. 511 (IX). *Reports from Committees. Growth of Cotton in India. 1847–48.*

C. NEWSPAPFRS

Anti-Slavery Advocate
Birmingham Daily Post
Daily News
Freeman's Journal
Hindoo Patriot
India
Indian News
Irish Tenant League
Manchester Examiner and Times
Morning Star
Nonconformist
Northern Whig
Spectator
The Bombay Times, and Journal of Commerce
The Spectator (*Madras*)
The Times
Truth

D. PAMPHLETS

BROWN, F. C., *The Supply of Cotton from India*, B.M. 08226 h 56 (8).
By one who knows him, *Mr. Lalmohun Ghose*, B.M. 10606 a 36.
CAIRD, J., *The Irish Land Question*, B.M. 8145 bbb 3 (8).
DIGBY, W., *Indian problems for English Consideration*, B.M. 8022 cc 17 (3).
HUTTON, H. D., *History, Principle, and Fact: in relation to the Irish Question*, B.M. 8145 bbb 5 (8).
Indian Reform Tracts, India Office Library, Tr. 565. No. 8.
Speech of Mr. Dickinson, B.M. 08023 aa 14 (8).
TOLLES, F. B., *Quakerism and Politics*, Friends Reference Library, Euston, 050 Social 11 (10 a).

E. OTHER PRINTED WORKS

The Amberley Papers, eds. Bertrand and Patricia Russell, 2 vols. (London: Leonard and Virginia Woolf, 1937).
ASHWORTH, H., *Recollections of Richard Cobden M.P. and the Anti-Corn Law League* (London: Cassell, Petter & Galpin, 1878).
BLUNT, W. S., *The Land War in Ireland* (London: Stephen Swift, 1912).
— *Secret History of the English Occupation of Egypt* (London: T. Fisher Unwin, 1907).
Cartoons by Sir John Tenniel (London: *Punch*, 1901).
CHAMBERLAIN, SIR AUSTEN, *Down the Years* (London: Cassell, 1935).
CHAMBERLAIN, J., *A Political Memoir 1880–92*, ed. C. H. D. Howard (London: Batchworth Press, 1953).
CHERRY, R. R., *The Irish Land Law and Land Purchase Acts 1860 to 1901* (Dublin: John Falconer, 1903).

Christian faith and practice in the experience of the Society of Friends (London: London Yearly Meeting of the Religious Society of Friends, 1960).

The Collected Works of Mahatma Gandhi, vol. i (Delhi: The Publications Division, Ministry of Information and Broadcasting, Government of India, 1958–).

Correspondence and Speeches of Mr. Peter Rylands M.P., ed. L. G. Rylands, 2 vols. (Manchester: A. Heywood & Son, 1890).

The Diaries of John Bright, ed. R. A. J. Walling (London: Cassell 1930).

DICKINSON, JOHN, *Last Counsels of an Unknown Counsellor*, ed. E. Bell (London: Whiting, 1883).

DUFFY, SIR CHARLES GAVAN, *The League of North and South* (London: Chapman and Hall, 1886).

— *My Life in Two Hemispheres*, 2 vols. (London: T. Fisher Unwin, 1898).

The Evolution of India and Pakistan 1858 to 1947, General ed. C. H. Philips (London: Oxford University Press, 1962).

Goldwin Smith's Correspondence, ed. A. Haultain (London: T. Werner Laurie, 1913).

GOWER, SIR GEORGE LEVESON, *Years of Content 1858–1886* (London: John Murray, 1940).

GREGORY, SIR WILLIAM, *Sir William Gregory K.C.M.G.*, ed. Lady Gregory (London: John Murray, 1894).

HARLOW, V. and MADDEN, F., *British Colonial Developments 1774–1834* (Oxford: Clarendon Press, 1953).

HEALY, T. M., *Letters and Leaders of My Day*, 2 vols. (London: Thornton Butterworth, 1928).

Journal of the Friends Historical Society, 1932, vol. 29, Letter to John Bright.

The Letters of Queen Victoria, eds. A. C. Benson and Viscount Esher, First series, 3 vols. (London: John Murray, 1907).

Letters of the Rt. Hon. Henry Austin Bruce G.C.B. Lord Aberdare of Duffryn, 2 vols. (Oxford: Printed for Private Circulation, 1902).

Life and Letters of John Arthur Roebuck, ed. R. E. Leader (London: Edward Arnold, 1897).

The Life and Letters of the Rt. Hon. Sir Charles Tupper, ed. E. M. Saunders, 2 vols. (London: Cassell, 1916).

MADDEN, F., *Imperial Constitutional Documents 1765–1952: A Supplement* (Oxford: Blackwell, 1953).

MILL, J. S., *Autobiography of John Stuart Mill* (New York: New American Library, 1964).

'My Dear Duchess', ed. A. L. Kennedy (London: John Murray, 1956).

PARKES, SIR HENRY, *Fifty Years in the Making of Australian History*, 2 vols. (London: Longmans, Green, 1892).

The Political Correspondence of Mr. Gladstone and Lord Granville 1868–1876, ed. A. Ramm, 2 vols., Camden Third Series, vol. lxxxi (London: The Royal Historical Society, 1952).

Proceedings of the Massachusetts Historical Society, 1911–12, vols. 45–6, Letters of John Bright.

The Public Letters of the Right Hon. John Bright, ed. H. J. Leech (London: Sampson Low, Marston & Co., 1895).

Selected Speeches of Sir William Molesworth, ed. H. E. Egerton (London: John Murray, 1903).

SHEE, W., *Papers, Letters and Speeches in the House of Commons on The Irish Land Question* (London: T. Richardson, 1863).

SMITH, ADAM, *An Inquiry into the Nature and Causes of the Wealth of Nations*, ed. E. Cannan, 2 vols. (London, Methuen, 1950).

Speeches of the Marquis of Ripon, ed. Kali Prasanna Sen Gupta (Calcutta: The 'Star' Press, 1883).

TORRENS, W. MCCULLAGH, *Twenty Years in Parliament* (London: Richard Bentley & Son, 1893).

WODEHOUSE, JOHN, First Earl of Kimberley, *A Journal of Events During the Gladstone Ministry 1868–1874*, ed. E. Drus, Camden Miscellany, vol. xxi (London: The Royal Historical Society, 1958).

SECONDARY SOURCES

A. BOOKS

ALLEN, G. C., *British Industries and Their Organization* (London: Longmans, Green, 1951).

AUSUBEL, H., *John Bright, Victorian Reformer* (New York: John Wiley & Sons, 1966).

BAILEY, S. D., *Ceylon* (London: Hutchinson's University Library, 1952).

BANERJEA, SIR SURENDRANATH, *A Nation in Making* (London: Oxford University Press, 1925).

BAY, C., *The Structure of Freedom* (New York: Atheneum, 1965).

BEARCE, G. D., *British Attitudes Towards India 1784–1858* (London: Oxford University Press, 1961).

BECKETT, J. C., *The Making of Modern Ireland 1603–1923* (London: Faber and Faber, 1966).

BENNETT, G., *The Concept of Empire, Burke to Attlee 1774–1947* (London: Adam and Charles Black, 1953).

BLACK, R. D. COLLISON, *Economic Thought and The Irish Question 1817–1870* (Cambridge: Cambridge University Press, 1960).

BLAKE, R., *Disraeli* (London: Eyre & Spottiswoode, 1967).

BODELSEN, C. A., *Studies in Mid-Victorian Imperialism* (Copenhagen: Gyldendalske Boghandel, 1924).

BOLTON, G. C., *The Passing of the Irish Act of Union* (London: Oxford University Press, 1966).

BRIGGS, A., *Victorian People* (Harmondsworth: Penguin Books, 1965).

BROWN, LUCY M., *The Board of Trade and the Free-Trade Movement 1830–42* (Oxford: Clarendon Press, 1958).

BURN, W. L., *The Age of Equipoise* (New York: W. W. Norton, 1965).

BURNS, SIR ALAN, *History of the British West Indies* (London: Allen & Unwin, 1954).

The Cambridge History of the British Empire, General eds. J. H. Rose, A. P. Newton and E. A. Benians. (vol. iii General eds. E. A. Benians, J. R. M. Butler, P. N. S. Mansergh and E. A. Walker), 9 vols (Cambridge: Cambridge University Press, 1929–59).

Chartist Studies, ed. A. Briggs (London: Macmillan, 1959).

CLAPHAM, SIR JOHN, *An Economic History of Modern Britain. Free Trade and Steel 1850–1886* (Cambridge: Cambridge University Press, 1952).

CONNELL, K. H., *The Population of Ireland 1750–1845* (Oxford: Clarendon Press, 1950).

COREY, A. B., *The Crisis of 1830–1842 in Canadian–American Relations* (New Haven: Yale University Press, 1941).

CREIGHTON, D. G., *Dominion of The North* (London: Macmillan, 1958).

CUMPSTON, I. M., *Indians Overseas In British Territories 1834–1854* (London: Oxford University Press, 1953).

CURTIS, E., *A History of Ireland* (London: Methuen 1952).

DUTT, R., *The Economic History of India*, 2 vols. (London: Routledge & Kegan Paul, 1956).

ENSOR, R. C. K., *England 1870–1914* (Oxford: Clarendon Press, 1936).

1859: Entering an Age of Crisis, eds. P. Appleman, W. A. Madden, M. Wolff (Bloomington: Indiana University Press, 1959).

FITZMAURICE, LORD EDMOND, *The Life of Granville George Leveson Gower, Second Earl Granville K.G. 1815–1891*, 2 vols. (London: Longmans, Green, 1905).

FRASER, PETER, *Joseph Chamberlain* (London: Cassell, 1966).

GASH, NORMAN, *Politics in the Age of Peel* (London: Longmans, Green 1953).

GOPAL, S., *British Policy in India, 1858–1905* (Cambridge: Cambridge University Press, 1965).

— *The Viceroyalty of Lord Ripon 1880–1884* (London: G. Camberlege, 1953).

GRAHAM, G. S., *The Politics of Naval Supremacy* (Cambridge: Cambridge University Press, 1965).

The Great Famine, eds. R. D. Edwards and T. D. Williams (Dublin: Browne and Nolan for the Irish Committee of Historical Sciences, 1956).

GRIFFITHS, SIR P., *The British Impact on India* (London: Macdonald, 1952).

GWYNN, S. and TUCKWELL, G. M., *The Life of the Rt. Hon. Sir Charles W. Dilke*, 2 vols. (London: John Murray, 1917).

HALÉVY, E., *A History of the English People in the Nineteenth Century*, 6 vols. (London: E. Benn, 1949–52).

HAMMOND, J. L., *Gladstone and the Irish Nation* (London: Longmans, Green, 1938).

HANCOCK, W. K., *Smuts. The Sanguine Years. 1870–1919* (Cambridge: Cambridge University Press, 1962).

HANHAM, H. J., *Elections and Party Management. Politics in the time of Disraeli and Gladstone* (London: Longmans, Green, 1959).

HARLOW, V. T., *The Founding of the Second British Empire. 1763–1793*, 2 vols. (London: Longmans, Green, 1952–64).

HARRIS, W., *The History of the Radical Party in Parliament* (London: Kegan Paul, Trench & Co., 1885).

HARRISON, R., *Before the Socialists* (Toronto: University of Toronto Press, 1965).

HIRST, M. E., *John Bright, A Study* (London: Headley Bros., 1945).

HOBSON, J. A., *Richard Cobden, The International Man* (London: T. Fisher Unwin, 1918).

Ideas and Beliefs of the Victorians: An Historic Evaluation of the Victorian Age (Talks broadcast on the BBC Third Programme; London: Sylvan Press, 1949).

Ideas and Institutions of Victorian Britain, ed. R. Robson (London: G. Bell, 1967).

ILBERT, SIR C., *The Government of India* (Oxford: Clarendon Press, 1922).

JENNINGS, SIR W. I., *Party Politics*, 3 vols. (Cambridge: Cambridge University Press, 1960–2).

JONES, W. D., *Lord Derby and Victorian Conservatism* (Oxford: Basil Blackwell, 1956).

KANE, R., *The Industrial Resources of Ireland* (Dublin: Hodges and Smith, 1844).

KAY, J., *The Social Condition and Education of the People in England and Europe*, 2 vols. (Longman, Brown, Green and Longmans, 1850).

KEENLEYSIDE, H. L. and BROWN, G. S., *Canada and the United States* (New York: A. A. Knopf, 1952).

KEIR, SIR D. L., *The Constitutional History of Modern Britain 1485–1951* (London: Adam and Charles Black, 1953).

KEITH, A. B., *A Constitutional History of India 1600–1935* (London: Methuen, 1936).

KITSON CLARK, G., *The Making of Victorian England* (London: Methuen, 1965).

KNORR, K., *British Colonial Theories 1570–1850* (Toronto: University of Toronto Press, 1944).

LANG, A., *Life, Letters and Diaries of Sir Stafford Northcote, First Earl of Iddesleigh* (Edinburgh: William Blackwood & Sons, 1891).

MACCOBY, S., *English Radicalism 1832–1852* (London: Allen & Unwin, 1935).

MACKAY, A., *Western India*, ed. J. Robertson (London: Nathaniel Cook, 1853).

MACLAGAN, MICHAEL, *'Clemency' Canning* (London: Macmillan, 1962).

MAJUMDAR, R. C., *The Sepoy Mutiny and the Revolt of 1857* (Calcutta: Firma K. L. Mukhopadhuay, 1963).

MANNING, H. T., *British Colonial Government After the American Revolution 1782–1820* (New Haven: Yale University Press, 1933).

MANSERGH, N., *The Irish Question* (London: Allen & Unwin, 1965).

MARLOWE, J., *Anglo-Egyptian Relations 1800–1953* (London: The Cresset Press, 1954).

MASANI, R. P., *Dadabhai Naoroji* (London: Allen & Unwin, 1939).

MCCORD, N., *The Anti-Corn Law League* (London: Unwin University Books, 1968).
MCDOWELL, R. B., *The Irish Administration 1801–1914* (Toronto: University of Toronto Press, 1964).
MEHROTRA, S. R., *India and the Commonwealth 1885–1929* (London: Allen and Unwin, 1965).
MILLS, J. T., *John Bright and the Quakers*, 2 vols. (London: Methuen, 1935).
MODY, H. P., *Sir Pherozeshah Mehta*, 2 vols. (Bombay: The Times Press, 1921).
MOORE, R. J., *Sir Charles Wood's Indian Policy 1853–66* (Manchester: Manchester University Press, 1966).
MORLEY, J., *The Life of Richard Cobden* (London: T. Fisher Unwin, 1906).
— *The Life of Willian Ewart Gladstone*, 2 vols. (London: Macmillan, 1905).
MUIR, R., *A Short History of the British Commonwealth*, 2 vols. (London: George Philip & Son, 1954).
NORMAN, E. R., *The Catholic Church and Ireland in the Age of Rebellion* (Ithaca, New York: Cornell University Press, 1965).
O'BRIEN, C. C., *Parnell and his Party 1880–90* (Oxford: Clarendon Press, 1957).
O'BRIEN, R. BARRY, *Fifty Years of Concessions to Ireland 1831–1881*, 2 vols. (London: Sampson Law, Marston, Searle, & Rivington, 1883–5).
— *The Life of Charles Stewart Parnell* (London: T. Nelson & Sons, 1910).
PALMER, J. A. B., *The Mutiny Outbreak at Meerut in 1857* (Cambridge: Cambridge University Press, 1966).
PARKER, C. S., *Life and Letters of Sir James Graham 1792–1861*, 2 vols. (London: John Murray, 1907).
PELLING, H., *A Short History of the Labour Party* (London: Macmillan, 1962).
PEMBERTON, W. S. CHILDE-, *Life of Lord Norton* (London: John Murray, 1909).
PHILIPS, C. H., *The East India Company 1784–1834* (Manchester: Manchester University Press, 1961).
POMFRET, J. E., *The Struggle for Land in Ireland 1800–1923* (Princeton: Princeton University Press, 1930).
PROWSE, D. W., *A History of Newfoundland* (London: Macmillan 1895).
READ, D., *Cobden and Bright* (London: Edward Arnold, 1967).
REDFORD, A., *Manchester Merchants and Foreign Trade 1794–1858* (Manchester: Manchester University Press, 1934).
ROBINSON, R. and GALLAGHER, J., *Africa and the Victorians* (London: Macmillan, 1961).
ROSTOW, W. W., *British Economy of the Nineteenth Century* (Oxford: Clarendon Press, 1948).
The Shaping of Modern Ireland, ed. C. C. O'Brien (London: Routledge & Kegan Paul, 1960).
SILVER, A. W., *Manchester Men and Indian Cotton 1847–1872* (Manchester: Manchester University Press, 1966).
SMITH, V. A., *The Oxford History of India* (Oxford: Clarendon Press, 1958).

SOUTHGATE, D., *The Passing of the Whigs 1832–1886* (London: Macmillan, 1965).

SPEAR, P., *India* (Ann Arbor: The University of Michigan Press, 1961).

STACEY, C. P., *Canada and the British Army 1846–1871* (Toronto: University of Toronto Press, 1963).

STOKES, J. E., *The English Utilitarians and India* (Oxford: Clarendon Press, 1959).

STRACHEY, SIR JOHN, *India, Its Administration & Progress* (London: Macmillan, 1911).

TAYLOR, A. J. P., *The Trouble Makers, Dissent over Foreign Policy 1792–1939* (London: Hamish Hamilton, 1957).

THOMPSON, J., *The Owens College: Its Foundation and Growth* (Manchester: J. E. Cornish, 1886).

THORNER, D., *Investment in Empire* (Philadelphia: University of Pennsylvania Press, 1950).

THORNTON, A. P., *The Imperial Idea and its Enemies* (London: Macmillan, 1959).

TREVELYAN, G. M., *The Life of John Bright* (London: Constable, 1913).

TYLER, J. E., *The Struggle for Imperial Unity (1868–1895)* (London: Longmans, Green, 1938).

UNDERHILL, F. H., *In Search of Canadian Liberalism* (Toronto: Macmillan Co. of Canada, 1960).

— *The Image of Confederation* (Toronto: C.B.C., 1964).

VINCENT, J., *The Formation of the Liberal Party 1857–1868* (London: Constable, 1966).

WAITE, P. B., *The Life and Times of Confederation 1864–1867* (Toronto: University of Toronto Press, 1962).

WALKER, E. A., *A History of Southern Africa* (London: Longmans, Green, 1957).

WALLACE, MARY ELIZABETH, *Goldwin Smith* (Toronto: University of Toronto Press, 1957).

WEDDERBURN, SIR WILLIAM, *Allan Octavian Hume, C.B.* (London: T. Fisher Unwin, 1913).

WHYTE, J. H., *The Independent Irish Party 1850–59* (London: Oxford University Press, 1958).

WILLIAMS, W. E., *The Rise of Gladstone to the Leadership of the Liberal Party 1859 to 1868* (Cambridge: Cambridge University Press, 1934).

WINKS, R. W., *Canada and the United States. The Civil War Years* (Baltimore: The Johns Hopkins Press, 1960).

WOODHAM-SMITH, CECIL, *The Great Hunger* (London: Hamish Hamilton, 1962).

WOODWARD, SIR L., *The Age of Reform 1815–1870* (Oxford: Clarendon Press, 1962).

YOUNG, D. M., *The Colonial Office in the Early Nineteenth Century* (London: Longmans for the Royal Commonwealth Society, 1961).

YOUNG, G. M., *Victorian England, Portrait of an Age* (London: Oxford University Press, 1953).

B. ARTICLES

AYDELOTTE, W. O. 'The Conservative and Radical Interpretations of Early Victorian Social Legislation', *Victorian Studies*, xi, no. 2 (Dec., 1967).

BECK, J. M., 'Joseph Howe: Opportunist or Empire Builder?', *Canadian Historical Review*, xli, no. 5 (Sept., 1960).

BIRKS, G. D. 'Industrialization in India', *The Annals of the American Academy of Political and Social Science*, ccxxxiii (May, 1944).

CUMPSTON, I. M. 'Some Early Indian Nationalists and their Allies in the British Parliament 1851–1906', *English Historical Review*, lxxvi, no. 299 (April, 1961).

GALBRAITH, J. 'Myths of the "Little England" Era', *American Historical Review*, lxvii, no. 1 (Oct., 1961).

GASH, N., 'Peel and the Party System', *Transactions of the Royal Historical Society*, 5th series, i (1951).

MACDONAGH, O., 'The Anti-Imperialism of Free Trade', *Economic History Review*, xiv, no. 3 (1962).

MANNING, H. T., 'The Colonial Policy of the Whig Ministers 1830–37', *Canadian Historical Review*, xxxiii, no. 3 (Sept., 1952).

MACPHERSON, W. J. 'Investment in Indian Railways 1845–1875', *Economic History Review*, Second Series, viii, no. 2 (Dec., 1955).

MCDOWELL, R. B., 'The Irish Executive in the Nineteenth Century', *Irish Historical Studies*, ix, no. 35 (March, 1955).

ROBINSON, O., 'The London Companies as Progressive Landlords in Nineteenth Century Ireland', *Economic History Review*, Second Series, xv, no. 1 (1962).

SINGHAL, D. P., 'Some Consequences of Nationalism in India', *Australian Journal of Politics and Economics*, vii, no. 2 (Nov., 1961).

C. THESES

SKINNER, J., *John Bright and The Representation of Manchester in the House of Commons 1847–57* (M.A. Wales, 1965).

WILLIAMS, J. A., *Manchester and the Manchester School 1830–57* (M.A. Leeds, 1966).

INDEX